MCLUHAN.
A GUIDE FOR THE PERPLEXED

MCLUHAN:
A GUIDE FOR THE PERPLEXED

W. TERRENCE GORDON

continuum

NEW YORK • LONDON

2010

The Continuum International Publishing Group Inc
80 Maiden Lane, New York, NY 10038

The Continuum International Publishing Group Ltd
The Tower Building, 11 York Road, London SE1 7NX

www.continuumbooks.com

Library of Congress Cataloging-in-Publication Data
Gordon, W. Terrence, 1942-
McLuhan: a guide for the perplexed / W. Terrence Gordon.
p. cm. – (Guides for the perplexed)
Includes bibliographical references and index.

ISBN-13: 978-1-4411-2629-0 (alk. paper)
ISBN-10: 1-4411-2629-5 (alk. paper)
ISBN-13: 978-1-4411-4380-8 (pbk. : alk. paper)
ISBN-10: 1-4411-4380-7 (pbk. : alk. paper)

1. McLuhan, Marshall, 1911-1980. I. Title. II. Series.

P92.5.M3G675 2010
302.23'092–dc22
2009022342

Typeset by Newgen Imaging Systems Pvt Ltd, Chennai, India
Printed in the United States of America

CONTENTS

PREFACE

Marshall McLuhan was dubbed a media guru when he came to prominence in the 1960s. The Woodstock generation found him cool; their parents found him perplexing. Today he is often referred to as a media ecologist, a phrase that would have pleased him for its resonance with James Joyce's *Echoland*. Joyce's kaleidoscopic verbal creativity stimulated McLuhan's vision for a unified explanation of everything from Woodstock to Wall Street, from woodcuts to weapons, in terms of media and their effects.

As an undergraduate student, McLuhan dismissed many of his teachers as myopic, less well read than him, and incapable of creative thinking. He vowed to eschew the academic life but became a professor in spite of himself, teaching English literature till the end of his career. Along the way, he found time to write about high literature (G. K. Chesterton, Wyndham Lewis, Ezra Pound, James Joyce, T. S. Eliot, and Thomas Nashe among others) and popular culture (movies, comics, and advertising), managing even to explore the link between them in reviewing the work of his arch-rival Northrop Frye ("Inside Blake and Hollywood"). By 1963 McLuhan was Director of the Center for Culture and Technology at the University of Toronto and would be a public intellectual on the international stage for more than a decade, then linked forever to his two best-known coinages: *the global village* and *the medium is the message*.

Both phrases express a paradox. We easily interpret the first as an image for our planet dramatically shrunken by the powerful media of instant communication. Broadband buzz and G3 gossip. For this we scarcely need McLuhan. But *the medium is the message* has an unsettling counter-intuitive quality that provoked critical commentaries—many of startling irrelevance to McLuhan's thrust and purpose.

Legions of bewildered students and intimidated faculty may have kept silent, and McLuhan's many interviewers often merely registered irritation, but Jonathan Miller and Umberto Eco were among the luminaries who lodged vigorous protests, stumbling over McLuhan's metaphor for how media operate and how they shape and control the speed, scale, and forms of human association and action. This was the key idea at the core of *Understanding Media*.

Even as *Understanding Media* was launched, McLuhan was raiding psychology, philosophy, structuralism, and taking second plunder from literary studies. By the end of his career, he had harnessed the complementarities of figure/ground, cause/effect, structure/function, and cliché/archetype to his earlier work. Their full and final expression was achieved in the posthumously published *Laws of Media*.

Taken as a whole, McLuhan's writings reveal a profound coherence and illuminate his unifying vision for the study of language, literature, and culture, grounded in the broad understanding of *any* medium or technology as an extension of the human body. *McLuhan: A Guide for the Perplexed* offers a close reading of all his major works with a focus on tracing the systematic development of his thought. The overriding objective is to clarify McLuhan's thinking, to consolidate it in a fashion which prevents misreadings, and to open the way to advancing his own program: ensuring that the world does not sleepwalk into the twenty-first century with nineteenth-century perceptions.

CHAPTER ONE

BACKGROUND, CONTEXT, DEFINITIONS, AND . . . STUMBLING BLOCKS

Norman Mailer said Marshall McLuhan had a mind that could only think in metaphors. The metaphor for McLuhan's life and life's work is a voyage of discovery, and it emerges from a literary classic that was one of his favorites: Edgar Allan Poe's *A Descent into the Maelstrom.*

The story tells of a fisherman caught in a fearsome whirlpool off the northwest coast of Norway, known to mariners as the Maelstrom. The narrator of Poe's tale recounts that he and his two brothers had spent years repeatedly risking their lives to cross this treacherous expanse of the Arctic Ocean in order to reach the rich fishing grounds beyond. They were skilled in timing their trips to coincide with slack waters, but they knew well that any miscalculation would put them at the mercy of a force strong enough to suck down trees, whales, boats and ships of all sizes. They had at times been stranded beyond the Maelstrom as it churned longer than usual; once they had nearly starved to death, as a full week of becalmed waters kept them from returning home.

After years of eluding disaster, the brothers find themselves heading for port as a monstrous hurricane brews with such great speed that they are driven into the dark and angry waters at the center of the whirlpool. One brother lashes himself to the mast for safety, but when it snaps he is carried overboard and drowns. The other brothers remain aboard their boat as it begins to descend into the spinning water. Amid total chaos, the one who would survive to tell of the experience sees both horror and beauty. As he notices which objects go most quickly to their destruction on the rocks at the bottom of the vortex, he discovers a pattern that offers a clue for a survival strategy.

When he fails to make his brother understand what must be done to escape a watery grave, he leaps overboard alone, lashed to a barrel that will keep him afloat. The other, trusting in the apparent safety of a ring-bolt aboard their vessel, vanishes with it.

As the Maelstrom's own force abates, the hurricane continues to rage, carrying the surviving brother down the coast, where he is rescued by other fishermen. Though the horror of the ordeal leaves him temporarily speechless, he is finally able to summon enough strength to relate what happened in full and explain how he came to understand the way to escape. But those who hear his account not only fail to understand but react with disbelief. Poe portrays himself as a traveler who is among those listening to the fisherman, whom he describes as broken in body and spirit and resigned already to retelling his story without any expectation of anyone believing him.

McLuhan first referred to the story of the Maelstrom in an article published in 1946, titled "Footprints in the Sands of Crime." It became a perennial favorite in his teaching and in his writing. It is given pride of place in his first book, *The Mechanical Bride*, where readers are told explicitly how much importance McLuhan attaches to it and precisely what place it occupies in his emerging method of analysis: "Poe's sailor saved himself by studying the action of the whirlpool and by cooperating with it. The present book likewise makes few attempts to attack the very considerable currents and pressures set up around us today by the mechanical agencies of the press, radio, movies, and advertising. It does attempt to set the reader at the center of the revolving picture created by these affairs where [s/]he may observe the action that is in progress and in which everybody is involved."[1]

McLuhan, like Poe's surviving fisherman, could say: "I became obsessed with the keenest curiosity about the whirl itself. I positively felt a *wish* to explore its depths, even at the sacrifice I was going to make; and my principal grief was that I should never be able to tell my old companions on shore about the mysteries I should see."[2]

And, like the survivor of the Maelstrom, McLuhan found amusement through rational detachment, as he surveyed new environments gathering enough force to endanger the cultural values he personally cherished. No less than the solitary figure of Poe's tale, McLuhan would meet with skepticism in offering his explanation of how to escape the maelstrom of the electronic age.

At age 17, Marshall McLuhan built and sailed a fourteen-foot boat. Some years later, writing to his mother, he would relate the experience explicitly to his conversion to Catholicism. "An innate distaste for spiritual perversion and incontinence would have kept me neutrally agnostic forever unless there had come opportunities for knowledge of things utterly alien to the culture—the grim product of life-denying other worldliness—that you know I hated from the time I turned from our pavements and wheels to boats and sails."[3]

The reference to pavements, wheels, boats, and sails also anticipates one part of the analytic framework that McLuhan would develop for examining the relationship between culture and technology: modes of transportation and their impact on social organization and interaction. McLuhan never limited his study of media to mass communication but defined a medium as any technological extension of body or mind. Inevitably, some readers were surprised that alongside chapters on radio, television, press, and film, *Understanding Media* offered many more dealing with clothing and clocks, comics and credit cards . . . Other readers were exasperated when McLuhan's late writings challenged them to understand what features safety pins and bulldozers shared with the metaphors of everyday language. Was this just an outrageous piece of rhetoric? Not at all, as we shall see in Chapter Five. McLuhan had too profound a respect for rhetoric to use it merely as a zapper.

At 19, he was an undergraduate student at the University of Manitoba, Canada. It was the 1930s, and the world of advertising caught his attention for the first time. He ventured the opinion that fifty years later the ads of that day would prove to be interesting cultural artifacts. Over those fifty years, McLuhan analyzed advertising repeatedly—first in *The Mechanical Bride*, then in journal articles, a major chapter of *Understanding Media*, and finally in *Culture Is Our Business*.

McLuhan earned a B.A. and M.A. from the University of Manitoba, a second M.A. in English literature from Cambridge University, where he then enrolled in the Ph. D. program. When he left Cambridge and took up his first teaching position at the University of Wisconsin, he experienced a shock effect. At age twenty-six he was barely older than his students, but he felt as though he was teaching them across a wide chasm. He recognized that this had something to do with ways of learning, ways of understanding, though he could not pinpoint it. But like Poe's sailor, he began observing what was happening around him, searching for a clue to a way out. He was on his way to the study of media that would absorb him for the rest of his life.

Media analysis was not a detour from literary studies for McLuhan. On the contrary, he constantly buttresses his academic publications on writers from G. K. Chesterton to T. S. Eliot with articles and books aimed not only at educators grappling with the same challenge he had first faced in Wisconsin but all readers with a stake in literate culture and its survival against the backwash of the electronic age. The writers of particular interest to McLuhan were those who galvanized language and inspired the development of his pivotal view of language as mankind's first technology. The list is long and runs from the Elizabethan era to the period of high modernism, from Thomas Nashe to Ezra Pound, from William Blake to Wyndham Lewis. James Joyce is the most frequently quoted author in *Understanding Media*; Harold Innis (*Empire and Communications, The Bias of Communication*) is absent.

Understanding Media is undoubtedly the best-known book by McLuhan. In print continuously since it first appeared in 1964, it has passed many publication milestones, with an anniversary edition dating from 1994 and the definitive critical edition released in 2003. Chapter Four below will provide a detailed analysis; the present chapter, intended as a gradual initiation to McLuhan's key terms and themes, is organized around critical reaction to the book. It is also intended to encourage newcomers and set all readers on the path to a fruitful reading of McLuhan by making an example of fine minds that stumbled there and identifying the stones that they failed to see.

The first edition of *Understanding Media* caused a splash, a deluge of reviews, commentaries, and reactions (a sampling will be given in Chapter Four) throughout North America and abroad. At first, the reception was somewhat muted in McLuhan's native Canada, even in the popular press, where he would later draw much attention. Fellow Canadian author Pierre Berton published *The Cool Crazy Committed World of the Sixties* in 1966, titling his introductory chapter "The Mood and the Medium" but without so much as mentioning McLuhan's name. Perhaps Berton did not wish to be the first to pronounce judgment on the significance of the man that the Haight-Ashbury generation would soon be embracing as cool.

4

McLuhan's arch-rival in the English Department at the University of Toronto, the already legendary Northrop Frye of *The Anatomy of Criticism* fame, showed no such reticence. Writing one year after Berton, his criticisms were pointed and broad-ranging, jabbing even at McLuhan's commitment to rhetoric, and perhaps subtly discounting the value of the inspiration that McLuhan had drawn from Canadian economist Harold Innis:

> The role of communications media in the modern world is a subject that Professor Marshall McLuhan has made so much his own that it would be almost a discourtesy not to refer to him in a lecture which covers many of his themes. The McLuhan cult, or more accurately the McLuhan rumor, is the latest of the illusions of progress: it tells us that a number of new media are about to bring in a new form of civilization all by themselves, merely by existing. Because of this we should not, in staring at a television set, wonder if we are wasting our time and develop guilt feelings accordingly: we should feel that we are evolving a new mode of apprehension. What is important about the television set is not the quality it exudes, which is only content, but the fact that it is there, the end of a vortical suction that 'involves' the viewer. This is not all of what a serious and most original writer is trying to say, yet Professor McLuhan lends himself partly to this interpretation by throwing so many of his insights into a deterministic form. He would connect the alienation of progress with the habit of forcing a hypnotized eye to travel over thousands of miles of type, in what is so accurately called the pursuit of knowledge. But apparently he would see the Gutenberg syndrome as a cause of the alienation of progress, and not simply as one of its effects. Determinism of this kind, like the determinism which derives Confederation from the railway, is a plausible but oversimplified form of rhetoric.[4]

Nearly twenty years later, French philosopher and social critic Jean Baudrillard would reflect on McLuhan and cast him not as a technological determinist but as a technical optimist:

> There is the technological optimism of Marshall McLuhan: for him the electronic media inaugurate a generalized planetary communication and should conduct us by the mental effect alone of new technologies, beyond the atomizing rationality of the Gutenberg

5

galaxy to the global village, to the new electronic tribalism—an achieved transparency of information and communication . . . In reality, even if I did not share the technological optimism of McLuhan, I always recognized and considered as a gain the true revolution which he brought about in media analysis (this has been mostly ignored in France).[5]

Whether McLuhan himself would accept the phrases *generalized planetary communication* and *achieved transparency of information* as accurate reflections of notions that he had framed is debatable. It might also be possible to argue that in spite of branding McLuhan a technological optimist, Baudrillard has allowed for an interpretation that is closer to the technological determinism that Frye laid to McLuhan's charge, at the point where Baudrillard speaks of *the mental effect alone of new technologies.*

Between Frye and Baudrillard came Arthur Kroker, whose *Technology and the Canadian Mind: Innis/McLuhan/Grant*, a detailed and insightful study that, like Baudrillard's, makes McLuhan the representative of technological optimism, reserving the label of technological determinism not for Harold Innis (the apparent implication of Frye's oblique reference to him) but for social philosopher George Grant. For Kroker, Innis represents technological realism.

McLuhan drew a reaction from one of England's high-profile persons about the arts, Jonathan Miller, when McLuhan traveled to London to do a radio broadcast for the BBC. He must have been satisfied that Miller had fully grasped a fundamental and crucial tenet of *Understanding Media* and flattered to find himself being whisked into the pantheon of twentieth-century intellectual giants when Miller declared that McLuhan was doing for visual space what Freud had done for sex: revealing its pervasiveness in the structuring of human affairs. (Soon after, Tom Wolfe would challenge readers to consider the consequences, if McLuhan was what he sounded like— the most important thinker since Newton, Darwin, Freud, Einstein, and Pavlov.)

But not long after McLuhan's return to Canada, he received a letter from Miller, declaring himself to be a disciple, offering suggestions to the master, along with his own reflections on television as a medium. Miller professed to be worried about McLuhan's use of the terms *cool* and *hot*, noting that four distinct meanings could be teased out of these terms in McLuhan's writings, though he did not quote chapter and verse. If Miller was indeed a disciple, he was questing after an orthodoxy that he found wanting in *Understanding Media*, an orthodoxy that McLuhan could not have woven into the tapestry of his text without violating the principle of probing his subject matter in a tentative manner that is comfortable with stretching meanings. In particular, Miller was keen to challenge McLuhan on his description of television as the cool medium *par excellence.*

Miller's cavil failed to take into account the full range of the defining features of television that McLuhan had carefully set out to show how the medium demands maximum sensory involvement from users, thus making it quintessentially cool. Of course, HDTV was unknown when *Understanding Media* first appeared in print, but that technical advance did not transform television into a hot medium. Much greater sharpness and clarity of the image on the screen has been accompanied by the decreased visual intensity of color transmission. For McLuhan, color was tactile, not visual, a matter discussed in his *Through the Vanishing Point.* From this point of view, color is cooler than black and white, ensuring that television retains the cool and tactile qualities that McLuhan ascribed to it, a state of affairs that Jonathan Miller apparently could not accept as the factor responsible for making television the coolest medium.

Television camera shots are most often close-ups, framed for viewing on a small screen. By contrast, postcards and photographs are also small, though not restricted to close-ups, because they are printed, and print is a *high definition medium.* The *low definition medium* demands close-up shots; television bathes the viewer's eye in a flow of images that remain in low definition, even on a large-screen set. Miller's reservations about McLuhan's take on television took no account of this fundamental point about the technology.

The image on a television screen is not photographic, like that of film. It is, as McLuhan constantly stressed, iconic and sculptural rather than pictorial. Whereas a reel of film is a series of visible and isolatable images permanently embedded in celluloid, no fixed image ever appears on the television screen. Nothing but a configuration of light of varying intensity and in a constant state of flux washes over the screen. It is produced by light *through*, not light *on*—by an endless barrage of electrons on the picture tube. HDTV has not changed this process. The television set of today has come a long way from the clunky cabinet of yesteryear, but it remains the cool medium it was when audiences watched the North American debut of the

Beatles in the same year that McLuhan published *Understanding Media*. Jonathan Miller was ready to challenge McLuhan on his understanding of the television medium.

McLuhan's metaphor for the image on a television screen was that of a *two-dimensional mosaic*. Because we watch television, we resist the notion that it is not fundamentally a visual medium with the same qualities as true visual media such as text and images on paper, photographs, movies (each of which get their own chapter in *Understanding Media*), paintings, cave drawings, fingerprints, or notes scribbled on a sandy beach. The TV mosaic does not have a visual structure comparable to the hot medium of the alphabet and its technological offspring of print, where the eye must constantly follow a straight line of sharply defined forms. Television does not extend sight, to the exclusion of the other senses, as print does. It compels the human eye to operate with great intensity to construct images from the flow on the screen. McLuhan called this *television's tactile quality*. TV does not have uniform, continuous, or repetitive features. On the contrary, it offers no images at all, in the conventional sense, but discontinuous and nonlinear patterns captured and *transformed into images* in the eye of the beholder. This is what gives the medium the features of a mosaic.

Television demands the use of what McLuhan later referred to as the *ear-view mirror*, meaning that the eye never receives a complete picture from the screen, just as the ear never receives a word in isolation from a stream of speech. When the eye and the ear, or the eye working like an ear, have to fill in what is missing, in order to get a complete and recognizable image, the medium is cool, the user is "hot"—the typical inverse correlation that emerges in the study of media and their effects.

McLuhan pushed his metaphor of the mosaic further, stating that the properties of the TV image create what he called *mosaic space*. He believed that the shift from the attitude of detachment and private, individual identity fostered by print to the involvement stimulated by television could be explained only by the differences between visual and mosaic spaces.

Television shifted the balance among our five physical senses and altered our mental processes. The shift was radical and irreversible. In the first place, the visual sense that had dominated Western culture for centuries, through the alphabet and the printing press, was suddenly dislocated by the new medium of television. Secondly, television ushered in an extension, a new intensity, for the sense of touch. Though received by the eye, the image on the screen has the type of texture associated with touch, which creates an interaction of all the senses.

Nonphonetic forms of writing that preceded the alphabet, as well as those that coexist with it in nonalphabetic cultures, are, like television, media that *integrate* the physical senses. Phonetic writing, by contrast, *separates* and fragments the senses. The low definition television image reverses this effect of phonetic writing and replaces the process of analytic fragmentation with a reintegration of sensory life.

The consequences of such a shift were particularly marked in North America and England, with their long traditions of literary culture. It was here that television pushed people toward the tactile model of continental European cultures. As for social trends and values influenced by television, McLuhan noted that Europe began Americanizing just as America began Europeanizing.

No sooner had television been made commercially available in the 1950s (its original applications were military thirty years earlier) than North Americans began acquiring new tastes for tactile involvement, in everything from the fad for skin-diving to the wrap-around space of small cars. The television western took on new importance (think about the extraordinary popularity of the show Bonanza), because the television image is highly compatible with the tactility of textures in saddles, buckskin clothing, and roughhewn wood. This fostered a new taste in the television-watching public for all experience *in depth*. The spill-over effect made itself felt in every domain of life from language teaching (where training in the spoken language was given priority to the point of displacing the emphasis on reading knowledge) to clothes (with a new emphasis on textured materials), food, wine, and car styles.

A television screen does not show a fixed image but a mesh of dots. Light shines through them with varying intensity and allows an image to form. But the spaces in the mesh need to be filled in for the image to take shape. Because touch is central among the senses, McLuhan defined tactility as the interaction of the senses, following St. Thomas's definition of touch as the meeting place of all the senses. (The resistance that McLuhan encountered to his ideas about television was not confined to Jonathan Miller and eventually led McLuhan to declare that his insight into the medium was only acceptable to Thomists.) There is, of course, no contact between the skin of the viewer and the television, but the eye is so much more intensely engaged by the television screen than by print that the *effect* is the same as that of touching. And it was the study of effects that interested McLuhan most. On these points, too, Jonathan Miller was to argue against him.

McLuhan cautioned that not even the type of insight he was trying to provide into the operation and power of media could offset the ordinary *closure* of the senses. Here *closure* refers not to the closing up of the spaces in the mesh of dots on the television screen, but to a shift toward a new balance among our senses, such as that performed while the eye views television images. Television simultaneously reawakened the tactile sense that had been impoverished by centuries of culture dominated by print and diminished the visual sense (impoverished because it was not integrated with the other senses), which had been the bias of print culture.

Sensory closure causes conformity to the pattern of experience presented by a medium. In making this observation, McLuhan sounded another caution, introducing medical metaphors and the principle of the numbing effect of media. The warning also shows us most clearly that to take McLuhan as a promoter of television is to miss an important part of his teaching about the noxious effect of television. (Privately, he pleaded with his eldest son not to let the grandchildren watch television, calling it a vile drug.)

The cool medium of television is unsuited to anyone who represents a type or a group with easily recognized features, because types deprive the viewer of the task of *closure*, in the sense of *completion of the image*. The nature of the medium itself, the sensory involvement it demands, and the habits of perception it imposes, conspire to make the viewer expect not a fixed image but one which must be fixed. Anyone whose physical appearance is a statement of role and status in life (this is high-definition stuff) overheats the cool television medium, with disastrous consequences for themselves. (Richard Nixon was a disaster on television; JFK was a success, because he was *cool* in McLuhan's sense.)

To be successful, television personalities require textured and sculptural qualities such as stylized hair, mustache, beard, small nose, large teeth, gapped teeth, craggy brow, chiseled bones . . . Merv Griffin hired Vanna White because of her large head. McLuhan offered observations and advice on such matters to public figures. Some got the message about the medium and their persona and welcomed McLuhan's insights. Canadian Prime Minister Pierre Elliott Trudeau became an enthusiastic McLuhanite; the Maharishi Mahesh Yogi declared that McLuhan was a seer. John Lennon and Yoko Ono came to visit him without making any declaration, but others were baffled, irritated, or dismissive. Some held convictions or intuitions that could not accommodate McLuhan's intuitions and clung to them as the brother of the Maelstrom survivor had clung to the ring-bolt aboard the perishing ship, and as Jonathan Miller had clung to his unyielding criticisms.

McLuhan readily acknowledged that persons who are neither shaggy nor craggy could project an acceptable television *persona* through cool and casual verbal skill. (Here already is an insight into the place that McLuhan assigned to language in relation to *all* other media, a point to which we will return in detail later.) Such was the case for *Tonight Show* host Jack Paar, in the earliest days of television. Paar's skill as an interviewer also played to the fundamental need of television for free-flowing chat and dialogue, which still informs it to this day. If Paar understood the medium intuitively, David Frost gained no insight into it from McLuhan; he appeared utterly baffled in their exchange.

McLuhan made no distinction between entertainment and education. The implications of the television medium for education are no different than those for any other area of social and cultural organization. Moreover, the consequences put as much at stake for the one as for the other, because the medium has imposed closure of the senses, as defined above. Teaching and learning techniques that developed spontaneously and inevitably out of the visual bias of print became less effective with the coming of the age of television. (We will learn much more about this in Chapters Four and Five), but the solution to this problem is not to let students learn from teachers teaching on television, for this is nothing more than an ineffectual overheating of a cool medium. Noting that television makes for myopia, McLuhan called for an understanding of the dynamics of the medium, its action on our senses, and its interaction with other media, stressing at the same time the futility of confining attention to the TV curriculum.

And so the conclusion that McLuhan draws as to what television can do that the classroom cannot, regardless of subject matter, is inherent in the medium itself. He notes that it is the educator's job not only to understand the television medium but to exploit its richness as a tool for teaching and learning.

Such are the points McLuhan makes in explaining television to the world in *Understanding Media*—illuminating points for some; debating points for Jonathan Miller. Miller differed with McLuhan above all on the nature of the image on the television screen, conceding only one point that would eventually be demonstrated by psychologist Herbert Krugman in support of McLuhan's view. But Miller insisted on a fundamentally different notion from McLuhan's in maintaining stoutly that television works by a series of frame-by-frame presentations. For McLuhan, this was only the case for the hot medium of film and one of the features that so radically differentiates television from film.

Miller dropped his frame-by-frame argument in his later writings about McLuhan's ideas, but in 1965 he dismissed what McLuhan had called *the iconic quality of television* as purely metaphorical and put it down to the small size of the screen making the television set akin to a tiny devotional object. McLuhan ignored the absurdity of this view and limited his response to explaining that his approach in *any* area of cultural investigation was to use language as a *probe* to open up his subject, rather than as a package to seal it. Miller declined McLuhan's implicit invitation to rethink the metaphor question, and events were to suggest that the lesson on the McLuhan method had been lost on him.

Four years later, McLuhan learned that Frank Kermode had commissioned Jonathan Miller to contribute to the Modern Masters series with a book about McLuhan. He described himself as enormously flattered. But Miller's book proved to be an outright attack on McLuhan, who did not read it until he realized that it was attracting much attention. Malcolm Muggeridge, British journalist, author, media personality, and, most famously in his later years, Christian convert, spoke confidently of McLuhan's "proneness to wild and sometimes crazy generalities," and, absolving himself of the intellectual's obligation to be counter-critical, declared confidently that "Jonathan Miller's *McLuhan* . . . does an effective demolition job."[6]

McLuhan wrote to Kermode with measured restraint, protesting that what Miller had offered readers was irrelevant to the lines of inquiry McLuhan had been trying to open up. But the little book captured public attention. McLuhan grew irritated and began to speak of an anti-McLuhan crusade launched by Miller. Eventually he dismissed Miller's work as a spoof, though he almost certainly knew that it had not been intended as such. At least this interpretation allowed him to react in good humor when Miller's book began to appear in translation and follow McLuhan around the world on his lecture tours.

Miller alone might not have provided the impetus to move McLuhan toward the investigation of linguistics that he had so long deferred, if it were not that he was adding his voice to that of the very high profile Umberto Eco. Here was a critic of McLuhan from the camp of semiotics. Unlike linguistics, the study of semiotics is not limited to human language but investigates all forms of communication. With such a broad scope of inquiry, semiotics might be expected to prove compatible with the interdisciplinary range of McLuhan's work, but this proves not to be the case, or at least not for Eco. Understanding the criticisms of McLuhan that Eco added to those of Miller, understanding how misguided the arguments of both scholars are, provides an important step to understanding McLuhan, and to appreciating the challenge he faced in communicating his ideas, even to the intellectually sophisticated.

The medium is not the message. This assertion stems from Eco's reflection on a cartoon showing a cannibal chieftain wearing an alarm clock as a necklace. Eco disputes McLuhan's view that the invention of clocks (a complete chapter, subtitled "The Scent of Time," is given to the subject in *Understanding Media*) universally fostered a concept of time as uniformly divided space. Eco will only concede that this happened in some instances, maintaining that the message of the clock could have different meanings, as it did for the cartoon cannibal. For Eco, this is the residual freedom of the individual to interpret in different ways. If we grant that such freedom exists, Eco says, "it is still equally untrue that acting on the form and contents of the message can convert the person receiving it."[7]

As an argument against the percept that the medium is the message, Eco's claim strays far from McLuhan in just a few flawed steps. It does not deal with the unperceived effects of technology acting on our physical senses, substituting instead conscious reflection on the technology. It also unites form and content, as if this were a standard state of affairs in McLuhan's view, when in fact he always separates them.

McLuhan uses the term *media* broadly. This part of Eco's discussion starts by presenting the technical apparatus of semiotics and then charging that McLuhan does not respect the distinctions required by that apparatus: "To say that the alphabet and the street are 'media' is lumping a code together with a channel."[8]

This is comparable to complaining that the cannibal (remember that it was Eco and not McLuhan who gave him the residual freedom as to how to interpret the clock) threatens the professional standards of the clock-makers' guild. Allowing McLuhan the freedom to define *media* broadly does not subvert the principles of semiotics. But Eco pursues his line of reasoning as if this were the case, noting that electric light can be signal, message, or channel, whereas McLuhan is concerned only with the third of these when he states that electric light is a medium without a message. At this point, Eco's objection is too narrow a focus rather than too broad a definition. His examples of the cases where light is a signal (using light to flash a message in Morse code) or a message in itself (light left on in a window as an all-clear to a lover) do not have any impact on the scale, speed, or patterns of organization in society as a whole (this is McLuhan's definition of *message*) and do not, therefore, damage Eco's view. McLuhan is concerned with the effect of light and the effect it produces, regardless of whether it is signal, message (in Eco's sense), or channel. Just as McLuhan's definition of *media* does not undermine semiotics, mandatory distinctions in a strictly semiotic analysis framework do not detract from McLuhan's observations to his own purpose—the study of media *effects*.

Eco concludes his comments on McLuhan's stretched sense of *media* by stating that "it is the code used that gives the light-signal its specific content."[9]

This neither undermines nor is undermined by any of McLuhan's observations. In fact, it has nothing to do with them.

All media are not active metaphors. Here Eco continues to protest that McLuhan ignores the all-important semiotic concept of *code*. The argument hinges on the observation that languages translate forms of experience by virtue of being codes but that a metaphor is simply a replacement *within* a code. On the one hand, Eco argues, the sense in which print is a medium needs to be distinguished from the sense in which language is a medium, therefore McLuhan's characterization of all media as metaphors is too all-encompassing. On the other hand, he argues that McLuhan's analysis would be improved by replacing the notion of media as metaphors with that of code, an argument which tacitly entails the possibility of a unified code of media.

But his admission that "the press does not change the coding of experience with respect to the written language"[10] undermines the prospect of establishing any such unified code capable of accounting for the cultural impact of the advent of the press. It would be irrelevant to McLuhan's purpose to analyze in terms of codes, when it is precisely the changes brought about by new media that he wishes to study. **"The medium is the message" has three possible meanings.** This is an entirely different matter than saying, as Eco did earlier, that the medium is *not* the message. Now Eco is concerned about contradictions among the potential meanings of McLuhan's phrase. He gives them as (1) the form of the message is the real content of the message; (2) the code is the message; (3) the channel is the message. And while these are only potential meanings, they are somehow proof for Eco that "it is not true, as McLuhan states, that scholars of information have considered only the content of information without bothering about formal problems."[11]

Language is not a medium. This criticism comes not from Eco but, once again, from Jonathan Miller, who laid to McLuhan's charge the untenable assumption that language can be conceived of as a medium existing independently of the mind of the language user. The evidence for such a view comes from Miller's labyrinthine discussion leading through the territory of linguistics to a destination that was never McLuhan's. Miller then speaks not of McLuhan's unacceptable assumption but "difficulties which arise when language is regarded as a medium."[12]

Just as Eco found fault with McLuhan's ideas in the absence of a conventional semiotic viewpoint, Miller condemns the absence of the distinction linguists make between knowing language and using it. Miller would like readers to believe that making the distinction undermines McLuhan's notion of language as a medium. This is impossible. The distinction made in linguistic theory between knowing language and using it has nothing to do with words as expression of thought. But Miller continues to rely on linguistic theory to buttress his argument, concluding that "[a]ny theory of human communication which does not take its implied differences into consideration has very little right to be taken seriously."[13]

McLuhan's purpose is not to offer a theory of communication but to probe the effects of any and every artifact that *mediates* (all media are intermediaries) between the human body and its physical environment, including language. This objective gains no advantage from the technical apparatus of linguistics, nor does linguistic theory undermine McLuhan's program. On the contrary, as we shall see shortly, when, late in his career, McLuhan discovered the foundational text of twentieth-century linguistics, Ferdinand de Saussure's *Course in General Linguistics*, he was enormously stimulated by it and distilled from it the ideas that were compatible with the media analysis he had already been refining for years.

McLuhan takes metaphors literally. Jonathan Miller quotes the following passage from McLuhan: "The TV image is not a *still* shot. It is not photo in any sense, but a ceaselessly forming contour of things limned by the scanning-finger. The resulting plastic contour appears by light *through*, not light *on*, and the image so formed has the quality of sculpture and icon, rather than of picture."[14]

Here Miller accuses McLuhan of interpreting a metaphor literally. This charge is based on Miller's own confusion. McLuhan does not refer to the television image as tactile because of a metaphorical finger scanning the screen, but because the image requires of the eye a degree of involvement as intense as that of touch. McLuhan characterizes involvement as tactile metaphorically; Miller takes a metaphorical term involving tactility and makes it into a mistake. The evidence that McLuhan does not give a concrete sense to the metaphors of tactility, sculpture, and iconicity is to be found in the same chapter that Miller quotes: "Iconographic art *uses the eye as we use our hand* to create an inclusive image, made up of many moments, phases, and aspects of the person and thing."[15]

Speech is as linear as print. In so saying, Miller believes he can disprove one of the most fundamental of McLuhan's percepts. The gist of Miller's argument is that sounds can be uttered only one at a time. Miller believes that he is trumping McLuhan with the observation that speech can be recorded on magnetic tape, implying that this is quintessential linearity. This lame line of thinking ignores the very different qualities of the marginal linearity that Miller describes and the much more powerful linearity of print, a linearity that constantly forces the eye to travel from left to right, from top to bottom, over visible figures against visible ground. (For figure/ground analysis see Chapter Five.)

Faced with such irrelevant criticisms from Eco and Miller, McLuhan could have countered them by arguing from his own position. And indeed he did, in the case of Miller, in both private correspondence and the popular press. But he also chose to explore linguistics to familiarize himself with the essence of the principles that Miller and Eco had invoked. If the initial impetus for this move was the negative one that they had provided, an equally important and much more positive influence came from a Brazilian anthropologist, Dr. Egon Schaden, visiting at the University of Toronto. He attended media seminars at McLuhan's Center for Culture and Technology and provided an entry point to Saussure's linguistics for McLuhan by explaining a key concept from the work of the anthropologist Claude Levi-Strauss.

Saussure's distinction between synchronic analysis (the state of the system under analysis limited to a specific moment in time) and diachronic analysis (the comparison of states of the system at different times) had found its way into Levi-Strauss's work. Upon learning this, McLuhan immediately linked synchronic versus diachronic to a concept on which he had long relied (and which he had inherited from Canadian economist Harold Innis), that of the interaction of center and margin in dynamic structures. McLuhan noted that diachronic analysis is the chronological approach to language and society, whereas the synchronic is the structural approach, in which any moment, or aspect of culture, can be made to reveal the whole to which it belongs, and in which all past cultures survive as *resonance* (a central phenomenon in the McLuhan view). This was a breakthrough for McLuhan, who had tackled the study of structuralism (Saussure's legacy to twentieth-century thought both in and beyond linguistics) on his own the previous year, with little success. Nevertheless, he came back to it over and over, studying treatments of the subject by William Wimsatt and Frederic Jameson. His conclusion was that the entire enterprise was sterile. But thanks to Schaden, structuralism was taking on a new look.

As soon as McLuhan began reading Ferdinand de Saussure's *Course in General Linguistics,* he detected the author saying that the medium is the message. He was also excited to find Saussure stating that language media are difficult to access, a notion coinciding with McLuhan's own teaching on *figure* (consciously noted element of a structure or situation) versus *ground* (the rest of the structure or situation, which is not noticed)—see Chapter Five below for a fuller treatment of the use McLuhan made of the complementary terms *figure/ground* appropriated from their original use in the psychology of perception. Saussure's discussion of perspective in painting, used to illustrate a point about synchronic versus diachronic analysis, appears to have jumpstarted McLuhan on a more fruitful way of thinking about linguistics and semiotics than anything that had emerged from the criticisms of Miller and Eco.

It had to do with the foundational definition in semiotics of a sign as *anything that stands for something other than itself*. In fact, Saussure's comments on perspective in painting are *not* linked to signs *per se*, but McLuhan quickly assimilates the gist of Saussure's teaching on signs to his own notion of sensory closure, noting that Saussure approaches all signs as *effects*, another key percept for McLuhan. A lesson on effects and closure is indeed implicit in the passage in which Saussure discusses perspective in painting. If it is left implicit, Saussure may perhaps be forgiven for insisting less strenuously on the matter than McLuhan, whose interests are elsewhere but whose reading of the *Course in General Linguistics* is entirely consistent with the principles set out by Saussure.

By way of exploring the limits of Saussure's framework of thought and its compatibility with his own, McLuhan puts zippers alongside Saussure's painting and treats them both as signs, or sensory closure. All of this is set in the context of McLuhan's emerging law of media that every figure obscures a ground of hidden forces, which are the effects of the figure.

Juxtaposing paintings and zippers, signs and sensory closure, provides the insight that when a painting is completed, alternative perspectives on space are preempted, in the same way that the surface concealed by a fastened zipper becomes a hidden ground, space transformed into a static entity by the zipper. In the same way, when the pure ground of thought and the pure ground of sound come together in the word (a sign), options are foreclosed. There is a further parallel to the way in which our physical senses are dulled to alternative input by the bias created by any medium that is becoming dominant and superseding a previously dominant medium.

McLuhan found much that was relevant to his own view in Saussure: the notion of language as a medium, including its effects and the creation of a service environment; vocal organs as hardware for the software of the language system; sound units as the sum of auditory impressions and movements of the speech organs, exemplifying the interplay of sensory input and sensory closure—all of these are hybrids of Saussure's concepts and McLuhan's percepts. The synchronic/diachronic distinction that is fundamental to Saussure is related by McLuhan not only to that of *center/margin* but to those of figure/ground and eye/ear orientation. Saussure's description of how the grammatical structures of language interact with word groups is assimilated to the interaction that McLuhan describes between *cliché and archetype*. (See Chapter Five for a detailed discussion.)

But it is, above all, the possibility of interpreting the definition of the sign as given by Saussure as compatible with his own core idea of unperceived sensory closure or media effect that gives value to Saussure's thought for McLuhan. It is surprising that Saussure's view of the sign as a link between thought processes and the continuum of sound is not developed further by McLuhan. In its full implication, Saussure's notion corresponds to McLuhan's characterization of media working in pairs, one veiling the operation of the other by creating the illusion of being its content. McLuhan's description of thought as pure process, articulated in *Understanding Media* more than a decade before he read Saussure, completely parallels the latter's description of the formless domain of thought before it achieves articulation through the creation of linguistic signs.

By the time McLuhan completed his study of the notions of system and sign in Saussure, he concluded that it was essentially a question of algebra. For his purposes, there was no need to pursue the matter further. But it had been very useful for the laws of media that McLuhan had not yet completed formulating. Saussure's views had served as a catalyst allowing McLuhan to say that he saw a new pattern of all technology as organized ignorance. He linked this pattern to four interlocking laws of media forming a *tetrad structure*, an idea central to his posthumous works of 1988 and 1989 (see Chapter Five). He describes the tetrad as a resonant structure and an update of "the ancient and medieval tradition of grammar-allied-to-rhetoric, in a way that is consonant with the forms of awareness imposed on the twentieth century by electronic technology."[16]

With the tetrad, McLuhan's adaptation of ideas from linguistics reaches its full form, late in his career. At the same time, the tetrad, offering a framework for media analysis of the broadest application, is directly and strongly linked, as the preceding quotation hints, to McLuhan's doctoral thesis, tracing the trivium of grammar, dialectics, and rhetoric through from antiquity to the work of Thomas Nashe in the sixteenth century. Central in the study of the trivium, dating back to classical antiquity, and in the work of Nashe is the concept of *chiasmus*—contrast by reverse parallelism. This notion grounds the McLuhan tetrad, as we shall see in Chapter Five.

Looking back beyond the 1970s, beyond the influence of Saussure, beyond the development of the tetrad, beyond the research program that produced the Nashe thesis, to McLuhan's Cambridge years, one discovers what might arguably be the most powerful and enduring influence on his work. It is the influence of Ivor Armstrong Richards, clearly evident in many key passages in McLuhan's writings: "All media are active metaphors in their power to translate experience into new forms. The spoken word was the first technology by which man was able to let go of his environment in order to grasp it in a new way."[17]

As his second term at Cambridge began in January 1935, a skeptical and critical McLuhan reported home on his course in the philosophy of rhetoric with Richards. *Practical Criticism: A Study of Literary Judgment* (1929) had sent shock waves through Cambridge, showing students their dismal and incoherent critical responses to a selection of unsigned poems, and shaming the faculty who had prepared them so poorly. Now Richards was repeating the experiment, asking students for their criticism of prose extracts. McLuhan had read *Practical Criticism* and saw what could counter its damning evidence. "I have some doubts about the method of giving *one* poem of any person as a test. A really cultivated taste might hit the nail most all the time, but uncultivated people can enjoy many things in a *volume* by one writer where the merits of his craft and ideas and feelings are permitted to permeate the consciousness from a 1000 different angles."[18]

Ideas, feelings, different angles. Here are some of Richards's key words in an argument undermining his own experiment. McLuhan's skepticism gave way to complete repugnance in the face of Richards's atheism. "Richards is a humanist who regards all experience as *relative* to certain conditions of life. There are no permanent, ultimate, qualities such as Good, Love, Hope, etc., and yet he wishes to discover objective, ultimate, permanent standards of criticism. He wants to discover those standards (what a hope!) in order to establish intellectualist culture as the only religion worthy [of] a rational being . . . When I see how people swallow such ghastly atheistic nonsense, I could join a bomb-hurling society."[19]

But Richards was giving McLuhan the powerful analytical tools he needed to explore the linguistic complexity and conceptual opaqueness of the modernist poetry he found so absorbing. As Richards's biographer, John Paul Russo, states "The Richardsian method, ana-lyzing the poet's sense, imagery and metaphor, rhythm, form, inten-tion, attitude, and irony, was fully prepared to handle compression, ambiguity, self-referentiality, obscurity, and allusiveness."[20]

From Richards, McLuhan learned how a poem works, learned it through a method calling for an analytical turn of mind. Richards taught that poetry "remains unintelligible so long as we separate words from their meanings and treat them as mere signs fitted into a sensory pattern."[21]

This was a fundamental principle from which McLuhan devel-oped his later observations and teachings on symbolism, patterns, cliché, archetype, and closure. Richards's approach was also perform-ance-based and opened new perspectives for McLuhan on principles of rhetoric. Long before "McLuhan" became synonymous with "media," he heard the message running through all of Richards's work about the power, the pervasiveness, the subtlety, the complexity, the interaction of media—and their effects.

Richards's ground-breaking approach to literary criticism pro-vided McLuhan with at least five key points:

(1) **The power of words**. Richards deplored the indefensible belief that word-meanings are fixed and independent of their use. He docu-mented the power of words to control thought, urging that thought should bring words under *its* control by determining meaning from context. This was the theme of Richards's book (with C. K. Ogden) *The Meaning of Meaning*. The principles set out in this book still imbue McLuhan's writings nearly forty years after he took lectures from Richards at Cambridge. As an example, *Take Today* (1972), where page one, distinctively McLuhan in tone, strikes an unmistak-able note from Richards: "Nothing has its meaning alone. Every *figure* must have its *ground* or environment. A single word, divorced from its linguistic *ground* would be useless. A note in isolation is not music. Consciousness is corporate action involving *all* the senses (Latin *sensus communis* or 'common sense' is the translation of all the senses into each other). The 'meaning of meaning' is relationship." The "meaning of meaning" was a much-used phrase in Cambridge circles before *The Meaning of Meaning* became a much-read book. Clearly, its title inspired McLuhan's own best-known saying.

In an interview from 1966, he stated: "Back in the 1920s, there used to be much concern about 'the meaning of meaning.' At that time,

the discovery that meaning was not statement so much as the simultaneous interaction of many things came as an exciting surprise.
When I say that 'the medium is the message,' I am merely stating the
fact that 'meaning' is a happening, the multitudinous interplay of
events. I have found sometimes that it helps to say 'the medium is
the message' [McLuhan spoke and intended the pun *massage* as indicated by what follows, but the typesetter restored the 'correct' word
message] because the medium is a complex set of events that roughly
handles and works over entire populations."[22]

(2) **An eye for an ear**. Richards was perennially confident that
pitfalls of language and problems of communication could be over-
come. Part of the solution came from the human body itself: "The
multiplicity of our channels is our best hope. The eye can check what
the ear hears, and vice versa."[23] This view shaped McLuhan's technological optimism. Neither he nor Richards was troubled by the paradox that intellectual power can only be derived from the very source
it needs to control.

(3) **Product versus process**. Richards attends to this distinction
in connection with language: "Though a few students of primitive
mentality or of the language of thought of the child have begun to
give serious attention to the evolution of thinking, on the whole our
historians of philosophy have been too much preoccupied with
results. Their eye has been on the thoughts as products rather than
on the thought processes."[24]

McLuhan applies Richards's concept here to his own observations
relating to environment, cultural contrasts, social history, and discourse: environment is process, not container; the West speaks of
space where the East speaks of spacing; historical descriptions of
change are mere narratives that offer no insight into dynamics; debate
packages knowledge for display, whereas dialogue organizes ignorance for discovery.

(4) **Understanding is a process of translation**. Richards conceived
of understanding and all acquisition of knowledge as a process of
interpretation and reinterpretation. The term for this was *translation*.
A key chapter of *Understanding Media,* entitled "Media as Translators," not only uses this concept but integrates it with Richards's
observations on the multiplicity of sensory channels: "Our very word
'grasp' or 'apprehension' points to the process of getting at one thing
through another, of handling and sensing many facets at a time
through more than one sense at a time. It begins to be evident that

'touch' is not skin but the interplay of the senses, and 'keeping in touch' or 'getting in touch' is a matter of a fruitful meeting of the senses, of sight translated into sound and sound into movement, and taste and smell."[25]

(5) **The probe.** Long after McLuhan had studied under Richards, he wrote to him to acknowledge that "I owe you an enormous debt since Cambridge days," adding that "your wonderful word 'feedforward' suggests to me the principle of the probe . . . "[26]

The probe is McLuhan's technique of choice in all his writings. It serves as an instrument for providing insight into media and their effects. It corresponds to Richards's *speculative instruments*, the set of key words whose meanings he stretched as a means of investigating meaning. Though there were other sources of influence on McLuhan's thought, few came so early in his career or proved to be as enduring as that of I. A. Richards.

McLuhan the media analyst sought to make his audiences ask: How can we escape the inevitable changes that new technologies bring? (The use that McLuhan made of Poe's tale of the mariner who escaped the Maelstrom undermines Frye's charge that McLuhan is a technological determinist.)

This McLuhan did with his probes. Like the speculative instruments of I. A. Richards—the words Richards used to expand his own understanding and that of his students—McLuhan's probes were drills. He used them to pierce the crust of mankind's dulled perceptions, but his principal interest was rarely, if ever, in getting a hole finished, for that would be a goal-oriented and linear activity. The drill, after all, is a spiral, and what it churns up was the important matter for McLuhan. The drill is the hardware counterpart to the spiral and the vortex, symbols of becoming, of pure process. Drill is to spiral is to vortex as hardware is to myth is to nature. The McLuhan probes raised charges against his ideas that came to be repeated frequently:

McLuhan makes mankind a prisoner of media. Not all of McLuhan's critics are easily pinned down. Take John Fekete:

McLuhan's critical theory . . . is effectively cut off from its genuine ontological basis in a similar fashion to any other objectivistic rationalism.[27]

According to this interpretation, McLuhan's observations make mankind powerless to escape media effects. If this were so, why would he write a book called *Understanding Media?* In fact, McLuhan says that media effects come about inevitably, as a result of altered sense ratios, but not that we are powerless to deal with them. Fekete knows, and eventually (mis)quotes, McLuhan's reference to bringing media into orderly service, but persists, even then, in painting McLuhan as a technological determinist. Other commentators, such as George Steiner, speak of McLuhan's "very powerful humanistic position."[28] And McLuhan himself describes his position by saying: "In the sense that these media are extensions of ourselves—of mankind—then my interest in them is utterly humanistic."[29]

A more balanced view of McLuhan than Fekete's is available in Arthur Kroker's *Technology and the Canadian Mind.* Kroker situates McLuhan in relation to two other thinkers, George Grant and Harold Innis, who represent for Kroker technological determinism and technological realism respectively, while McLuhan emerges as the champion of technological optimism.

McLuhan misrepresents the role of the visual sense. Fekete seems to be disappointed, even exasperated, that McLuhan left the strict confines of literary criticism to explore media analysis. When Fekete grudgingly meets McLuhan on his new turf, he misinterprets him: "Not only is [McLuhan's] vision-tactility opposition phony, but the hand and sight, combined in the work process and tool formation, were both crucial variables of human evolution from the pre-human. By minimizing the role of vision before the alphabet, McLuhan makes his own claim that man is a tool-making animal (*Gutenberg Galaxy,* p. 4) unintelligible."[30]

McLuhan does *not* minimize the role of the visual sense before the development of the alphabet; he simply observes that it became powerfully privileged by the alphabet. As a new technology, the alphabet required a new set of habits that carried over from reading to virtually every area of human thought and endeavor: media effects. How could this state of affairs make the claim for the tool-making animal unintelligible? Vision and tactility are integrated for the tool-maker, but they are separated for the book-reader, to the point where the visual sense dominates the world and experience of it.

Electricity has not unified the world into a global village. Where McLuhan speaks of the global village, his key word is *interdependence*, a far different matter from *unity*.[31] Here is McLuhan himself on this question: "There is more diversity, less conformity under a single roof in any family than there is with the thousands of families in the same city. The more you create village conditions, the more discontinuity and division and diversity. The global village absolutely insures maximal disagreement on all points. It never occurred to me that uniformity and tranquility were the properties of the global village . . . The tribal-global village is far more divisive full of fighting—than any nationalism ever was. Village is fission, not fusion, in depth . . . The village is not the place to find ideal peace and harmony. Exact opposite. Nationalism came out of print and provided an extraordinary relief from global village conditions. I don't *approve* of the global village. I say we live in it."[32]

Linguists are fond of saying that their discipline is the most human of the sciences and the most scientific of the humanities. This observation may have held some appeal for McLuhan, though it appears to be of little use in answering some of the criticisms brought against him and reviewed here. What are the criteria of scientific theory that Jonathan Miller found lacking in McLuhan's work? It must be formal (i.e., formulated independently of language), capable of empirical validation, and have the power to predict, or show itself to be universally applicable. In *Laws of Media* McLuhan follows the method implicit in this provisional definition of scientific theory, but the discoveries emerging from the application of those laws challenge the first part of the definition, because the laws of media prove not to require formulation independently of language: "Utterings are outering (extensions), so media are not *as* words, they actually *are* words."[33]

In the decade following the publication of the first edition of *Understanding Media*, McLuhan's star continued to shine. His subsequent disappearance from public view, as illness took its toll, may have left a void, but by then the academic world, at least, was in thrall to postmodernism and deconstruction. It would be years before any serious inquiry would be made into McLuhan's place in intellectual history. These include S. D. Neill's *Clarifying McLuhan* (1993), Judith Stamps's *Unthinking Modernity: Innis, McLuhan and the Frankfurt School* (1995), Glen Willmott's *McLuhan, or Modernism in Reverse* (1996). But McLuhan's place had long since been assured and his influence indelibly stamped on programs in media studies that had been established in the interim around the globe.

When McLuhan's *Understanding Media* appeared in 1964, one American reviewer obscurely titled his comments "Reverse Canadian."[34]

The title of Willmott's book invokes both that long-forgotten review and McLuhan's fourth law of media (see Chapter Five). Willmott's two-part study traces the roots of McLuhan's modernism and the evolution of his postmodernist impulses. The notion of reversal is fundamental to both. In the first instance, under the influence of critics and artists including I. A. Richards, F. R. Leavis, Sergei Eisenstein, and Wyndham Lewis, McLuhan developed the strategy of communicating a reversing structure of experience, of developing a language of retracing or counter-learning. In the second instance, according to Willmott, McLuhan simply illustrated that reversal by acting out its dictates.

Willmott displays admiration for McLuhan in the early going, comparing *The Mechanical Bride* favorably to Roland Barthes's *Mythologies* (1956), noting that the former appeared at an earlier date. But what Willmott perceives as a shift in McLuhan's critical aesthetic is marked by a move on Willmott's part toward guarded skepticism. This is somewhat puzzling, given that Willmott's engagement with the perlocutionary aesthetic is clearly as strong as the one he imputes to McLuhan.

Though the book is far from massive, the author covers an astonishing amount of ground, ranging over the influence of the figures noted above, as well as that of T. S. Eliot, Ezra Pound, the French symbolist poets, Lewis Mumford, Sigfried Giedion, and Harold Innis in discussing the early McLuhan. Part two focuses on McLuhan's oeuvre after the publication in 1962 of *The Gutenberg Galaxy*, with particular emphasis on points of connection to Jacques Lacan, Martin Heidegger, and George Grant (for the latter see also Arthur Kroker, *Technology and the Canadian Mind: Innis/McLuhan/Grant*).

Willmott discusses much in McLuhan's work that has previously received little commentary. Thus, for example, the discussion of McLuhan's collaboration with Ted Carpenter, decisive in moving McLuhan toward his key notions of acoustic space and sensory typologies, is also evocative of the theme of word magic and the rich vein of semiotic reflection which has still to be mined in McLuhan's work. Willmott detects the trends in McLuhan's major works as they first emerge in the minor writings, and he displays a talent for pithy summary of complex points that rivals the aphoristic style McLuhan favored.

By the midpoint of his book, Willmott is simultaneously deconstructing McLuhan (for valorizing the kind of response in G. K. Chesterton that he excoriated in Henry James, for his flip on Robert Hutchins) and giving him credit for a unique manipulation of modernist ideology. At the same time, Willmott points out that one of his purposes in focusing on McLuhan's early work is to interpret its enduring traces in his later writings. This remark is characteristic of the balance Willmott strives constantly to achieve. Coupled with his own commitment to the tenets of postmodernism, his orientation produces a suspended judgment.

Set off against the various strengths of Willmott's work is its weakness in forcing McLuhan into the postmodern mold. The claim that modernism flips into postmodernism is hardly controversial, but Willmott situates McLuhan at the rupture point, a view that repelled McLuhan himself when one commentator suggested it to McLuhan himself.[35] Since McLuhan offered his reaction to this initiative only in private correspondence, it lacks the potential for satirical force required to buttress Willmott's argument. But Willmott rescues McLuhan from deconstruction by deconstructing himself, first by characterizing McLuhan as one of those postmodernists who see in a totalizing consciousness of the break the utopian conditions for a new world order and then dismissing as satirical the most utopian of passages in McLuhan's writing.

Or is it McLuhan himself who deconstructs his utopianism, his satire, and his Saussure-turned-Toynbee formalism and rescues his historicism? Willmott casts his own fear about a misguided rediscovery of "practical critical ideology" as being of a piece with McLuhan's own fears about the popular audience for *Understanding Media*, but detaches that fear from the hope that McLuhan linked to it—a link Willmott himself has already pointed out. It is a hope that allows discovery of a practical diacritical technique of intellectual investigation free of any ideology.

Willmott concludes with a comment on McLuhan's style, characterizing it as neither message nor theory but a medium. This is an important observation, illuminating the original McLuhan probe and anchoring McLuhan in the postmodern aesthetic.

But this is precisely the aesthetic from which McLuhan unwittingly dissociated himself by reading Saussure selectively, whereas much in postmodernism has arguably stemmed from a radical misreading of Saussure. McLuhan's inattention to Saussure's use of the *coincidentia oppositorum/coincidentia differentiarum* complementarity was a happy accident. It allowed him to build on Saussure when he might otherwise have dismissed him as a practitioner of sterile dialectics. *McLuhan, or Modernism in Reverse* allows readers to build on McLuhan, when they might otherwise dismiss him as a practitioner of sterile postmodernism.

Among recent commentators, Judith Stamps examines McLuhan in relation to Harold Innis, Theodor Adorno, and Walter Benjamin. Some of her claims are startling: (1) McLuhan had a theory of negative dialectics; (2) he shared with Innis and Adorno a difficulty in coming to grips with reason and civilization in the post–World War II period; (3) he had a commitment to understand the relations between classifying and colonizing; (4) he was a social scientist; (5) he wrote a work on the history of the Western world. Stamps candidly admits that she is pursuing ephemera and making a radically innovative reading of McLuhan—indisputably true, particularly when she labels him as a latter-day practitioner of dialectics. Stamps marginalizes McLuhan the media analyst in order to deal with him primarily as a historiographer. She speaks of McLuhan challenging positive theory, reading history negatively, and developing new methods as the innovative synthesis that marks his work. It is difficult to determine how this synthesis is achieved, given that Stamps offers only scant and unconvincing documentation. She also speaks of a tension between historicism and ahistoricism in McLuhan's early writings giving way to outright ahistoricism in his later work, but the supporting argument is unconvincing. Stamps characterizes her four subjects as having understood history as an open-ended series of qualitative changes that emerged at the margins of dominant institutions, but she herself has not understood the history of McLuhan as an open-ended series of qualitative changes that emerged at the margins of his dominant metaphors. The tension between historicism and ahistoricism becomes irrelevant in light of the internal dynamics of the classical trivium, the unifying element of all of McLuhan's writings from his Cambridge thesis to the posthumously published *Laws of Media*.

CHAPTER TWO

LITERARY LINKS

G. K. CHESTERTON

In 1936, McLuhan published his first scholarly article in *The Dalhousie Review*, challenging readers to look afresh at the writings of Chesterton, to rethink the views of dismissive critics who saw him as nothing more than a showman. McLuhan had detected a paradox in Chesterton that made him a practical mystic. This was the insight that McLuhan offered to his readers. The Chesterton who had for thirty years been "examining current fashion and fatalism," who "fears lest certain infinitely valuable things, such as the family and personal liberty, should perish," is evoked in the opening paragraph. In retrospect, the same paragraph, and much of the entire text that follows, evokes the McLuhan who would do likewise for another thirty years and more.[1]

McLuhan identifies Chesterton with true mystics: those who reveal mysteries rather than hiding them. His preliminary discussion of this point anticipates the groundwork of the approach to media that he would later develop himself. He called the mysteries revealed by Chesterton the daily miracles of sense and consciousness. The inexpressible value of existence that for Chesterton transcended any argument for optimism or pessimism was transformed in McLuhan's work, beginning with *The Mechanical Bride*, into the suspended judgment that so disoriented and irked his commentators.

Applying to Chesterton the words that French Catholic philosopher Jacques Maritain spoke of Arthur Rimbaud ("The Eucharistic passion which he finds in the heart of life"), McLuhan observes that Chesterton transcended poetry.[2]

McLuhan quotes Chesterton describing one of his own literary creations as someone who "had somehow made a giant stride from babyhood to manhood, and missed that crisis in youth when most of us grow old," words that McLuhan transfers to Chesterton himself. [3] They are just as aptly transferred to McLuhan himself.

From his "more than ordinary awareness and freshness of perception," McLuhan declares, Chesterton drew his "extraordinarily strong sense of fact," a sense possessed no less by McLuhan and derived from the same source.[4] That sense of fact required humility, dubbed by McLuhan as "the *very* condition of honest art and all philosophy."[5]

If these words of McLuhan dating from 1936 convinced readers that Chesterton was humble, it would prove much more difficulty in later years to successfully project such an image of himself, when he carried on Chesterton's legacy by transforming the latter's practical mysticism into media analysis. But few commentators would deny McLuhan's originality—a quality he identified in Chesterton, adding an important qualifier that characterizes his own work, in both literary analysis and media studies: "In short, he is original in the *only* possible sense, because he considers everything in relation to its origins."[6] McLuhan consciously emulated Chesterton, who "consciously causes a clash between appearances in order to attract attention to a real truth transcending such a conflict."[7]

Any observer, if prepared to allow (or at least tolerate) the broad-ranging line of inquiry that McLuhan invariably took, could apply his words about Chesterton to McLuhan himself: "There is no hint or hue of meaning amidst the dizziest crags of thought that is safe from his swift, darting, pursuit."[8]

McLuhan rises to the defense of Chesterton against those who saw him as a medievalist (a charge that would later be leveled at McLuhan): "The merest reference to anything prior to the Reformation starts a clockwork process in the minds of the nineteenth-century journalists who still write most of our papers."[9]

Speaking from the perspective of the broad historical sweep that would mark his doctoral thesis on Thomas Nashe, McLuhan invokes "the conspiracy . . . to ignore history, which in practice meant the Middle Ages," noting that it "had not generally been found out when Mr. Chesterton began to write."[10]

McLuhan never defended himself against charges of relying on overblown rhetoric, though he easily could have with the words he applies to Chesterton: "In fact, that he turns a few cart-wheels out of sheer good spirits by way of enlivening his pages has annoyed a certain type of person, and is sure to puzzle a lazy or fatigued mind. Such, for instance, is his unparalleled power of making verbal coincidences really coincide."[11]

Any critic reluctant to accept this point would need to admit a parallel between Chesterton and McLuhan along the lines the latter describes in the former, saying: "The fact is that Mr. Chesterton has always that additional human energy and intellectual power which constitute humor."[12]

As for Chesterton's capacity to "focus a vast range of material into a narrow compass,"[13] this same quality, so appealing to McLuhan, proves to be an admirable (or bewildering—according to one's taste) trait of the later McLuhan. Chesterton's "great labor of synthesis and reconstruction"[14] was McLuhan's own, focusing on the present and the past "because he is concerned lest our future steps be blindly taken."[15]

McLuhan stresses the progression and coherence in Chesterton's work but leaves it unspoken in the case of his own. He describes the contrast between Chesterton's use of alliteration (a device turned to vice, in the eyes of some of Chesterton's harsher critics) as "something quite different from a Swinburne lulling the mind by alliterating woolly caterpillar words,"[16] maintaining that in Chesterton's hands cumulative consonance complemented clarity of concepts. Chesterton's enthusiasm for the detective story, shared by McLuhan, was, the latter explains, "based upon the poetry of fact which Mr. Chesterton has explained so well."[17]

McLuhan concludes his Chesterton essay with an observation recognized, even in his own lifetime, as pertaining to himself: "He has become a legend while he yet lives. Nobody could wish him otherwise than as he is."[18]

WYNDHAM LEWIS

Lewis, who poured his prodigious energy in equal parts into painting and writing both novels and essays, was the most prominent artist in the British movement known as Vorticism. The term derived from Ezra Pound's use of *vortex* as an epithet for the art world of London in the period preceding World War I. Lewis too found it apt as a description of the swirling energy that characterized the emerging forms of art in that period. Typically, his paintings feature bold and dramatic geometric forms.

Lewis's profound influence is indelibly stamped on McLuhan's work. The conception of media as extensions of the physical body, the use of the myth of Narcissus to illustrate media effects (see Chapter Four for details), among other fertile ideas, finds a source in Lewis's writings.

Lewis served McLuhan as a model for avoiding categorical judgments. McLuhan's impetus toward the principles of integration and synthesis in all his work resonates with Lewis's ideal of reintegrating the arts of sculpture, painting, and architecture. In the first volume of the journal *Blast*, Lewis, as editor, articulated the principle that the Vorticist is not the slave of commotion but its master; McLuhan, the navigator of the electronic maelstrom, would teach the principle that understanding media provides the means of keeping them under control. Lewis understood the fragmenting effects of technology and spoke of them in terms that would be closely paralleled in McLuhan's writings, beginning with *The Gutenberg Galaxy*. Lewis's concept of space contains the core of the idea that McLuhan would develop as the distinction between visual and acoustic space. Like Lewis, McLuhan would move beyond his original interests in the world of the arts to understanding the relationship between art and technology. McLuhan shared Lewis's concept of the artist being inextricably linked to the inevitable encroachments of technology. Both men accepted the necessity of facing the effects of technological advances as detached observers of their causes. Lewis's notion of the vortex as a mask of energy in relation to both art and technology was applied by McLuhan to language *as both art and technology*.

In spite of so many parallels between their work, and McLuhan's clear recognition and acknowledgment of them, he did not hold Lewis above criticism. In terms of the analytical framework for understanding culture and technology that McLuhan grounded in the interplay of our physical senses, he saw Lewis's work as falling short: "Another person to whom I owe a good deal in terms of structural awareness is Wyndham Lewis, the painter. He spent his life defining what he considered to be the values of the eye by which he meant the audible, tactile, boundary line of abstract and sculptural form. He, by the way, did not understand that cartoon and sculpture are not visual forms. Since Lewis never got this straightened out, it is not surprising that students of his have trouble too."[19]

Such criticism does not undermine the value of Lewis's achievement for McLuhan, who enthusiastically embraced Lewis's deflation of the twentieth-century myth of progress and his identification of shamanistic tendencies in science and philosophy beginning with Newton and Kant. The opening of McLuhan's essay on Lewis's theory of art and communication cites the passage from *Time and Western Man* where Lewis states: "For me art is the civilized substitute for magic; as philosophy is what, on a higher or more complex plane, takes the place of religion. By means of art, I believe Professor Whitehead and M. Brémond wish to lead us down and back to the plane of magic, or mystical, specifically religious, experience."[20]

It is pertinent to note that in spite of Lewis's deprecating reference to mystical experience here, McLuhan will, within a few pages, refer to him as a mystic (compare McLuhan's characterization of Chesterton as a practical mystic above), but in so doing he makes a crucial distinction and qualification: "[Lewis] is a mystic or visionary *of the comic*, moving toward the pole of intelligibility instead of that of feeling" (emphasis added).[21]

McLuhan establishes a qualified resonance between Lewis and Joyce and dissonance between them and Eliot: "Joyce tends like Lewis to reject the way of connatural gnosis and emotion favored by Bergson, Eliot, and theosophy, in which the emotions are used as the principal windows of the soul."[22]

At the same time, he casts his net wider still to encompass Pound and offer an insight into the Vorticism movement: "But Joyce, Lewis, Eliot, and Pound are perhaps nearer in agreement on the subject of the vortices of existence. If 'the world of the "pure present" of the Classical Ages is obviously the world that is born and dies every moment,' it is clear that it is such a world that Lewis seeks to arrest in his paintings (and novels) . . . If we can elucidate the vortex concepts in Lewis we shall be finally in a position to see his grounds for rejecting the thought and work of the Time and Flux school of this century."[23]

Like all of the authors from whom McLuhan distilled insights that took him beyond literature *as* literary production purely for esthetic appreciation, Lewis takes his place in *Understanding Media*: "Mental breakdown of varying degrees is the very common result of uprooting and inundation with new information and endless new patterns of information. Wyndham Lewis made this a theme of his group of novels called *The Human Age*. The first of these, *The Childermass*, is concerned precisely with accelerated media change as a kind of massacre of the innocents. In our own world as we become more aware of the effects of technology on psychic formation and manifestation, we are losing all confidence in our right to assign guilt."[24]

Quoting Lewis's observation that the artist is always writing a history of the future because he alone is aware of the nature of the present, McLuhan adds:

> Knowledge of this simple fact is now needed for human survival. The ability of the artist to sidestep the bully blow of new technology of any age, and to parry such violence with full awareness, is age-old.[25]

This ability in Lewis, and in all the writers to whom McLuhan paid particular attention, is precisely the ability that McLuhan sought to jumpstart in his own audience.

EZRA POUND AND T. S. ELIOT

Written at an interval of nearly thirty years, McLuhan's publications on Ezra Pound show his preference for an integrating approach to be as pronounced in literary studies as in media analysis. In both essays, the discussion of Pound's creative work and editorial work, as well as his critical prose, develops around Pound in relation to T. S. Eliot. But this complex and powerful relation also draws into its orbit further connections with Mallarmé, Poe, Lewis, Joyce, and others. The later essay also makes full use of the analysis of rhetoric that McLuhan had developed as an essential part of the ground work for his doctoral dissertation on Thomas Nashe. And, inevitably, reference to Vorticism occurs prominently, not only linking the writers that McLuhan studies to each other but linking all of them as sources of his own principles of media analysis.

Even before he underscores radical differences between Pound and Eliot, McLuhan hints at the conclusion that those differences are dwarfed in their significance for literature *as literature*—the private preserve of the *literati*—by their significance as tell-tales of the unique cultural shift engendered by technology at the beginning of the twentieth century. Thus: "By contrast with Pound's sharp and alert sentences the gentle rhythms of Eliot's paragraphs are a balm for minds which find only distress in the violence of intellectual penetration. Mr. Eliot has said the same things, for example, about Dante and the French Symbolists as Mr. Pound. They share an immense interest in verbal technique and poetic structures. But whereas Mr. Pound has been vehement and explicit about these things, Mr. Eliot has been unobtrusive and casual. Mr. Eliot has adjusted the 'frequency modulation' of his prose so that it causes little perturbation in foolish ears, but Mr. Pound insists on his reader's attention even where no likelihood of understanding is present. And for this he has not been forgiven by the literate."[26]

The literate are those who remain in the mind-set of nineteenth century visual culture and resist attempts such as Pound's to create an awareness of the dawning age of postliterate culture.

Just as McLuhan's first publication, the essay on Chesterton dating from 1936, contains observations that apply equally to himself, so too does the earlier of his publications on Pound (1950), where he speaks of the latter's "fascination with technological discovery coexisting with erudition and sensitivity in language and the arts."[27]

Allied to that erudition and sensitivity is the preference for analogical presentation which Pound and McLuhan also share, a method that makes demands on readers and disappoints them, because McLuhan, like Pound, "seldom translates himself into ordinary prose."[28]

It is also at the end of his earlier essay on Pound that McLuhan subtly evokes the divisions of the classical trivium that will find full expression in the later essay as the framework for a fuller discussion of the Pound-Eliot relationship: "Mr. Eliot has held the interest of a whole generation of readers by making basic concessions in his prose to their demand for dialectic and persuasive charm. What he has to say, however, is neither dialectical nor charming, but profoundly analogical and even unpleasant. Mr. Pound's prose on occasion follows the procedure of Mr. Eliot's poetry when it is for most readers extremely obscure, just as the organization of the sections of *The Waste Land* employs the analogical 'music' of [Pound's] *Mauberley.*"[29]

In his comparison of Pound's "Portrait d'une Femme" and Eliot's "Portrait of a Lady," McLuhan focuses on a line from the former—"Your mind and you are our Sargasso Sea,"—calling it "a sort of vortex of inclusive consciousness," which allows him to link it simultaneously to Vorticism, to Poe's Maelstrom, and to the poetic form that Pound and Eliot share:

The pattern of the London vortex . . . reappears structurally in the Cantos themselves. Both Pound's "Portrait" and Eliot's constitute a kind of epyllion [a narrative poem with romantic and mythological themes] which, we shall see, is a pattern they used a great deal the parallel actions function as a plot and counterplot which enrich each other by their interplay, Poe's "Descent into the Maelstrom" has structurally much in common with the vortices of the Cantos, Similarly, the "Sargasso Sea" is a vortex that attracts multitudinous objects but which also tosses things up again in recognizable patterns which serve for survival. Survival for Poe's sailor had meant attaching himself to one of the recurring objects in the whirlpool. The same strategy applies to Pound's readers who need to be alert to the resonance of recurring themes. Apropos the same kind of awareness, Lewis wrote in Blast magazine that the vorticists defined their art as an art of the energized present, an art which has captured the point of maximum intensity.[30]

In his discussion of possible revisions that Pound suggested to Eliot, McLuhan observes that *The Waste Land* had originally been structured in four parts, in anticipation of Four Quartets, and that this division applied to the seasons, the ancient concept of the elements of fire, air, earth, and water, as well as to the convention of four levels of interpretation. Although this constituted a link between Eliot's work and Pound's own writings, the latter found the liturgical pattern at the basis of Eliot's composition repelling enough to suggest a radical recasting in terms of the five-part division of classical oration, so familiar to McLuhan from his preparatory background study for his dissertation on Thomas Nashe.

McLuhan's final essay on Pound and Eliot, published in 1979, just one year before his death, is vintage McLuhan, the literary scholar still practicing close reading as he had learned it in the Cambridge English School more than forty years earlier, offering readers a detailed analysis explicitly relating the divisions of oratory to the textual passages under his critical microscope:

Pound's five divisions are: invention, or the finding of the theme or matter: "For three years, out of key with his time" (Personae, p. 187); the arrangement (disposition) of that matter: "The age demanded an image" (p. 188); elocution or ornament in accord with the occasion: "What god, man, or hero/ Shall I place a tin wreath upon" (p. 189); memory: "frankness as never before . . .

trench confessions" (p. 190); and delivery: "There died a myriad, . . ./For a botched civilization, . . ./Quick eyes gone under earth's lid". (p. 191)[31]

At the same time, McLuhan links key elements of his Nashe study to some of his most recently acquired analytical apparatus. In the first instance, linguistics:

> As already remarked, both patterns [of composition in The Waste Land] are synchronic and simultaneous, rather than diachronic or sequential. The simultaneity of the four levels, as used by the grammarian constitutes the resonance of the Logos, just as the five divisions, when used by the orator, constitute the presence of the word. This is what the linguists now call *la langue*, and Eliot calls "the auditory imagination," The "auditory imagination" includes both the four levels and the five divisions . . .[32]

In the second instance, it is the subtle linking of the internal dynamics of the classical trivium to the analytical framework of figure vs. ground (see Chapter Five for details). "Eliot's attachment to the four-part structure involved his devotion to Grammatica and its figure/ground structure included in the text itself. By contrast, Pound's insistence on the primacy of the public outside the poem as the real ground, led him to prefer the use of rhetoric."[33]

MCLUHAN AND JAMES JOYCE

McLuhan's interest in James Joyce dates from his Cambridge years when he attended lectures by F. R. Leavis. It was an interest that endured till the end of his career. Mentioned once only at the end of McLuhan's doctoral dissertation of 1943, published as *The Classical Trivium: The Place of Thomas Nashe in the Learning of His Time* (2006), Joyce became the most frequently quoted writer in *Understanding Media* (first edition, 1964; critical edition, 2003). Like Chesterton and Lewis, Joyce shaped McLuhan's notion of language as technology. Eventually, he cast Joyce in the role of the architect responsible for the detailed blueprints from which McLuhan constructed his laws of media. He also linked Plato's *Cratylus*, with its notion of language as the key to an inclusive consciousness of human culture, to the inseparability of substance and style, of medium and message, in Joyce's *Finnegans Wake.*

McLuhan apprenticed at Joyce's forge, learning to fashion puns that educated as they entertained. Easily his favorite among those that the master had struck was the one linking language, technology, and media effects: *allforabit* as a pun on *alphabet.* The echo here mimics the insight that it opens, that of the alphabet as a technology impoverishing the fullness and richness of experiencing the world through all of our five senses simultaneously, a richness exchanged for the visual alone, skewing the integrated balance of the senses, fostering the private point of view of literate society. McLuhan frequently quoted Joyce's puns such as "Who gave you that numb?" as he taught about the numbness, the sensory closure, brought on by print technology and the associated loss of perceptual acuteness and awareness. Through puns, through all the linguistic inventiveness of *Finnegans Wake,* Joyce shows the way to transcending numbness and making a breakthrough into new types of awareness. His constant objective in *Finnegans Wake* of making language physical matched up completely with the overriding objective of all McLuhan's teaching: to provide a program of training in perception.

Here are some of McLuhan's references to Joyce in *Understanding Media* (2003).

Regarding puns:

> The title of his *Finnegans Wake* is a set of multi-leveled puns on the reversal by which Western man enters his tribal, or Finn, cycle once more, following the track of the old Finn but wide awake this time as we re-enter the tribal night. It is like our contemporary consciousness of the Unconscious. (55)

Regarding phonograph and radio:

> James Joyce . . . made *Finnegans Wake* a tone poem that condensed in a single sentence all the prattlings, exultations, observations, and remorse of the human race. He could not have conceived this work in any other age than the one that produced the phonograph and the radio. (378)

Regarding the alphabet and print:

Cervantes devoted his *Don Quixote* entirely to this aspect of the printed word and its power to create what James Joyce throughout *Finnegans Wake* designates as "the ABCED-minded," which can be taken as "ab-said" or "ab-sent" or alphabetically controlled. (383–384)

Regarding unity in the age of electricity:

Humpty-Dumpty is an obvious example of integral wholeness. The mere existence of the wall already spelt his fall. James Joyce in *Finnegans Wake* never ceases to interlace these themes, and the title of the work indicates his awareness that "a-stone-aging" as it may be, the electric age is recovering the unity of plastic and iconic space and *is* putting Humpty-Dumpty back together again. (250)

Regarding television:

The mode of the TV image has nothing in common with film or photo, except that it offers a nonverbal *gestalt* or posture of forms. With TV, the viewer is the screen. He is bombarded with light impulses that James Joyce called the "Charge of the Light Brigade" that imbues his "soulskin with sobconscious inklings." (418)

Regarding television:

James Joyce in *Finnegans Wake* headlined TELEVISION KILLS TELEPHONY IN BROTHERS BROIL, introducing a major theme in the battle of the technologically extended senses that has, indeed, been raging through our culture . . . With the telephone there occurs the extension of ear and voice that is a kind of extrasensory perception. With television came the extension of the sense of touch or of sense interplay that even more intimately involves the entire sensorium. (357)

Regarding photography:

[T]he world of the movie that was prepared by the photograph has become synonymous with illusion and fantasy, turning society into what Joyce called an "all-nights newsery reel," that substitutes a "reel" world for reality. Joyce knew more about the effects of the photograph on our senses, our language, and our thought processes than anybody else. His verdict on the "automatic writing" that is photography was the *abnihilization of the etym*. He saw the photo as at least a rival, and perhaps a usurper, of the word, whether written or spoken. But if *etym* (etymology) means the heart and core and moist substance of those beings that we grasp in words, then Joyce may well have meant that the photo was a creation from nothing (*ab nihil*), or even a reduction of creation to a photographic negative. (262)

Regarding telegraph and radio:

> Telegraph and radio neutralized nationalism but evoked archaic tribal ghosts of the most vigorous brand. This is exactly the meeting of eye and ear, of explosion and implosion, or as Joyce puts it in the *Wake*, "In that european end meets Ind." The opening of the European ear brought to an end the open society and reintroduced the Indic world of tribal man to West End woman. Joyce puts these matters not so much in cryptic, as in dramatic and mimetic, form. The reader has only to take any of his phrases such as this one, and mime it until it yields the intelligible. Not a long or tedious process, if approached in the spirit of artistic playfulness that guarantees "lots of fun at Finnegan's wake." (404)

Sandwiched neatly halfway between the sole mention of Joyce at the end of McLuhan's Nashe thesis (1943) and the compass rose of Joycean quotations in *Understanding Media* (1964) came McLuhan's 1953 article (reprinted in McNamara 1969) "James Joyce: Trivial and Quadrivial." The title refers to Joyce's use of a pun to reply to a critic of his puns! He conceded that some of them were trivial and some quadrivial. McLuhan explains that Joyce "means literally that his puns are crossroads of meaning in his communication network, and that his techniques for managing the flow of messages in his network were taken from the traditional disciplines of grammar, logic, rhetoric [making up the trivium], on the one hand, and of arithmetic, geometry, music, and astronomy [the quadrivium], on the other."[34]

McLuhan quickly moves from his metaphor of the crossroads of meaning for the Joycean pun in question to a historically grounded explanation for why Joyce's vision and method compels him to linger constantly at those crossroads. At the same time, McLuhan's explanation reveals his own emerging interest in the intersection of culture and technology, his conception of language as mankind's first technology, and the all-encompassing concept articulated at the end of his career, that of all media as sharing the four-part structure of metaphor:

> At the time when Joyce was studying the trivium with the Jesuits there had occurred in the European world a rebirth of interest in the traditional arts of communication. Indirectly, this had come about through the reconstruction of past cultures, as carried on my nineteenth-century archeology and anthropology. For these new studies had directed *attention to the role of language and writing in the formation of societies* and the transmission of culture. And the total or gestalt approach natural in the study of primitive cultures had favored the *study of language as part of the entire cultural network. Language was seen as inseparable from the toolmaking* and economic life of the peoples. It was not studied in abstraction from the practical concerns of society. (emphasis added)[35]

McLuhan sees the result of the work in anthropology and psychology as a revitalization of the classical trivium and a rebalancing of its three components, grammar, logic, and rhetoric, after a long period of neglect and the dominance of logic alone. An integrated trivium had been the norm among ancients such as Cratylus, Varro, and Philo Judaeus. It was a tradition passed down to the Fathers of the early Christian church but lost during centuries of conflict among grammarians, logicians, and rhetoricians (see later in this chapter for details).

Not only had the trivial arts been practiced in equilibrium by the Fathers, they had been integrated with the quadrivial arts: "In the milieu of St. Augustine it was natural to consider metrics in relation to numbers and arithmetic, for the entire order of the cosmos was supposed to be based on numbers, just as all earthly music was but an approximation to the music of the spheres. Music was, esthetically speaking, the meeting place of poetics and mathematics, of *grammatica* and astronomy."[36]

It was natural too for Joyce to transpose this ancient vision of the link between terrestrial and celestial harmony *and* its ideal expression through the linking of the trivium and quadrivium. McLuhan demonstrates how the recurring musical motif of the ellipse between empty fifths and the octave in *Ulysses* reflects this double linking of theme and rheme, concluding with a quotation from one of the Joycean passages where it occurs: "The longest way round is the shortest way home."[37]

Though the quotation is from *Ulysses*, it is an apt summary of the whole of *Finnegans Wake* (where Joyce's principles of composition are no less a marriage of the trivial and the quadrivial than in his earlier work), with its *commodius vicus* linking the last line of the book directly to its opening words. The paradoxical symbiosis of interval or gap and direct link first came to McLuhan's attention as a stylistic device in the background studies for his dissertation and resurfaced prominently in the final expression of his laws of media.

The quadrivial art of astronomy surfaces in *Ulysses*, providing, in this instance, an example of how Joyce was comfortable both with emulating the erudition of the ancients, as he did for the music-arithmetic link, and creating what at first appears to be an improbable link between his hero (Leopold Bloom) and a bar of lemon soap. It is the soap itself that articulates the link:

> We're a capital couple are Bloom and I;
> He brightens the earth, I polish the sky.

McLuhan notes: "At another level the soap is a sign of grace uniting earthly and stellar, hermetic and astrologic, East and West labyrinths. These two levels of reality, which are in conflict all during Bloomsday, are thus reconciled among the stars."[38]

McLuhan emphasizes that Joyce portrays Bloom as the perfect rhetorician and a representative of Homer's ideal of the man of many rhetorical devices. There is, thus, a link between Joyce himself and Bloom, as a man of encyclopedic knowledge whose learning precedes his eloquence and fashions it—the link between grammar and rhetoric to which McLuhan was so attuned. Stephen, on the other hand, being an artist, is exempt from respecting any principles of decorum that would put him in the mold of the ideal man. Such observations underline the complexity and complementarity of Bloom and Stephen on the one hand, Joyce and Stephen on the other. Perhaps more importantly, they underscore Joyce's belief that, unlike the orator, the true artist cannot speak with his own voice, cannot develop a style of his own, but must allow the multiple facets of reality to speak for themselves, to be *utteringly pure*. This was already implicit in the closing lines of *A Portrait of the Artist as a Young Man*. There Stephen goes "to encounter for the millionth time the reality of experience," not to finally capture it and put his own stamp upon the expression of it, but to "forge in the smithy of my soul the uncreated conscience of my race." In place of his subjective expression *per se*, the artist offers a retracing of any moment of cognition as the unique artistic form of that moment.

McLuhan's comments on this aspect of Joyce's vision, linking it subtly to the French Symbolist poets and explicitly to Thomist philosophy:

> [Joyce] seems to have been the first to see that the dance of being, the nature imitated by the arts, has its primary analogue in the activity of the exterior and interior senses. Joyce was aware that this doctrine (that sensation is imitation because the exterior forms are already in a new matter) is implicit in Aquinas.[39]

McLuhan goes so far as to declare that Joyce constructed virtually every line that he wrote on "the dual labyrinths of stone and water."[40] This observation is, once again, intimately linked to McLuhan's emergent overview of fundamentals of media operation and the way that they are illuminated by Joyce.

"Since, moreover, the letters of the alphabet are easily polarized in the same way, it is a matter of main consequence to recognize their hermetic signature in order to get around in the *Wake*."[41] The polarization in question subtly shifts the *allforabit* pun into one of all for two bits and then even more subtly deconstructs it with the notion of hermetic signatures that recall Joyce's rhetorical question: "For why sign anything, when every word, letter, pen stroke, paper, space, is a perfect signature of its own!" Perfect signatures linked to a short inventory of media that range from the semiotic reduction of the alphabet through the support media of ink and paper to the signifying absence of empty space.

Far from being limited to a presence obscured by the signs that are the letters of the phonetic alphabet, the element of stone is in plain view in *Ulysses*. McLuhan is alert to how Joyce configures it as a symbol of the medium that shaped and dominated centuries of literate culture: Gutenberg's press:

> The [Aeolus] episode opens with the evocation of the stone-steel labyrinth of the Dublin tramway system and then shifts to the analogous network of movable type and the world of spatial communication controlled by the press.[42]

McLuhan typically underlines simultaneous similarity and contrast between *Ulysses* and *Finnegans Wake*:

> The doctrine of decorum, the foundation of classical rhetoric, is a profoundly analogical doctrine, so that to discuss it is as it operates in Joyce is to be at the center of his communication network. In *Ulysses* each character is discriminated by his speech and gestures, and the whole work stands midway between narrative and drama. But the *Wake* is primarily dramatic and the techniques proper to this form are taken from the fourth part of rhetoric, *pronuntiatio*, or action and delivery. This division of rhetoric was a crux of communication theory in former times, being the crossroads of rhetoric, psychology, and other disciplines.[43]

With respect to his principal theme of delineating the interaction of the trivium and the quadrivium in Joyce, McLuhan stresses that it is grounded in the grammatical division of the trivium and, in particular, in philology. For his definition of philology, McLuhan looks not to linguistics but to T. S. Eliot, from whose writings he quotes the definition of words "as a network of tentacular roots linking all human culture, and 'reaching down into the deepest terrors and desires . . .'"[44] Against the background of such a definition, words are not the representatives of things but the things themselves. This explains, for McLuhan, why Joyce can choose to use the conventional meanings of words or disregard them at will, because he is concerned above all with concentrating on "the submerged metaphysical drama which these meanings often tend to overlay."[45]

If the interaction of the trivial and the quadrivial privileges the former because of the importance of grammar, the key, as ever, is equilibrium, as the original Joycean quip on the subject emphasized. And in spite of McLuhan's own predilection for privileging the interaction of grammar and rhetoric, he gives full due to the role of dialectics in Joyce, noting, for example, that dialectic, the third member of the trivium, appears as "technic" in the ninth episode [of *Ulysses*]. At the same time, he stresses that dialectics shuns the way of these nets of analogies that were so crucial for Joyce.

Thus, dialectics is presented in terms of strife in *Ulysses*, Joyce's book of the day. In his book of the night, *Finnegans Wake*, full integration of the trivial and the quadrivial is achieved, as they must for Joyce, for whom they are the "keys to dreamland."[46] (47)

FROM *THE GOLDEN BOUGH* TO THE HOLLYWOOD BOWL

Hollywood too provides the keys to dreamland, as McLuhan noted in a publication of 1947, reviewing both Northrop Frye's *Fearful Symmetry: A Study of William Blake* and Parker Tyler's *Magic and Myth of the Movies*. McLuhan singles out a passage from Tyler for quotation: "The rudimentary camera trick, for instance, that of appearing and disappearing persons, which occurs in the wink of an eye, is a visualization of the correspondence between matter and spirit that was a cardinal tenet in the beliefs of primordial savages."[47]

In making this observation, Tyler is ostensibly on McLuhan's turf, offering an explanation *of* analogy (the correspondence between matter and spirit) grounded *in* the analogy between a modern technological trick and an ancient belief, but this does not satisfy McLuhan. He comments on the quotation, concluding "This sets *The Golden Bough* in the Hollywood Bowl."[48]

The reference to *The Golden Bough*, the master work of social anthropologist and folklorist Sir James Frazer, is deceptively casual and risks dismissal as little more than a modest rhetorical flourish linking *bough* to *bowl* to underscore the review's improbable juxtaposition of Blake and Hollywood. But, in the best tradition of the trivium, McLuhan never uncoupled the exploratory power of rhetorical form from the explanatory function of grammar, and a glance back at the title he chose for his review, "Inside Blake and Hollywood," shows us that the alliteration of *bough/bowl* is an alert both to the deficiencies that McLuhan will detect in Tyler and to the symbiosis of inside/outside that runs as a theme throughout the review, grounding McLuhan's criticism of Frye, linking Tyler's work to Frye's, and opening on the perennial McLuhan theme of the *interior landscape*.

The Frye/Tyler review, published originally in *Sewanee Review* 55, October 1947, pages 710–715, makes use of some of the broad-ranging material that McLuhan gathered in preparation for writing his Ph.D. thesis on Thomas Nashe. So, for example, his references to the medieval notion of the *translatio studii*, the continuity in transmission of culture from Greece to Rome, from Rome to Britain, and from Britain to the court of Charlemagne, sit Janus-like between the critical-historical-literary perspective of the work on Nashe and its distilled elements in the cultural-technological framework that overarched thirty ensuing years of reflection and writing from McLuhan. Such references as "the awareness of the mythopoeic activity in history and art"[49] become less explicit in McLuhan's later writings, though they do not cease to be part of his own perspective or to be integrated in modified form in his analytical procedures and the implicit program of educational reform he will perpetually advocate. His idea of pairing Blake and Hollywood, high literature and popular culture, before they had separated, came before the *audiences* had separated. His opening sentences signal the inseparability of his concerns: "[The books under review] serve to remind us that one of the principal intellectual developments of the past century or so has been the supplanting of linear perspective by a multi-locational mode of perception."[50]

McLuhan's manifold teachings around this topic unified his entire career. Here the young professor displays his command of a remarkable range of studies. Particularly noteworthy, in his opening paragraph, as a formative influence on McLuhan, is the reference to the magisterial work of his colleague Etienne Gilson, *The Unity of Philosophical Experience*. The unity cited in Gilson's title, and developed by him as a tool of intellectual analysis, is assimilated by McLuhan beyond the confines of philosophical writings to those of Freud in psychology and to the accomplishments of the cubists in the domain of visual arts. As was also the case for James Joyce, all these thinkers and artists advance what McLuhan refers to alternately as a *multi-locational mode of perception* or *circulating point of view*. Similarly, Blake took the view that "history as linear time is the great apocrypha or mystery which has to be rejected" since "the whole of human life is seen and understood as a single mental form."[51]

These observations lead McLuhan to trace and explain the development of what he dubs the obsessive metaphor of linear perspective in Western civilization, justifying what might appear to be a digression from the principal topic of Blake precisely by the pairing of Frye's study with Tyler's study and the reminder that the metaphor in question warrants attention "especially since we are now deep in the process of extricating ourselves from it."[52]

And yet the turning point in this extrication is coming more than two hundred years after Giambattista Vico sought to loosen the hold of the metaphor of simple linear perspective by offering what McLuhan calls "a complex genetic metaphor that becomes the intellectual means of being simultaneously presenting all periods of the past and all mental climates of the modern world as well."[53]

McLuhan clearly admires Blake for his vision, as cited by Frye, of "the machine as the symbol of a new kind of human existence developing in his own time. His poetry is an imaginative mechanism designed to fight the machine age . . ."[54]

But McLuhan's admiration for Blake is not unqualified: "Unlike Vico and Joyce, but like Freud, Blake mistook a psychology for metaphysics and theology."[55] And though he compliments Frye ("[R]eading Professor Frye is a more satisfactory thing for most of Blake than reading Blake himself . . .")[56] it is not without suggesting a corrective: "Professor Frye's *inside* view of Blake . . . is perhaps in need of some further development from the *outside*."[57] Such a development would entail situating Blake within an unbroken tradition of allegory stretching back to the ancients such as Philo of Alexander and forward to the Cambridge Platonists.

Just as Frye takes his readers inside Blake, Tyler takes his audience "inside Hollywood with its mushrooming symbolism."[58] McLuhan gives Tyler his full due for giving serious attention to a form of culture that is dismissed as low art and demonstrating that its psychological complexity rivals that of so-called high art. But Tyler gets full marks from McLuhan only for providing a preliminary to opening up a plenary critique. And like Frye, Tyler comes in for criticism: "[H]is tools of analysis do not carry him to the point where he can isolate the *cliché* and timidity as rooted in the death of all intellectual impulse. This in turn is related to Mr. Tyler's lack of expressed awareness of the perennial uses and necessity of art in maintaining social viability."[59]

Cliché is product—fixed, frozen, immutable for ever. Tyler's shortcoming is in failing to identify the process behind the product, failing to utilize the multi-locational mode of perception or circulating point of view, as defined earlier by McLuhan. Moreover, just as Frye's undeniable achievement of taking readers inside Blake stopped short of developing the complementary "outside" view to which McLuhan refers above, Tyler virtually weds his strength to his weakness: "Mr. Tyler's great merit is that he explores the multiple modes of the movie night-dream as it is his limitation seldom if ever to emerge from that dream."[60]

Emerging from the dream of *Finnegans Wake* is what Joyce invites his readers to do. (He is mentioned prominently even in the review under discussion, along with T. S. Eliot, as McLuhan continues to develop his theme of inside/outside.) The keys that Joyce offers could not be more unlike the keys to dreamland that Hollywood offers, keys that unlock a door opening on a store room full of *clichés*. Joyce's keys take us outside, liberate us from the interior landscape of daily nightmares.

THOMAS NASHE

McLuhan was always concerned with the big picture. In *The Classical Trivium: The Place of Thomas Nashe in the Learning of His Time*, predating by twenty years the analysis of media that put McLuhan on the world stage, he is a literary historian, an intellectual historian surveying classical culture, a reader of Thomas Nashe, applying all that he had learned from I. A. Richards about literary criticism, a teacher with a program for the education of future generations. And he is a gardener tending hybrid seeds of stock with ancient philosophical roots—seeds that would germinate in his media analysis of the 1960s and 1970s.

When McLuhan's reflections returned to Nashe during that later period, he recorded voluminous notes, many explicitly linking what he had written about Nashe to his more recent work. So, for example, he outlines correspondences between his laws of media, Aristotle's typology of causes, and the divisions of classical rhetoric. He speaks of "multimedia exegesis of both Scripture and the Book of Nature." *Multimedia exegesis* offers a convenient working definition of both the dynamics and the purpose of the trivium in fully integrated form, as found in classical antiquity, and as revealed in McLuhan's study of Thomas Nashe.

Nashe had scarcely come to McLuhan's attention as he searched out a topic for his doctoral dissertation at Cambridge University. His impulse to range as broadly as possible over as much as possible of what he had learned of English literature at Cambridge drew him at first to Raymond Wilson Chambers's *On the Continuity of English Prose* (1932), and he planned to expand Chambers's coverage beyond Thomas More to the end of the sixteenth century. This would bring Thomas Stapleton, Cardinal William Allen, Robert Parsons, Edmund Campion, and others within the scope of the survey that Chambers had made. McLuhan was stimulated and challenged by the prospect of examining a vast array of literature from a variety of authors—theologians, preachers, pamphleteers, historians, romancers, annalists, including Thomas Nashe.

Chambers had provided an inspiration and a model by the breadth of his survey, but McLuhan quickly grew dissatisfied with what he perceived as convenient assumptions grounding the thesis and the title of the work. Chambers appeared to be dismissing the rich variety in the prose writers of the sixteenth century as nothing more than an anomaly in relation to a longer tradition in English literature. Once McLuhan had narrowed the scope of his projected dissertation to a study of Thomas Nashe, he discovered the origins and the relevance of multiple traditions to a full understanding of Nashe's writings that had escaped Chambers. Ezra Pound had already published *How to Read*, Mortimer Adler would soon publish *How to Read a Book*, and I. A. Richards was about to trump Adler's approach with his *How to Read a Page*. By then, McLuhan, with his dissertation at an advanced stage, had a trump card of his own and must have been tempted to subtitle his work *How to Read Thomas Nashe*.

During the nineteenth century, scholars of Elizabethan literature had marginalized Nashe, viewing him merely as useful for documenting and illustrating editions of stage plays and historical research. By the time McLuhan delved into Nashe, the prevailing view of him had reduced his status to that of the journalist *par excellence* of his day and little, if anything, more. McLuhan realized that this view was at odds with the richness and the subtleties of Nashe's style. The majority of commentators had seen Nashe in a trivial light; McLuhan would see him in light of the classical trivium.

In the sparkling brilliance of such works as *The Anatomie of Absurditie* and *Pierce Penilesse*, McLuhan suspected, there was more than a dash of studied casualness. His suspicion was confirmed when he read Morris Croll's work on Nashe's contemporary John Lyly, and this led him to an investigation of patristic and medieval writers as sources for models of rhetoric that compelled a profound revision in how Chambers had viewed the continuity of English prose. At the same time, the evidence that the critical reception of Nashe had shortch-anged him continued to mount, as McLuhan turned to the standard edition of Nashe's work by Ronald McKerrow. There he discovered McKerrow's impatience with Nashe's verbal pyrotechnics and an unwillingness to set them in any larger context. McLuhan tackled a systematic study of the theory and practice of rhetoric in Nashe's time. This became the first of the three-part framework required to give Nashe his due.

McLuhan elaborated a sweeping survey of rhetoric as it was con-ceived and practiced in every form of literature in the sixteenth cen-tury. His investigation ranged over English writers and then extended to teachers and practitioners or rhetoric in Italy, France, Spain, and Germany. The sheer scope of this investigation buttressed the con-clusion that had begun emerging early on, namely that the sixteenth century was an age of rhetoric. In itself, this discovery did nothing to rescue Nashe from obscurity. But McLuhan widened the scope of his inquiry still further, moving beyond the history of the standard rhetorical canon to encompass the modes of education over the cen-turies from Cicero to Nashe. This tactic inevitably illuminated the complementarity of rhetoric, dialectic, and grammar, the three com-ponents of the integrated trivium that had endured complex vicissi-tudes since classical antiquity. It was this perspective for the study of the arts that became the full framework for McLuhan's doctoral dissertation.

So vast was this framework that it threatened to crowd Nashe himself out of the study, as McLuhan quickly realized and candidly admitted. But he believed he had no option, if he was to achieve his goal. The imperative was to develop an analysis in which awareness of the internal dynamics of the trivium would enlighten an educated reader, just as it had guided Nashe in composing his works. The inspired innovation that McLuhan began to elaborate was essentially Practical Criticism, as he had absorbed it at Cambridge, linked to the scholarly spade work of the intellectual historian. This approach held the prospect of rectifying the inadequacies characteristic of the work of Chambers, McKerrow, and others, thus ensuring that Nashe could enjoy the reputation he deserved.

McLuhan set his sights higher still. The programmatic call for whole-sale educational reform that would mark his work for years to come was already set out in essence in his dissertation. It was McLuhan the author of *Understanding Media*, the director of the University of Toronto's Center for Culture and Technology, the calm and detached observer of the social upheavals of the 1960s who declared that the cultural confusion surrounding modernism was favorable to the rebirth of grammatical studies, in the full sense of the art of interpretation that the term had within the classical trivium. He characterized the *grammatica* of the trivium as the pursuit of psychological order in the midst of material and political chaos and equated modern symbolism in art and literature with ancient allegory. At the same time, he conceded that *grammatica* fell short of its mark whenever it neglected to avail itself of support from dialectics and philosophy. Such statements amount to a call for a radical fundamental revision of education based on the noble and broad-ranging ideal of reintegrating the classical trivium.

Grammatica, or grammar, as we will see, is not to be understood simply in the sense of parts of speech, sentence structure, or any other narrow sense typical of prescriptive grammar or modern linguistics. In its widest meaning, and crucially in relation to dialectics and rhetoric, with which grammar constitutes the three dimensions of the classical ideal of learning, it is the art of interpreting not only verbal language but all phenomena. Above all, classical grammar entails a fully articulated science of exegesis, or interpretation. Dialectics is, variously, a way of testing evidence or the study of kinds of proofs for an argument, a method of dialogue, or simply logic. Rhetoric, of course, includes the rhetorical devices such as alliteration that are most commonly associated with it in general usage today, but as set out in McLuhan's comprehensive study of the trivium, it proves to be a very complex feature of discourse, involving five divisions. These are *inventio* (discovery), *dispositio* (arrangement), *memoria* (memory), *elocutio* (style), and *pronuntiatio* (delivery). The structure and function of the classical trivium both presupposed the interpretive component of *grammatica* and predisposed authors to engage in the historical controversies surrounding the dynamics of the trivium. McLuhan systematically treated all this material in *The Place of Thomas Nashe in the Learning of His Time*.

McLuhan constantly emphasizes the interpenetration of the trivial arts, describing the complex evolution of the topic. Dialectics is described in grammatical terms from a rhetorical point of view by the Greek Sophists; dialecticians subordinate grammar and rhetoric to their art; rhetoricians subordinate dialectics to *inventio* and *dispositio*. But harmony marks certain periods: in the treatises on physics by the Stoics, grammar is virtually inseparable from dialectics.

But such cases are exceptions, far more often than they are the norm. Typically, polemics deliberately subvert the integral operation of the trivium. Or misunderstandings split it apart. McLuhan delineates one such instance in which the major European historians of rhetoric after the Renaissance unwittingly impoverished their studies by retaining the bias of that period and neglecting the contributions to rhetoric made during the Middle Ages. McLuhan redresses the balance here by offering evidence that the Ciceronian ideal of the Renaissance did not spontaneously develop out of an impulse to retrieve the great orator's teachings but from a tradition that had continued throughout medieval times. On the evidence he musters for an enduring tradition, McLuhan recasts the inaccurately named quarrel between the ancients and the moderns as the continuation of Cicero's clash with philosophers and the medieval conflict between dialecticians and grammarians.

Even in the earliest pages of the Nashe thesis there emerge themes that McLuhan would continue to evoke throughout his career: "The great alchemists . . . were grammarians. From the time of the neo-Platonists and Augustine to Bonaventure and to Francis Bacon, the world was viewed as a book, the lost language of which was analogous to that of human speech. Thus the art of grammar provided not only the sixteenth-century approach to the Book of Life in scriptural exegesis but to the Book of Nature as well."[61] Here McLuhan articulates for the first time what would become the core idea, more than four decades later, in his posthumously published *Laws of Media.*

Similarly, in developing his revisionist view of intellectual history, McLuhan articulates the observation he will eventually use as a cornerstone in his media analysis: "A consideration of the Ciceronian ideal and tradition . . . has claims to being one of basic importance in the history of western culture, and its comparative neglect must be ascribed to impercipience of the ubiquitous, rather than to mere indifference on the part of scholars."[62] *Impercipience of the ubiquitous.* Here McLuhan's own rhetoric has the ring of his writings from the 1930s, polysyllabic pronouncements that gave way over the years to a style favoring punchy aphorisms; the grammar was retained by the McLuhan of *The Mechanical Bride* and through to *Laws of Media.*

As McLuhan builds his vast backdrop for the sixteenth-century humanism of Nashe, he incorporates a full account of the role of the late medieval church in maintaining the ideals of classical learning: "Grammar and classical culture had been preserved by the Church after the fall of the Empire because grammar was then the indispensable mode of theology. The advent of dialectics was, therefore, sheer gain for theology but almost a total overthrow for grammar."[63] Here too McLuhan is obliged to provide rereadings of the patristic scholars from the perspective of an integrated trivium. Thus, for example, Hugh of St. Victor, if seen as belonging to a tradition of grammar that spans the ages from Plato to Francis Bacon, can be read coherently as an opponent of radical scholasticism.

McLuhan constantly hunts out critical bias and seeks to redress errors that have arisen from distorted perceptions of the legacy of friction and opposition between those who were partisans of grammar or dialectics to the mutual exclusion of the other. "The modern view that allegory is a product of medieval scholasticism is the precise contrary of the facts. The modern distrust of allegory and parable is demonstrably rooted in the prevalence of the mathematical modes of abstraction which becomes general in the seventeenth century but is no less typical of Abelard and the dialecticians. It is the Cartesians who distrust fancy with its metaphors, allegories, and similes. Just as the grammarians distrusted abstraction, so the dialecticians contemned the concrete models of language."[64]

If McLuhan's dissertation is intended to provide a new tool for scholars, it also challenges them to undertake very large tasks. By facilitating the understanding of the full implications of the basic distinction between grammar and dialectics, it opens the way to recasting the histories of European literature from the fifteenth century onward. So, for example, the entire golden age of Spanish literature can be reinterpreted as an expression of patristic rhetoric and exegesis. Such a revision requires looking beyond questions of style to more fundamental issues of method and undertaking an entirely new study in the broad perspective offered by McLuhan.

With his history of the trivium in place, McLuhan gives his full attention to describing Nashe's writings. But the description also serves as a test of the critical apparatus that McLuhan's revisionist history entails. He begins by reviewing sources for Nashe's method and style, an issue opening onto the larger one of his aims as a member of the patristic party in the Anglican Church. Nashe's opponents prove to be the Calvinist partisans within the church, armed with scholastic method in theology and defending the territory staked by Peter Ramus in dialectics and rhetoric. McLuhan quickly establishes correctives for the conventional interpretation of the antagonism between Nashe and Gabriel Harvey: "It is a mistake to suppose that, in opposing Harvey, Nashe appeared reactionary to his contemporaries; for in the sixteenth century Harvey seemed to be tied to the scholastic Ramus, whereas Nashe belonged to the party of the ancients who were defending the cause of the reformed grammatical theology of Erasmus."[65]

McLuhan offers a solution to one conundrum: the link between Nashe and the Parnassus plays proves to be their anti-Ramistic view of the arts. Another so-called puzzle he dismisses: Nashe's disavowal of the pseudo-eloquence that he himself called "bragging blanke verse"[66] is no anomaly when the principal themes of his writing are seen as part of an overarching commitment to the union of poetry, eloquence, and theology. For McLuhan, Nashe is a "fully enlightened protagonist in an ancient quarrel,"[67] namely the battle for supremacy between dialectics and grammar—the central narrative of McLuhan's history of the trivium.

In this battle, as McLuhan makes clear, doctrine was not at issue, rather methods of interpretation in theology and preaching. Some Catholics and some Protestants held patristic views, while others took up scholastic positions. As a consequence, Nashe could align himself with Erasmus, More, and Rabelais, for example, without opening himself to the charge of holding Catholic views. At the same time, and with complete consistency to his patristic position, Nashe could decry the "drifat duncerie"[68] and "dunsticall inkhorn Calvinism"[69] of Harvey as vestiges of medieval scholastic philosophy.

McLuhan returns repeatedly in the final section of his work to the elaborate framework he erected to study Nashe, demonstrating how it clarifies his writings and how, in turn, the writings consolidate the framework: "Nashe's defence of Aristotle is always with reference to Ramus. It never commits Nashe to the monopoly which Aristotle held in some of the late medieval schools . . . The responsible historian should guard himself from repeating the opinion that the 'authority of Aristotle' was absolute at any time in the history of European thought."[70] Even in specific textual commentary, McLuhan's scrutiny of Nashe is rooted in the trivium and its place in intellectual history. And the variety of Nashe's writing styles are also explained in historical terms. So, for example, McLuhan views *The Unfortunate Traveller* as a satire on medieval romances, forming part of Nashe's attack on Duns Scotus and the Calvinists.

It becomes clear that Nashe simultaneously validates McLuhan's history of the trivium and personifies the case for its indivisibility. This conclusion stems not from any argument developed by McLuhan but from the cogency of his close reading of Nashe's texts. McLuhan sensed that Nashe's power as a writer extends beyond simple mastery of a deliberate variety of styles to skill in remolding his array of verbal tools. In this respect, Nashe may have provided at least part of the early inspiration for the aphoristic formulations that the later McLuhan would call his *probes*. At any rate, as McLuhan's dissertation draws to a close, amid illustrations of Nashe's allegory, hyperbole, paradox, metaphors, and dramatic devices, the echo of McLuhan's Cambridge mentor I. A. Richards is strong: "Perhaps more than enough has been said to indicate that the locus of any solution for the problem of the professional and artistic status of Nashe must be sought in the character and purpose of his rhetoric."[71]

The dialogue between art and scholarship which McLuhan considered to be both inevitable and indispensable is clear as he summarizes the prospects he has facilitated for transcending conventional views of Nashe and the literary production of his day: "It required, perhaps, the advent of such a successful devotee of the rhetoric of the second sophistic as James Joyce to prepare the ground for a scholarly understanding of Elizabethan literature."[72] Armed with his doctoral dissertation on Thomas Nashe, McLuhan went on to prepare the ground for a scholarly understanding of James Joyce and much more.

Whether McLuhan's interest in Nashe and the unique approach of studying him in the context of the patristic legacy coincides by chance with McLuhan's then recent conversion to Catholicism must remain a matter of speculation. But it is clear from archival material relating to the dissertation that McLuhan had a massive study of rhetoric underway before Nashe became the focus of his attention. Scores of names for figures of speech, their Latin-derived names carefully cross-referenced with their Greek-derived counterparts, form part of this material. Only a handful of the cumbersome terms eventually found their way into the Nashe dissertation. But a large amount of potential material for a study of Sir Philip Sidney is assembled and arranged in essentially the same format that McLuhan retained when he settled on Nashe.

The references to Sidney in the following pages suggest that a dissertation centered on him would have given little opportunity to go beyond rhetoric to grammar and dialectics. Nashe fairly demanded a three-part study and set a massive intellectual challenge of the type that instinctively appealed to McLuhan. (The authors mentioned in the introductory chapter as being equally suitable as Nashe for McLuhan's purpose are Bacon and Donne, not Sidney.) His focus on the history of the church and its role in education over the centuries, whether incidental or the primary motivation for the final choice of the dissertation topic, was, from the beginning, as central to it as Nashe himself. Archival material indicates that by the time McLuhan drafted his dissertation, he had assembled far more material on all aspects of the patristic heritage than he was able or willing to use.

Among the most important material to be retained and reworked in the text of the dissertation was the mass of reading notes on the writings of Catholic philosopher Etienne Gilson. All of Gilson's books published by the time McLuhan had completed writing his dissertation are carefully annotated in his resource files, and all but *Reason and Revelation* (New York: Scribner's, 1938) are referred to in the dissertation. Gilson and McLuhan would eventually become faculty colleagues for over thirty years at St. Michael's College, University of Toronto. Their mutual respect and admiration did not prevent McLuhan from badgering Gilson in the same way that he might prod a hapless undergraduate student into thinking, nor did it prevent Gilson from becoming exasperated with McLuhan's rhetoric.

The influence of Gilson on McLuhan the doctoral candidate is perhaps most clearly seen in the realm of the Logos, or universal reason, which placed grammar at the center of both Stoic physics and the earliest Christian theology. In discussing the dynamics unifying grammar, dialectics, and rhetoric, McLuhan stresses that while the reception of the doctrine of the Logos into Christianity was regularly noted by scholars, the intermediate stages of that reception through training in the grammatical arts was, for the most part, overlooked. He also stresses the metaphysical character of the Logos, and it is in this respect that Gilson's work influenced him, as he readily acknowledges. The fundamental difference between the grammatical and dialectical schools, for example, begins to emerge in McLuhan's presentation with the help of a key quotation from Gilson on the philosophy of St. Bonaventure.

Gilson observes that the role of things as sign in the order of reve-lation sanctions the same role for them in the order of nature. Once this transfer is in place, it functions by a method distinguishing it radically from dialectics. McLuhan characterizes the contrast: "M. Gilson proceeds to show that these guiding principles of interpre-tation are managed in their application not by the logic of dialectics of Aristotle, which are adapted to the analysis of a world of natures and leave us 'without the means to explore the secrets of a symbolic world such as that of the Augustinian tradition,' but by the reasoning of analogy."[73] Here one can detect a source of both McLuhan's principle of the probe and his preference for the analogical over the logical, as well as a worldview demanding the investigative technique of closure based on relationships—a worldview shared by McLuhan and the ancients of the grammatical school. He freely acknowledges this link in noting that the history of the trivium is essentially a history of the rivalry amid practitioners of grammar, rhetoric, and dialectics, adding that it cannot be written without adopting the viewpoint of one of them. The analogists viewed words and pheno-mena as interrelated by proportions and etymologies—a view retained and reworked by McLuhan long after he wrote his Cambridge dissertation.

McLuhan's brief introductory chapter scarcely requires any com-mentary. The emphasis it lays on modes of education and educational traditions clearly signal the purpose of his work as going beyond an analysis of Nashe's writings. He evokes the integrity of the trivium and pinpoints the period during which it broke down: "In the eight-eenth century there still persisted a significant remnant of those dis-ciplines, sufficient to make Nashe more comprehensible to [Thomas] Warton than to [Nashe's twentieth-century editor, Ronald] McKerrow; but the rapid displacement of the linguistic disciplines by the mathe-matical, and those related to mathematics, has been carried on so much in an atmosphere of controversy that even scholars have come to the point of patronizing sixteenth-century writers and sixteenth-century education."[74] At one point, McLuhan's words apply as much to himself as to his subject: "Nashe has never been considered on his own terms, and today he is praised for reasons which would have baffled and annoyed him."[75]

McLuhan begins his chapter on the trivium up to the time of Saint Augustine by offering a compressed history of intellectual inquiry

from Plato's *Cratylus* to Korzybski's *Science and Sanity*, as it bears
on the grammatical component of the trivium. The survey reinforces
the observations from the introductory chapter regarding the negative effects of the "displacement of the linguistic disciplines by the
mathematical."[76] No less important than the evidence offered in
support of this, a key component in McLuhan's overarching thesis,
is the evidence his argument structure provides for his own method.
Between Plato and Korzybski, McLuhan ranges comfortably *over*
the domains of philosophy, linguistics, and semiotics, as a grammarian, rather than shuttling back and forth *among* them, as among
territories staked out in dialectic mode. What linguist then or now
would set aside the label of *general semantics* that Korzybski himself
attached to his work and simply call it "linguistic study?"[77] But then,
what linguist has ever positioned himself as McLuhan does with the
qualifier "grammar in the old sense?"[78]

When McLuhan points out that until Descartes language was
viewed as the linking among all the intellectual and physical functions of man and of the physical world, he is evoking the empty language of mathematics, the language of pure form, to underscore
the eclipse of grammar *as method*, but without implicitly denying the
grammar of forms. The McLuhan of *Understanding Media* would
later define the spoken word as "the first technology by which man
was able to let go of his environment in order to grasp it in a new
way"[79] and fully explore the grammar of pure forms, the message of
media as media, in a fashion which remains consonant and consistent with McLuhan the expositor of the classical trivium.

Much space is devoted in this chapter to the concept of the Logos.
It is inseparable from the continuum of natural causes and the order
of nature; it is indispensable in understanding the ancient world's
concept of the connection between language and physics; it is universal reason; it is the counterpart in the philosophy of antiquity to the
Trinity of Christian theology; it is simultaneously the life and order
in all things *and* in the human mind. From McLuhan's perspective,
understanding the Logos in all its dimensions provides a corrective
for the misconception, all too popular among scholars, that ancient
grammarians regarded language as a product of nature and onomat-
opoeia as the origin of language. Such a misreading of ancient texts
regularly entails the wholesale dismissal of science in the grammatical mode as a primitive worldview. But metaphysics rescues grammar-
based science from mere animism, and for this reason McLuhan can

say of the Stoics that their doctrines stood to mythology not in a relation of derivation but application. (One could say of the later McLuhan that his observations on media effects did not derive from disciplines as diverse as philosophy and psychology but rather applied them to his purpose.)

As this chapter draws to a close, its orientation and emphasis are decidedly semiotic. St. Augustine is cited in the matter of the vestigial signs in nature and their translation into simple signs and formulae by the liberal arts governed by grammar. St. Bonaventure too is cited on the question of things as signs in the order of nature. The discussion provides McLuhan with a transition to the first of his chapters on dialectics by way of reference to Gilson, who demonstrates how the principles of interpretation are impoverished by the dialectician's denial of the symbolic world, whereas ancient grammarians made that world accessible by reasoning from analogy.

Preliminary working definitions of dialectics as reasoning or probable argumentation come from Aristotle. As the chapter progresses, the full concept of dialectics proves to be substantially more complex than this. McLuhan stresses the inseparability of dialectics from rhetoric with respect to the origins and history of both in the early pages of this exposition and later gives prominence to quotations from Aristotle explicitly characterizing rhetoric as the counterpart of dialectics and as an outgrowth of dialectics. This is so because inventing and discovering all the arguments for or against any position (the *inventio* and *dispositio* of rhetoric) were subordinate not to the discovery of truth but to rhetorical persuasion. To the extent that dialectics functioned as a technique of argument and discourse, it was automatically subsumed under rhetoric—by rhetoricians. But dialecticians rigorously subordinated rhetoric *and grammar* to their art.

These are not simply statements of historical facts about the trivium; they have explanatory value from the standpoint of literary analysis, in particular with respect to the principles of composition to which the writers of antiquity adhered. McLuhan cites the dialectic basis of early rhetoric as explaining the dynamics of the highly patterned form of prose known as gorgianics. The discourse of the Sophists developed certain features such as *commonplaces* (general themes) and *mnemonics* that became standard in dialectics *and* rhetoric throughout the Middle Ages and Renaissance.

McLuhan states plainly that he is writing his history of the trivium from a grammatical point of view, *because* the analysis and interpretation of the doctrines under discussion are a grammatical problem. He points out that with the exception of Aristotle's fragmented account, there is no history of dialectics written from a dialectical point of view. Aristotle and Plato are bracketed as McLuhan continues to demonstrate both the inherent inseparability of the components of the trivium and the inseparability of its history from the rivalry among them: "Plato and Aristotle were the greatest enemies of the rhetoricians, not so much in rejecting rhetoric, as in asserting that as an art it had no power to control dialectics."[80]

Thomas Nashe, waiting in the wings until McLuhan can train his spotlight on him, takes his place in a thumbnail sketch of the great battle at the center of the pageant of the trivium:

DIALECTICS	< >	RHETORIC
MACHIAVELLI	< >	CASTIGLIONE
GABRIEL HARVEY	< >	THOMAS NASHE

There is much rich material touching in varying degrees on perennial topics in philosophy and in particular the philosophy of language: nominalism, word magic ("words condense and translate the most ancient effect of things upon us"[81]), the relation of logic to syntax, formalism, Francis Bacon on keeping knowledge in a state of emergent evolution (a concept that McLuhan himself embraced and privileged through the use of the aphoristic formulations he called *probes*). Relegated to the extensive footnotes are such vital questions as the distinction between figures of language and figures of thought.

As for the massive documentation from which McLuhan quotes so abundantly, a passage from Léon Robin on the fundamental question of defining dialectics is of particular interest: "With reference to a given question, from a 'probable' answer—that is, one approved by an imaginary interlocutor, or by some philosopher, or by common opinion—you deduce the consequences which it entails, and you show that these consequences contradict each other and the initial thesis, and lead to an opposite thesis, no less 'probable' than the first . . ."[82] The passage suggests that the foundational premise of deconstruction can be traced to classical antiquity. As such, it opens an avenue for "translating" the quarrel between Nashe and Harvey into the framework of deconstructive discourse *and,* following McLuhan's lead, making an attempt at a fresh interpretation of the Nashe-Harvey affair as a test-case for deconstruction.

McLuhan deals extensively with the doctrine of the Logos in his chapter on rhetoric in the period culminating with the work of St. Augustine, emphasizing that it is both a spiritual and material phenomenon, noting that adherence to the doctrine entails the ideal of universal erudition, commenting on the translation of Greek *logos* into Latin *ratio atque oratio*. He continues to teach the distinctions and complementarities that hold among the departments of the trivium: "Just as for the adherent of the doctrine of the Logos, grammar is a science, and dialectics a part of philosophy, itself, rather than a mere technique of testing evidence, so rhetoric is a virtue, and one which is almost synonymous with wisdom."[83] Nashe's writings are cited for the first time, and he is given his due as providing an eloquent account of the Ciceronian ideal of encyclopedic wisdom and oratory.

In the opening pages of the chapter dealing with the period from Saint Augustine to Peter Abelard, McLuhan is in historical mode, spanning centuries, and providing the documentation for the correctives his thesis delivers. If we keep in mind the introductory chapter, the account of the origins of the dissertation, and the flaw that McLuhan detected in Chambers's *On the Continuity of English Prose*, the unifying thread of his work is clear as a subtext throughout; here we are explicitly reminded of it at the end of his second paragraph: "to render the continuity of the trivium evident."[84] This objective achieves its own intensified unity in passages succinctly drawing together all three domains of the trivium: "[Fourteenth-century Italy's] schools show an uninterrupted tradition of grammar and rhetoric, untouched by the great dialectical developments of the twelfth and thirteenth centuries."[85]

A footnote, perhaps to be construed as equal parts appeal and promise to readers impatient for the appearance of Nashe, also reemphasizes the unity of McLuhan's subject: "Education continued to be based on the cycle of the liberal arts until the days of Thomas Nashe. Our problem is at once to show this and to explain some of its more important literary consequences."[86] A subsequent note quotes E. C. Thomas (*History of the Schoolmen*) describing antiquity's division between the arts (the trivium) and the sciences (the quadrivium of arithmetic, geometry, music, and astronomy).

A chapter on dialectics for the same period and the corresponding chapters for other periods may suggest that McLuhan overdisciplined himself in conciseness only when dealing with dialectics, but much of the subject is dealt with in chapters on grammar and rhetoric.

The brevity of the presentation should not obscure the emphasis it gives to a variety of important points.

McLuhan pronounces on a principle of historiography in the early pages: "For the historian of culture the matter of significance is not so much to determine the precise content of this teaching [of logic] as to note how it functioned in relation to the disciplines of grammar and rhetoric."[87] The remark comes after a lengthy quotation from one of McLuhan's principal sources, McKeon's "Rhetoric in the Middle Ages" (*Speculum* 17 (1942), 1–12). McKeon studied under Gilson, making his scholarship congenial to McLuhan by its implicit support for his own call for a revisionist approach that unmasks "history as disguised philosophy."[88]

A crucial paradigm shift in the teaching of logic, upsetting the traditional subordination of dialectics to rhetoric, is set out by McLuhan, with full documentation promised for the next chapter on rhetoric. A lengthy footnote provides details on the revival of Old Logic in opposition to New Logic, because "there are the greatest consequences at the literary level."[89] There are consequences not only for the generations of writers following the upheavals in question but for the present generation of students unschooled in the evolving legacy of antiquity: "The basic difficulty in discussing such matters today is that we, inevitably, are attempting to deal with the complex and sophisticated intellectual disciplines provided by the trivium, in the terms of the naïve literary and linguistic culture of our own day."[90]

Important new dimensions of rhetoric are presented, adding to the vast tableau of the trivium that will emerge in all its fullness before it is applied to the work of Thomas Nashe. McLuhan opens his discussion by explaining the notion of *colors of good and evil* and how it is relates to *figures of thought*, mentioned first in the discussion of dialectics in the period from antiquity to Saint Augustine. The latter topic then receives fuller treatment. McLuhan offers convenient working definitions of various terms in the rhetorician's intimidating array of intellectual tools: *effictio* (physical traits), *notatio* (psychological traits)—used in the ancient practice of portraiture—*pathos* (representation of human suffering), *ethos* (characterization), *ethopoiea* (the imitation of other persons' characteristics), etc. Two references to works on *the second sophistic* are given here. The topic assumes its full importance in the closing lines of the dissertation, where McLuhan will link the notion to the work of James Joyce.

The key word *continuity* is to be found repeatedly in conjunction with a reminder of the author's purpose: "to indicate the continuity and wide influence of the rhetorical tradition in medieval and Renaissance times."[91] In support of this objective, McLuhan quotes again from McKeon, on the subject of what McLuhan himself has elsewhere called "the interfusion of the trivium." The passage from McKeon is couched as a warning against formulating a definition of rhetoric that confines it to style, literature, or discourse, to their mutual exclusion, precisely because doing so obscures the history of the subject in the medieval period and contributes to the fragmentation of the trivium. The discussion extends to legal rhetoric and judicial oratory. Just as McLuhan had in an earlier chapter offered the prospect of making a test-case juxtaposition of dialectics and deconstruction, he offers a starting point for juxtaposing rhetorical analysis in a long view of the trivium with rare contemporary treatments of legal language from the perspective of linguistics, such as Lawrence Solan's *The Language of Judges.*

McLuhan refers to a separate monograph he had undertaken on the subject of Francis Bacon's scientific program in relation to grammar, dialectics, and rhetoric, welcoming confirmation of the views he expressed there by way of McKeon's "Rhetoric in the Middle Ages." The holograph version of the monograph in question is an expansion and synthesis drawn from many sections of the Nashe thesis. It was eventually submitted for publication to an editor who made suggestions for reducing the length of the submission from over forty to under twenty pages by omitting the condensed history of the trivium, the detailed comparison between Roger Bacon and St. Bonaventure, and all discussion of Francis Bacon in relation to rhetoric. McLuhan, of course, found these suggestions uncongenial, and the work was never published. As for his projected "sketch of early medieval sermon technique,"[92] mentioned in passing, the compiled material was never brought to publication form.

The final chapter dealing with the period from Augustine to Abelard draws to a close with a discussion of the paradox of grammar and rhetoric in the service of the codifiers of Canon Law producing a renaissance of dialectics in the twelfth century. McLuhan concludes: "This emphasizes once more the complex bonds which join together the rival sisters of the trivium."[93] Given that the laws of media articulated by McLuhan at the end of his career apply to many dimensions of language, it is pertinent to ask if and how the present work suggests the possibility of articulating a tetrad of the trivium.

The opening of the section devoted to the trivium from Abelard to Erasmus follows the pattern of an initial chapter on grammar to be followed by complementary chapters on dialectic and rhetoric. McLuhan begins by identifying a paradox of a different type from that discussed at the end of the preceding chapter. There the paradox is to be explained in part, at least, by the internal dynamics of the trivium; here it is essentially a matter of historical accident. McLuhan's opening comments on the rationale of choosing Abelard as a turning point in the history of the trivium show his skill in simultaneously illustrating grammatical and rhetorical modes operating in combination and using that combination to justify his argument. McLuhan draws on the case Gilson made for Abelard (whose name is most frequently associated with "the early triumphs of dialectics"[94]) as a humanist "in the full Renaissance sense of the term."[95] Following developments from Abelard to Erasmus, therefore, allows McLuhan to reinforce his thesis that the trivium endured intact, even during those periods when obvious ascendancy of one component appeared to eclipse another. As for Erasmus, the grammarian, McLuhan rejects the notion that he viewed the Middle Ages "as given over to the barbarities of the schoolmen."[96] Instead, McLuhan makes the case for both Abelard and Erasmus as committed to "the use of the three arts."[97]

As a cultural historian McLuhan is impartial; as a grammatical historian he expresses his bias. He deems the application of dialectics to the resolution of apparent contradictions of authorities as inevitable, but continues: "It was not inevitable, nor was it fortunate for the history of thought and culture, that the dialecticians should have spurned the aids of grammatical method and that they should have insisted upon an exclusively dialectical method for the solution of every kind of problem, even those of metaphysics."[98] But McLuhan is not impervious to flaws in the fabric of grammatical thought over the centuries: "We shall see that the basic error of the grammarians sponsoring the patristic tradition was to mistake scholasticism for a surrogate for, rather than a fulfillment of, the work of the Fathers."[99] That fulfillment is explicitly summarized as "the complete patristic ideal in which all the liberal arts harmoniously collaborated with eloquence and theology."[100]

It is at this point that McLuhan refers to the organization of his own work as a framework for studying Nashe and the necessity of beginning with an account of a "large party within the late medieval church"[101] to whom the ideals of sixteenth-century humanism can be traced, in order to explain what was self-evident to Nashe but invisible to commentators who have failed to understand him. "More specifically, the work of Nashe and his contemporaries is inexplicable except as a consistent development of the aims and interests of that party—a debt so pervasive that Nashe, Bacon, or Donne would have been puzzled by any demand for explanation."[102]

Given the historical period under review, the interaction of grammar and dialectics is a substantial focus for McLuhan: mnemonic grammars and the influence of dialectics in grammar becoming a speculative study; the role of theology in relation to the rise of dialectics and the decline of grammar, etc.

A remarkable passage in the middle of the long chapter on grammar relates an instance of theological doctrine being a catalyst for optical experiments. McLuhan uses this case to illustrate the place that analogy occupied simultaneously in scriptural exegesis and science. The quotations from St. Bonaventure around which the discussion develops deal with light in both the physical and spiritual sense and relate light to our five senses. As such, the entire passage relates to both the privileged position that the later McLuhan will accord to light as a medium and the relationship he will describe between media ecology and the human sensorium. The passage also anticipates the role that analogy will play in McLuhan's thought and writings throughout his career. A passage McLuhan chooses to quote from McKeon on the subject of Francis Bacon also has anticipatory resonance: "The study of Bacon is chiefly the study of this theory of knowledge and of the details of reform to which knowledge of languages and of the various sciences is to be subjected."[103] It requires only the expansion of *languages* to *languages of the media* for the observation to characterize the media ecology studies of McLuhan twenty years on.

As this rich chapter draws to a close, McLuhan draws attention to how basic facts in the history of culture can be skewed, linking the problem to the revisionist views he is advancing: "When Erasmus is seen to be of this ancient [patristic] party, then it is, for example, easy to see why Swift is not a 'modern,' and Descartes, the child of scholastic culture, is."[104] He implicitly sets a challenge for any investigator wishing and willing to build on the groundwork offered here: "Just why the Renaissance gradually lost interest in the fourfold interpretation of myth and Scripture has never been explained."[105]

As for Nashe, McLuhan simply identifies him here as an upholder of traditional patristic culture, alongside Thomas More, Francis Bacon, and Sir Thomas Browne.

In surveying the trivium from Abelard to Erasmus, McLuhan comments on the interaction of the departments of the trivium, focusing on the virtual inseparability of grammar and dialectics for Abelard. This leads to an important discussion of dialectics as "the province of concepts and authority, but not of equal authorities."[106] Aristotle, for example, would be a dialectician's authority for postulating probable conclusions for an argument, but citing him would be a different matter from citing a text of Scripture, the authority of which was absolute. The latter was, therefore, "the object of dialectical investigation rather than dialectical proof."[107] The whole concept of authority, McLuhan stresses, is radically different for dialectics and for philology. If grammar and dialectics were both put into service by Abelard, it remained for Saint Thomas to reconcile them, as McLuhan points out, drawing heavily on Gilson.

McLuhan provides much useful orientation for the reader by way of concise overviews:

– the grammarian is concerned with connections; the dialectician with divisions;
– the four dialectical functions are hermeneutic, apologetic, polemic, and theological;
– grammarians distrusted abstraction; dialecticians distrusted concrete modes of language.

McLuhan the revisionist is still hard at work here: "[T]he modern view that allegory is a product of medieval Scholasticism is the precise contrary of the facts."[108] And he is still issuing challenges: "[T]he history of Renaissance education . . . is still badly needed."[109]

The closing pages seem to promise the reader that awaiting the completion of the panopticon McLuhan is erecting will be worth the advantage of seeing Nashe fully illuminated: "The celebrated satire of Agrippa on human learning, from which Nashe drew so frequently, is pointless except it be seen against the background of a decadent scholasticism under attack by patristic theologians."[110]

With McLuhan's history of the trivium drawing to a close, the ideal of the broadest possible perspective toward which he has been working is now in sight. It informs his commentary and invites the reader to adopt the same perspective. He explains that even though grammar and rhetoric joined forces "against the barbarous subtleties and vermiculate divisions of the dialecticians,"[111] there was a long-standing dispute between grammar and rhetoric. This is relevant to both literary issues (the opposition between poetry and rhetoric is fictitious and vanishes when full definitions of grammar and rhetoric are kept in view) and theological questions (inexhaustible literal meaning in the patristic view versus multiple meanings cancelled by rhetorical functions in the Calvinist view is a *parti pris* opposition that cannot be reconciled).

It was John of Salisbury who turned the ancient Stoic use of etymology for philosophical and scientific purposes (grammar) toward rhetoric, urging the study of the origins and nature of things to increase understanding of words. This, as McLuhan observes, was a restoration of the "full status of the Ciceronian position,"[112] in which eloquence was a virtue and inseparable from wisdom, but rhetoric declined into empty verbiage once philosophy and rhetoric were separated.

Commentary on authors here is systematically related to the framework of the trivium that has been developed: Playfere's style is ascribed to the dominance of patristic exegesis; Bacon's *Essays or Counsels Civil and Moral* are described as being founded on the colors of good and evil; Hamlet's paralyzing circumspection is considered in relation to the rhetorical concept of civil prudence in the ideal prince; Machiavelli is characterized as consciously anti-Ciceronian.

As for Nashe, his rhetoric is said to be, like Bacon's, inseparable from its moral aim and inseparable from the notion of colors of good and evil.

McLuhan continues to outline the work still to be done by literary scholars willing to apply the appropriate distinctions between grammar and rhetoric. The mention of the impoverished view of rhetoric as "merely stylistic embellishment,"[113] a view that conveniently supports dismissive criticism of Nashe, is McLuhan's lead to the conclusion of his work and the intensive scrutiny it will give to Nashe's writings.

And in a rare annotation to the holograph manuscript of this work in McLuhan's own hand, dating from the period when he was giving full attention to media ecology, he ponders the connection between features of rhetoric and the phenomenon of the flip between figure and ground.

The application of Nashe as a test case for McLuhan's history of the trivium is undertaken by exploring the thesis that the conflict between Nashe and Harvey parallels the clash between the school of Erasmus and the partisans of Scholasticism.

McLuhan broaches a variety of absorbing questions, emboldened by his vision of the interdependent trivial arts, advancing reasons why it is of no consequence if Nashe was not directly familiar with the texts of Rabelais of which his work is so often evocative, why Nashe proceeded with caution (he did not), why Nashe said nothing explicitly about patristic theology (it was unnecessary and dangerous).

Ramist rhetoric ("Ramistic *reductio ad absurdum*"[114]), McLuhan observes, was a great boon to the rationalists, "for, once all figures had been planed away from the text, it could mean anything or nothing."[115] Leaving aside, once again, an intriguing connection with postmodernism, this state of affairs implies that the attacks on Nashe's works by his enemies is of a piece with uninformed readings of Nashe such as McKerrow's. Both ignore the cohesive force of his work, which McLuhan calls an "almost uninterrupted texture of patristic implication."[116] Nashe, for his part, attacked Ramus by name and condemned his separation of words from matter. Nashe was fully conscious of and fully aligned in an ancient dispute, but, as McLuhan notes, that dispute cut across the lines between Roman Catholic and Protestant theology.

As a stylist, Nashe combined high style with low images in the service of satire. In the same service, he invented fantastic etymologies, spoofing the etymological absurdities proposed by dialecticians for whom grammar was speculative rather than empirical. McLuhan mentions these facts here, reserving more complex issues pertaining to rhetoric for his concluding chapter.

McLuhan explains the reason for Nashe's contempt for plain style by reference to the technique deriving from Ramus whereby "[t]he rhetorician simply whittled away all the figures from a text, delivering a simple abstract statement which was as useful in one language as in another."[117] In the typescript version of the dissertation, McLuhan's handwritten annotation summarizes this matter and sharpens the issue with the rhetorical terminology "concept vs. percept," adding a phrase to recall that in the issue at stake, theology is inseparable from language study: "the heresy of paraphrase."

If the rivalry between dialectics and rhetoric was, as noted earlier, so often and so essentially a rivalry with respect to authority, it is relevant to learn from the final chapter devoted to dialectics, with respect to *methodology*, and the full implications of this for a revitalized and integrated trivium, the proportional analogy that McLuhan presents: exemplum: rhetoric::induction:logic.

Nashe's status must be determined in the "character and purpose of his rhetoric,"[118] McLuhan affirms, an observation recalling the foundational principle of the literary criticism he learned from I. A. Richards and others at Cambridge: analysis guided by context and purpose. He offers massive documentation from Nashe's texts, amid which, somewhat obscured, is the demonstration of how Nashe traps Harvey and protects himself, the notion of figures of emotion (added to the previously presented distinction between figures of speech and figures of thought), the criteria for finding method and clarity in Nashe.

Passing reference to the second sophistic movement of Roman literature (circa 0–400 CE), made much earlier in the work, is now made explicit in several passages and assumes a privileged place in the closing lines, where James Joyce is dubbed "a successful devotee of the second sophistic."[119] McLuhan's phrase "fantastic grandness,"[120] used earlier in the chapter to characterize the second sophistic, constitutes a link between Joyce and Nashe. For McLuhan the advent of Joyce is a harbinger of hope that Nashe, and all Elizabethan literature can be revitalized by the recognition that they are most profitably studied in the context of a revitalized trivium.

CHAPTER THREE

FROM MADISON, WISCONSIN TO MADISON AVENUE: *THE MECHANICAL BRIDE* AND HER ELECTRICAL BROOD

A whimsical McLuhan once declared Madison Avenue to be the Archimedes of our time. Travelling in McLuhan's time machine, the venerable scientist arrives in the electronic age and declares "Well, I'll be fulcrummed."[1]

McLuhan felt more than a little fulcrummed himself, when he took up his first teaching position as a professor of English in Madison at the University of Wisconsin, in the same year that he broke into print with his article on Chesterton (see Chapter Two above). He sensed an unsettling gap between himself and his students, though they were not much younger than him. He suspected that some sort of cultural erosion was at work and began to record his reflections on the matter. He concluded that if the function of studying literature was to grip the emotions of readers, the thrill of reading Byron was no match for the thrall of watching Bogart. To this he added a second *if:* the possibility of carrying on the study of literature and philosophy by immunizing young readers against an environment keeping them awash in Bogart and Bergman, Harlow and Hayworth, Lamarr and Leigh . . .

Before long he was pondering a work to be titled "Guide to Chaos." McLuhan intended to construct his book like a vortex, where readers would be compelled to make their own observations and discover a way out of the maelstrom of modern culture by making connections for themselves: "When the interrelatedness of many things is made plain, then the mind is freed from any watchful fretting over any one of them."[2]

In this respect, McLuhan had predecessors, to whom he called attention: eighteenth-century political theorist and philosopher Kenneth Burke, twentieth-century historian and architectural critic Sigfried Giedion, and twentieth-century painter, photographer, and Bauhaus academic Laszlo Moholy-Nagy. All of these thinkers had detected the interrelatedness of apparently disparate objects in a manner which served McLuhan as a model of perceptual acumen.

The "Guide to Chaos" aimed at nothing less than the rescue of rationalism: "In any age which boasts of its extension of reason to everything, is it not strange that reason has so seldom been allowed to explore the assumptions and attitudes of daily life? . . . After studying the exhibits in this book, the man who is concerned about the political chaos of the world will readily see why the most reasonable plans are bound to fail. The gap between political pronouncements on one hand and the jungle of lethal appetites daily aroused and propitiated by current entertainment illustrates why people are not basically convinced by reasonable policies. Reason is not an accepted criterion. Reason imposes limits. And there is nothing limited about Sherlock Holmes or Superman . . . Certainly [exhibits presented] were never intended for rational consumption, since that destroys their value as anodyne, dope, or directive. Rather they are intended by their authors to be absorbed by a sort of osmotic inattention . . . "[3]

Deceptively and deliberately amorphous, full of luminous fragments that appeared and disappeared in various drafts as randomly as electrons and photons, "Guide to Chaos" nevertheless had a carefully wrought four-part structure: 1—Know-How or Daedalus; 2—Sex and Technology or Pasiphae and the Minotaur; 3—Jitterbugs of the Absolute or Dionysus; 4—Sixty million mama boys—or Typhon.[4] McLuhan explained the rationale as follows: "The American immersion in matter is shown at four levels of existence in the USA . . . The four levels go progressively deeper into the effects of mechanism and technology on the total human response to what in the first section appears as a whimsical vagary."[5]

This intricate structure was eliminated from the version of the work eventually published as *The Mechanical Bride*. The loss might have disturbed McLuhan less than the delay in publication, had he been able to foresee either one when he had begun to plan the book. As for its purpose, McLuhan emphasized that his attack on advertising was not intended to galvanize the public into boycotting commerce, "a frivolous expenditure of effort which would only land the reader deeper than ever in the emotional morass of irrational reactions."[6]

His intent was much more radical. "Nothing less, in fact, than fully conscious awareness of the multiple inter-relations of all these things."[7] McLuhan declared that writing the "Guide to Chaos" had been fun, and that he intended readers to share it. He qualified this as "fun through intelligibility,"[8] though he fully expected that reviewers would brand it a "bilious book."[9]

When the reviews of *The Mechanical Bride* appeared, it would be called everything from "brilliant" to "baloney," but not "bilious."

As his ideas crystallized, the titles he had provisionally chosen for sections of the work were considered for the whole: *Typhon in America*, a reference to a hundred-headed monster from Greek mythology, *Sixty Million Mama's Boys*, a reference to what McLuhan saw as the mushy psyche beneath the faux machismo of the North American male. A manuscript of the work, in gestation for fifteen years, came to publication form as *The Mechanical Bride*, the title inspired by the Marcel Duchamp painting, *The Bride Stripped Bare by Her Bachelors, Even*. McLuhan linked *The Mechanical Bride* to the Duchamp work by declaring that his theme was the decimation of sex by fragmentation or mechanization.

Comic strips engage McLuhan's attention in *The Mechanical Bride*, less as examples of what he would later serve as a prime example of a *cool medium* than as a mirror of popular culture. Comics also fit McLuhan's educational program, because their dramatic pictorial form provides clues to the powerful tide of visual-auditory bias of magazines, radio and television that began to wash over the twentieth century and displace literary culture. McLuhan alternately condemns and praises the world of comics (compare the comments on Li'l Abner and Dagwood below), but his purpose is always to create awareness of their bias and the values they perpetuate. He reads Little Orphan Annie as the American success story with a psychological twist: the drive to succeed by both pleasing parents and outdoing them. Annie is an orphan by choice. Her isolation and helplessness are potentially frightening, but offset by her innocence and goodness—to say nothing of the campaign she wages so successfully against incompetence, interference, stupidity, and evil.

In the hybrid of science-fiction and drama portrayed in the adventures of Superman, McLuhan detects the dominant theme of the psychological defeat of technological man. Superman achieves victory through sheer force but remains the alter ego of the ineffectual and downtrodden Clark Kent. In this respect, Superman is nothing more than the wish fulfillment of a man whose personality reveals the true significance of the strip for McLuhan: society's reaction to pressures created by technological advances, the rejection of due process of law, and recourse to violence.

Tarzan too has an alter ego in Lord Greystoke. But unlike the hapless Clark Kent, Greystoke represents a vestige of feudal times. The contrast between the noble savage and the civilized man does not apply to him; an aristocrat, he renounced the trappings of society in favor of life in the jungle. In McLuhan's interpretation, Greystoke combines the ideals of the YMCA, Rudyard Kipling, and the Boy Scouts.

McLuhan is thoroughly irritated by Blondie in the *Mechanical Bride,* because the strip is pure formula and cliché. Dagwood, a frustrated victim trapped in suburban life, gets little respect from his children and none from McLuhan. Readers might find Dagwood's snacking comical, but McLuhan finds it contemptible—a symbol of the abuse that Dagwood endures and the insecurity it engenders. This psychological take on Dagwood is rounded out in terms that revert to the *Mechanical Bride's* emphasis on society's values. McLuhan explains that, unlike the character of Jiggs ("Bringing Up Father"), who belongs to the first generation to realize the American dream, Dagwood is second generation and lacking the competitiveness that assured his father's success. McLuhan's speculation that Dagwood's dilemma would continue playing out in an age alien to it has been borne out: Blondie has endured and entered the twenty-first century.

The dreary and inescapable world of Dagwood is offset for McLuhan by the delightful predicaments in the Dogpatch of Al Capp's Li'l Abner. Satirical, ironic, free of the shallow sentimentality that repelled McLuhan, Capp's strip works toward the same purpose as McLuhan himself—the development of sharpened perceptions. Just as McLuhan approaches his objective by the use of what he called *the mosaic technique* (multiple points of view), Capp makes the Li'l Abner character a mosaic of hero images. For McLuhan, the real hero is Capp, seeking endlessly to expose the delusions and illusions foisted on society by politicians, business, and the media. McLuhan made no predictions for the future of Al Capp's strip, and unlike Blondie, Li'l Abner has not survived, confirming McLuhan's observation that society prefers somnambulism to awareness.

McLuhan had already published a dozen or more major articles on literary themes when he made his first foray into commentary on advertising, in *Horizon*, No. 93–94, October 1947, pp. 132–141. (Reprinted in Bernard Rosenberg and David Manning White, eds., *Mass Culture: The Popular Arts in America*, New York: The Free Press, 1957, pp. 435–442 and in W. Terrence Gordon, ed., *McLuhan Unbound*, Corte Madera, CA: Gingko Press, 2005.) The essay anticipates many of the themes of *The Mechanical Bride*, already in draft form at that time. The writing style in the essay still carries a whiff of Cambridge University wit, a donnish tone, but there are also strong hints of McLuhan's later style, his ability to juxtapose areas of culture, his willingness to plunge into popular culture at a time when this was still unheard of in academic circles. McLuhan takes kitsch seriously here. But perhaps most remarkable is the suggestion on his opening page that the proliferating forms of American advertising could be a healthy thing for the nation's social and political life. The undercurrent of moral indignation that marks *The Mechanical Bride* is absent in this earlier publication, where McLuhan simply catalogues symbols and wit in rich proliferation, behavior patterns in revealing evidence of social transformation. He regards all this as containing an opportunity for an educational program directed toward self-knowledge and self-criticism. It is an outlook that puts him closer to the McLuhan of the 1960s and 1970s than to the father of *The Bride*, makes him unequivocally optimistic in his outlook, as he concludes that America can still fulfill its Utopian promises, because its Jeffersonian tradition and its psychological vigor remain intact. By the time *The Mechanical Bride* reached publication form, its treatment of advertising was marked throughout by a sarcastic tone that is in stark contrast to the McLuhan readers had met in the pages of *Horizon*.

McLuhan moves from his description of the sweet, nonsexual, innocent, clean, and fun-loving gal of a vintage Coca Cola poster to commentary on a quotation from a Coke executive discussing the company's marketing strategy and concludes that there "would seem to be a very small gamble, with the globe itself becoming a coke sucker."[10]

Though the Duchamp painting that inspired the title of *The Mechanical Bride* is not shown in the book, nor even alluded to, it is referenced repeatedly in the reproductions of ads for nylons, beauty preparations, Bayer Aspirin (featuring a drum majorette), and more, including a Four-in-One Proportioned Girdle that anchors McLuhan's comments headed Love-Goddess Assembly Line. As in each section of the book, he opens with questions intended to move the reader toward a conclusion about the message of the ad in question: Did you notice the Model-T bodies of the women in that revived 1930 movie last night? Can the feminine body keep pace with the demands of the textile industry? His own conclusions, to the end of his career, emerged from what such questions might reveal about the interplay of medium and message: Nickelodeon platter all samee as *Digest* yatter? Can you see through his adnoise? You've heard money talking; did you understand the message?

McLuhan is relentless in his attacks, constantly ferreting out the absurdities of the ads he analyzes. *Reader's Digest*, the National Association of Manufacturers, the educational establishment, Quaker State Motor Oil, haberdashers, and candy companies all take their licks. Nobody is safe: John Wayne and Humphrey Bogart are roasted on the same fire as Henry Booth Luce and Mortimer Adler.

In the fiftieth anniversary edition of *The Mechanical Bride* (Gingko Press, 2002), the new introduction by Phillip Meggs notes that "McLuhan searches for semiotics beneath semiotics—levels of meaning beyond the messenger's intent or the recipient's awareness."[11]

This observation, rich and condensed, deserves as much attention and reflection as McLuhan's own aphorisms. Explored fully in the context of intellectual history, it invites readers to evaluate *The Mechanical Bride*, subtitled *The Folklore of Industrial Man,* in relation to the contemporaneous series of publications by Roland Barthes on what he dubbed "mythologies," ranging over automobiles, detergents, movie stars, food, and other subjects. Barthes took the programmatic call for developing semiotics from the founder of structuralism, Ferdinand de Saussure, and applied it to popular culture. McLuhan's study of the same culture heeded no such call, because he came to Saussure first hand only late in his career (refer back to Chapter One above), but Saussurean semiotics can be viewed legitimately as of a piece with the long tradition stemming from the French Symbolists, running through Pound, Eliot, and Joyce, the tradition that McLuhan had absorbed and assimilated before coming to Saussure himself. Meggs's notion of "semiotics beneath semiotics" not only links McLuhan to Barthes through Saussure but resonates with the least known, least studied, and least understood aspect of Saussure's own work—an intensive phase of research on hidden meanings in literary texts. (See Jean Starobinski, *Words Upon Words: The Anagrams of Ferdinand De Saussure*. Translated by Olivia Emmet. New Haven: Yale University Press, 1979.)

If skepticism, irony, whimsy ("Is it a smoke screen or just the fog from a confoosed brain?"—p. 5), and Joyce-like puns (*Ballet Luce* for *Ballet Russe*—p. 9) dominate *The Mechanical Bride*, it is without obscuring illuminations from a gallery of thinkers summoned by McLuhan in support of his thesis. Margaret Mead (50, 145), Alfred North Whitehead (97), Edgar Allan Poe and T. S. Eliot (106), James Joyce (107), Sigfried Giedion (50, 134), and Wyndham Lewis (92, 143) take their place alongside those who take their licks. The latter include Mortimer Adler (43), Emily Post (51), and Dale Carnegie with his "jackal strategy" (78).

A final example from the closing pages of *The Mechanical Bride* serves to show that McLuhan the cultural critic is just as insightful in the role of cultural historian:

> Certainly the West of Buffalo Bill which attracted movie patrons in 1894 was not the same as the one that appeals to suburban kids today. The frontier as presented to the contemporary child is a world full of lessons in citizenship and business enterprise. Roy Rogers portrays a combination of Quaker Oats salesman and Mr. District Attorney. On the other hand, the idea of the West that appealed to the patrons of 1894 and still lives in the imagination of French, German, and English boys is the West not of Gary but James Fenimore Cooper; that is, a world of fantastic adventure and noble savages. It was directly related to the romantic ideals of revolutionary France and the attack on feudal civilization.[12]

McLuhan refers to his subtitle for *The Mechanical Bride: The Folklore of Industrial Man* in the closing pages of the book, inviting readers to find their own answer to the question: Are ads themselves the main form of industrial culture?

But for all its vigor, *The Mechanical Bride* had lost some of its grit in the transition from the draft version of "Guide to Chaos." Much of the earlier manuscript was cut altogether. Despite the retention of the key-phrases *know-how* and *man of distinction* as titles for exhibits in the book, the following passage appears only in the original draft:

Know-how and technology isolate man at work and play just as much as a big city and unemployment do. But this fact is also the basic condition of science. A scientific experiment has to be carefully isolated from normal conditions. And the success formula certainly sets you apart. A man of distinction. Sing Sing or a padded cell couldn't be more effective in this respect. By making each cell (home, hotel, blonde, car) in the world exactly alike, technological man manages to create the illusion of being at home everywhere and with everybody. At the same time he has created a bright and salubrious hell from which, as Sartre noted, there is "No Exit."[13]

The passage repays attention. The comment on the requisite of scientific experimentation encapsulates McLuhan's reason for choosing the analogical and integrating techniques of classical learning over the logical and isolating techniques of modern science. As for the reference to technological man's illusion of being at home everywhere and with everybody, it anticipates much more than McLuhan's later pronouncements on the global village and the retribalization of Western culture. Twenty years after the original publication of *The Mechanical Bride*, McLuhan would grow even more concerned and speak more forcefully of electronic technology turning that illusion into the reality of discarnate mankind, at home nowhere and sustained by no illusion.

McLuhan collected and carefully filed dozens of reviews of *The Mechanical Bride*. According to one, he had buried a good idea amid much rubbish. Another observed that McLuhan had used the huckster techniques he condemned in the admen. But other reviewers dubbed these same techniques full-blooded thumps and pronounced the work a significant social document. The *New York Times* found the book full of righteous anger, nearly as solemn as Nazi propaganda, and regretted its lack of humor. But the Toronto *Globe and Mail* was prepared to nominate *The Mechanical Bride* for the Stephen Leacock prize for humor. The *New York Herald Tribune* objected to McLuhan's excessive use of bold metaphors and found them smart alecky. The reviewer for *The New Republic* recoiled from McLuhan's puns, finding them altogether bloodcurdling, while *Advertising and Selling*, the organ of the vested interests whose machinations McLuhan had unveiled, greeted the whole production as something of an Arabian

Nights entertainment opening on a new world of popular culture and mythology. Walter Ong, who would later become McLuhan's student, produced the only review to offer a detailed analysis of the book, and, as far as McLuhan was concerned, it was the only review to make any sense. As we will see in the next chapter, McLuhan became his own critic, nearly a decade after *The Mechanical Bride* was published, more than two decades after he first conceived the project.

If the sustained sarcasm of *The Mechanical Bride* is at odds with earlier and later McLuhan, the book's objectives are not. The origins of words were often instructive clues for McLuhan to their full meaning and application. *Sarcasm* is no exception. Derived from the Greek, meaning *to rip off the flesh*, the term has obviously lost its original force, but its root word is an apt metaphor for McLuhan's practice of tearing off the hide to reveal the hidden, the medium under the message.

CULTURE IS OUR BUSINESS

Compared with *The Mechanical Bride*, *Culture Is Our Business* reveals much more ambivalence on McLuhan's part toward the world of advertising, the perpetrator of somnambulism, and its arsenal of techniques, as amazing as they are insidious. If McLuhan appears to have more admiration than condemnation for these techniques, it is only because he deliberately holds the latter in check. When McLuhan's disapproval of advertising becomes clear, it is disapproval of the end, not the method, which is after all his own: "[Making someone ill, then selling the cure is] the way advertising is done. They start off with the effects then look for the causes. That's how I prophesy. I look around at the effects and say, well, the causes will soon be here."[14]

In *Culture Is Our Business* McLuhan identifies advertising as the cave art of the twentieth century; neither is intended to be examined in detail but to create an effect. There is a further similarity in that cave art and advertising both express corporate aims rather than private thoughts. McLuhan comments on the social and emotional upheavals brought about by twentieth-century technology but continues to withhold judgment: "It would have been self-defeating for me to have said years ago 'the medium is the mess-age': such judgments distract attention from the events and processes that need to be understood."[15]

Culture Is Our Business does for the advertising of the 1960s what *The Mechanical Bride* did for the advertising of the 1940s. The effect of television made this update necessary. The title was a deliberate put-on of the nineteenth-century idea in North America that "business is our culture." With the advent of radio, movies, and television, culture had turned into the biggest business in the world. Only rarely does McLuhan comment on the hundreds of ads reproduced in the book. His preferred method, as in *The Mechanical Bride*, is to put the ads side by side with statements probing their significance, questions to the reader, or quotations and observations from writers as diverse as James Joyce, T. S. Eliot, William Congreve, Alfred North Whitehead, Ashley Montagu, and Karl Polanyi. A bumper crop of McLuhanisms sprouts like figures over the ground of Joyce's puns: "costume is custom," "the end of the muddle crass," "Jung and easily Freudened," "freedom from the press."

Culture Is Our Business pushes the mosaic approach found in virtually all of McLuhan's works to its most playful and thought-provoking extremes. A section entitled "Rear-View Mirror" begins by juxtaposing James Joyce's observation that "pastimes are past times" with a travel ad showing a British beefeater under the caption "On a clear day you can see a long, long time ago." Then the mosaic quickly takes on the quality of intellectual sandpaper: a banana ad headed "this page is dedicated to the proposition that all bananas are not created equal" sits across from a quotation from Pierre Trudeau's *Federalism and the French Canadians* to teach us that the concept of nationhood has been made obsolete by the electronic retribalization of Western culture. At the same time, the cliché "banana republic" is tossed back on the compost heap of language. McLuhan also slips in a word about gaps and interfaces—as much a part of his method as of the new environment he evokes.

McLuhan was less than enchanted with the book when it appeared. "Did I tell you about the McGraw-Hill blooper with *Culture Is Our Business?* It may be a collector's item, since the book appeared before it had been proofread by anybody at McGraw-Hill and before I had seen any galleys or proofs. It is packed with errors and omissions. The jacket was botched, like everything else. It was intended to be a cyclops, that is the image of the hunter in the new world of the information environment."[16] Instead, the book designer had parodied a well-known advertisement for Hathaway shirts showing a man with an eye-patch.

Joe Keogh, McLuhan's former student and assistant, friend, and sometime collaborator, drafted a review and sent it to him.[17] Keogh saw the book as "a sort of *Bride* stripped bare by the x-rays of color tv,"[18] noting that it "reads as if, by a commodius and vicarious recirculation, the excreta of *Finnegans Wake* were finally making a splash in the dry waste land of Madison Avenue."[19]

French philosopher and social critic Jacques Ellul had written to Keogh to say that because of McLuhan all was not lost. Though this was the thrust of Keogh's review, and included his pointed observation that the book was free of moralism, McLuhan was not entirely pleased with the passage that put him at the end of the tradition begun by Eliot and Joyce, or with finding himself compared to George Orwell.[20]

When McLuhan indicated this to Keogh, he replied: "What *you* assume is that the conventional poses in my review represent *me*; I am sure you've never reacted that way to Mr. Eliot. Of course your approach is not 'moral'—but in my little metaphysics, there are two other categories, and 'truth' is only one of them. 'Good(s)' count for a lot, and you've obviously got the goods on twentieth-century culture. If you weren't a Catholic and didn't respect the sacramental system, you couldn't do it. (But you didn't expect me to say that in a review for a secular magazine.)" McLuhan's deep and abiding Catholic faith never showed as more than a tip of an iceberg in his writings, and Keogh was merely respecting his wishes to keep it that way. The review was never published.[21]

Ten years after the appearance of *The Mechanical Bride*, twenty-five years after his first teaching assignment in Madison, Wisconsin, had prompted all the reflections that led him to write the book, out of concern for the humanities in the electronic age, he chose precisely this phrase for an article he contributed to *The Humanities Association Bulletin* (1961). It provides one of the richest commentaries on educational reform to be found anywhere in McLuhan's writings. His programmatic call to action summons the distilled wisdom of management studies visionary Peter Drucker, Bertrand Russell, A. N. Whitehead, Harold Innis, and Teilhard de Chardin, a mix that ensures a balanced new perspective for overhauling the study of the humanities. Central ideas from *Understanding Media* are evident in the text in advanced stages of gestation: the definition of media as outer senses, the subtle assimilation of media of commercial production to language as a medium for the externalization and exchange of the products of thought and experience, the "globally dilated senses" of mankind in the electronic age. And it is here that McLuhan conjures Archimedes experiencing twentieth-century culture shock: "Archimedes had rightly observed; 'Give me a place to stand and I will move the world.' Today, looking at our globally dilated senses, he would comment, 'Well, I'll be fulcrummed. Why I can stand on your ear, on your eye, on your skin and move the world as I wish'."[22]

McLuhan hails Peter Drucker's discovery of the true meaning of liberal education when he entered the field of management consulting, viewing this as an indication of the imminent return of the Ciceronian ideal of the *doctus orator*. It is the supremacy of design in product creation and marketing that explains this revival for McLuhan. Other factors include the provision of advance models of future development through artist's designs and the necessity of coping with the speed of the new technology. McLuhan concludes: "So the artist moves from the Ivory Tower to the Control Tower in modern industry."[23]

McLuhan cites Whitehead with respect to his observations on the nineteenth-century discovery of the technique of discovery, relating this to Bertrand Russell on the twentieth century's achievement of the technique of suspended judgment. McLuhan interprets this as "the discovery of the process of insight itself, the technique of avoiding the automatic closure of involuntary fixing of attitudes that so easily results from any given cultural situation. The technique of open field perception."[24]

The technique in question is McLuhan's own; the technique that served as the organizing principle of *The Mechanical Bride*, the technique he invited educators and students to adopt to parry the effects of new technologies and the environments they create, the technique of the navigator of the maelstrom.

Pursuing Whitehead's observation that the great discovery of the nineteenth century was the discovery of the technique of discovery, McLuhan adds that Whitehead does not explain his point, whereas Edgar Allan Poe does in his "Philosophy of Composition." The explanation hinges on understanding that the "technique of invention is to begin with the *effect* one wishes to achieve and then to go *backwards* to the point from which to begin to produce that effect, and only that effect. In a sense this technique of starting with the effect, before seeking the causes and means of the effect, is the per-fection of the assembly-line method."[25]

The assembly line, in turn, is the legacy of the mechanization of print. McLuhan was already at work on *The Gutenberg Galaxy*, when he offered in the present article his account of how that legacy would be undone by the advent of the electronic age and how such an upheaval could still be countered with help from the reliable quarter from which it had come before in the face of similar disloca-tions: "And assembly-line methods imply complete analysis and total reconstruction *backwards* from the end-product. This power of advance segmental analysis of each phase of a complex operation was bequeathed to us by Gutenberg and his moveable types. It is a technique made obsolete by electrically recorded tapes. The assembly-line yields now to galaxy clusters of simultaneous operations which are made possible by the exact synchronization of the information on tapes. The humanist will observe, however, that no matter what period or technology is in question, the artist has always solved the new problem both for the engineer and for the human community, by his new advanced models for sensibility and awareness."[26]

McLuhan reprises Bertrand Russell's point about the technique of suspended judgment, linking it to the work of his sometime mentor Harold Innis: "Innis' concern in *The Bias of Communication*, and later, is with the technique of the suspended judgment. That means, not the willingness to admit other points of view, but the technique of how not to have a point of view. This is identical with the problem facing physicists in correcting the bias of the instruments of research, and it draws attention to the fact that the historian, the poet, the critic, and the philosopher, now as always, face exactly the same situ-ations as the scientist."[27]

From Teilhard de Chardin's work, McLuhan cites a passage in *The Phenomenon of Man*:

> It has been stated over and over again. Through the discovery yesterday of the railway, the motor car and the airplane, the physi-cal influence of each man, formerly restricted to a few miles, now extends to hundreds of leagues or more. Better still, thanks to the prodigious biological event represented by the discovery of electro-magnetic waves, each individual finds himself henceforth (actively and passively) simultaneously present, over land and sea, in every corner of the earth.[28]

McLuhan permits himself a strong note of optimism in drawing to a close, but it is an optimism that is contingent on educators understanding that the mechanical age has yielded to the electronic age, understanding the full consequences of that transition, and formulating answers to questions that it entails:

> Our existing ideas of educational organization are still of the centre-margin pattern of institutionalized structure that is taken for granted by the baffled administrator as he meditates on the explosion in student population and the explosion in learning. How is this centre-margin pattern to be maintained *and* TV fitted into it? How is the entire community to receive a higher education *and* present standards of instruction to be maintained? The answer is simple and it has been rendered many times by other new structures in the electronic age: decentralize. Create multiple new centres. Abandon centre-margin patterns of the old hierarchy of specialties and functions. Enthrone the living dialogue in centres and between centres, since the entire new technology of our age demands this greatest of all humanist forms of instruction, not as an ideal, but as a daily necessity of action in every area of our communities.[29]

The echoes of Joyce and the classical trivium are strong as McLuhan looks to the future: "The humanities, then, are about to enter their greatest period of cultivation and expression in the electronic age. But they will assume different relations to each other than we have latterly known them to have. In the ancient world and in the medieval period the trivial and quadrivial studies were, in the main, centres without margins. They are returning as such, but where they were seven before, they may soon be seventy."[30]

CHAPTER FOUR

FROM MEDIA AS POLITICAL FORMS TO
UNDERSTANDING MEDIA

EXPLORING . . .

More than ten years before McLuhan came to prominence with the publication of *Understanding Media*, he and a group of colleagues at the University of Toronto were engaged in an interdisciplinary seminar whose work would eventually lead to the formation of the Center for Culture and Technology under McLuhan's direction. Members of the seminar represented disciplines ranging from anthropology to architecture, from psychology to economics. A lively publication titled *Explorations* gave the seminar high-profile exposure. McLuhan's own contributions to this journal reveal the development of his thought in the period between the appearance of *The Mechanical Bride* and *Understanding Media.*

An essay from *Explorations 3* (1954), titled "New Media as Political Forms" complements "Notes on the Media as Art Forms," published earlier in the same year. The resonance between the two titles provides a typical instance of McLuhan privileging integration over differentiation. If establishing a distinction forecloses the prospect of making a synthesizing discovery, McLuhan resists any impulse to favor the distinction. A reader will look for one in vain if s/he approaches the two essays under discussion with the assumption that art and politics are as two different worlds. McLuhan opens his discussion of media as political forms by heralding James Joyce's optophone principle in art as "the key for future literary *and* social education."[1]

McLuhan characterizes the Joycean principle in question, the overriding principle of composition for *Finnegans Wake*, as a technology for turning images into sounds. (This makes the principle a phenomenon comparable to but infinitely more complex than the invention of the phonetic alphabet and at the same time reverses the alphabet's "all-for-a-bit" effect.) As such, it is a medium for helping mankind, retribalized by electronic technology, to adjust to a civilization no longer dominated by the rational, linear, orderly world of print. In making these preliminary observations, McLuhan has not yet moved his discussion explicitly from art form to political form. Before doing so, he documents the transfer of pictorial imagery to the printed page beginning three centuries before Joyce, in order to provide the fullest understanding and appreciation of the latter's optophonic innovation. The survey begins in 1600, when "print was in the ascendant and the old pictorial 'Bibles of the Poor,' painted cloths, dumb shows and popular spectacles were in decline. Today the reverse process obtains."[2]

It is precisely because the reversal occurred and because Joyce's "radar" (McLuhan's analogy for any artist's capacity to detect the effect of technological change before they are widely understood) picked it up that he developed the optophone principle. McLuhan cites William Hazlitt's *Spirit of the Age* and the author's discussion of the relationship between book culture and painting, where a comment on the poet George Crabbe (1754–1832) aligns him with Joyce as a painter in the verbal medium: "He is the very thing itself; he paints in words instead of colours."[3]

Hazlitt, writing a century before Joyce, seems not only to have anticipated the latter's all-for-a-bit thesis about the impoverishing effect of the alphabet on the integrated functioning of our five senses but taken it a step further in impugning literary culture for the decline of visual acuity: "Book-learning, the accumulation of wordy common-places, the gaudy pretensions of poetical fiction, had enfeebled and perverted our eye for nature."[4]

But a subsequent decline of literary culture itself occurred, dealt a double blow by the popular press and then television. To these twin factors McLuhan adds an account of historical happenstance to describe the full consequences in the political terms promised by his title: "The American Government was the first to be founded on public opinion . . . It was the new medium not of the book but the press which shaped the U.S.A. And this creates a political crisis with the passing of the press into the entertainment limbo, and with the rise of TV as a political shaper."[5]

Read more than fifty years after they were written, these words are confirmed by today's realities.

McLuhan concludes that if "politics and the citizen are to survive the new media, we must alter our entire sighting and range-finding apparatus, which is still oriented to the printed page alone."[6]

The printed page in question is the comforting page of the popular press, not the unsettling pages of *Finnegans Wake*. The former lulls us with transparent messages and creates an invisible environment of media effects; Joyce creates a visible environment of media effects intended to jar us awake with apparently opaque messages. (He characterized a typical audience as one "whose idol is common sense, and whose torment is to be confronted with a clear work of art that reflects every obscurity like a mirror.")[7]

Earlier in the same year that McLuhan offered his take on the impact of media on political life, *Explorations Two* (1954) had featured an embryonic version of *Understanding Media* titled "Notes on the Media as Art Forms." Between the appearance of this essay and the publication ten years later of the book, he would say for the first time that the medium is the message. In the essay, the same principle is articulated at the end of the opening paragraph as a corollary to the observation on the widespread inattention to communication as involvement in a shared situation: "[I]t leads to ignoring the *form* of communication as the basic art situation which is more significant than the information or idea 'transmitted.'"[8]

And so the theme announced in the title, the link between medium as message and art forms, is established and opens the way to the manifold illustrations of the link in the text that follows. Even before this valuable paraphrase and expansion of basic McLuhan are introduced, his opening sentence—"The use of the term 'mass media' has been unfortunate"—is an explicit caution against the excessively narrow interpretation of the term to which commentators would fall prey in discussing *Understanding Media*. McLuhan's objective is to head off such interpretation with his blunt dismissal of the content-view of culture as a "gratuitous assumption that communication is a matter of transmission of information, message or idea. This assumption blinds people to the aspect of communication as participation in a common situation. And it leads to ignoring the *form* of communication as the basic art situation which is more significant than the information or idea 'transmitted.'"[9]

As is the case for all of McLuhan's writings, careful and reflective reading of "Notes on the Media as Art Forms" is repaid by insights gleaned from the reworking of themes from other pieces: "Every medium is in some sense a universal, pressing toward maximal realization. But its expressive pressures disturb existing balances and patterns in other media of culture."[10]

Among the condensed riches of this brief essay, it is possible to detect a preliminary formulation of a notion that would ultimately appear as the principle of reversal in McLuhan's posthumously published *Laws of Media*: "The intensely abstract character of the printed page was to be the matrix of the technology of America. But paradoxically, the new technology was to produce a new set of arts and a new architecture which was anything but abstract."[11]

In the course of little more than ten pages, McLuhan's exploratory spirals solve the riddle of why European immigrants readily accept America's inferior style of bread, ranging then over classrooms without walls, Erasmus, Dylan Thomas, Hitler, Goebbels, jazz, bebop, and jive. But the core of the spiral is the notion announced in the title: media as art forms. Technology is assimilated to literary art: "Like the short story or the lyric poem, cinema works best with the single mood, state of mind or metaphor."[12]

Advertising is assimilated to magic: "[V]isual ads are in themselves magical in their habit of transforming ordinary objects and situations."[13]

References to Joyce are even more extensive than in "Media as Political Forms," as in the discussion following the observation: "James Joyce was the first to exploit the multiple revolution of telegraph, press, radio, cinema, and TV."[14]

McLuhan's concluding page anticipates the focus on politics that he would give to the complementary essay, discussed above, and shows why he began developing his key ideas from both essays into book-length treatment in *Understanding Media*: "The existing cultural paralysis engendered by orthodox elite-theories of culture are greatly to their advantage. But we might consider how far we have evaded the direct political control of the media by the expedient of indifference to the impact of the media so long as they can be exploited for public fun and private profit. This may prove to have been a piece of unconscious political wisdom. But so far it has been based on the dubious assumption that 'control the message and you control all.' The actual history of any of the media suggests the reverse."[15]

Seldom does McLuhan weave a finer tapestry than the one to be found in "Myth and Mass Media" (1959), with its warp of media analysis and woof of language and literature. His signature style, a kaleidoscopic offering of themes, is firmly in place:

(1) *formal* causality is explicitly linked to *form* (as postulated and explored in the two complementary essays discussed above) and to McLuhan's best-known dictum: "[T]he formal causes inherent in . . . media operate on the matter of our senses. The effect of media, like their 'message' is really in their form and not in their content;"[16]

(2) media analysis is linked to rhetoric: "The oligarchic reign of these figures [of rhetoric] was swiftly liquidated by printing;"[17]

(3) the development of nationalism under print is described in fuller detail here than in *Understanding Media*;

(4) a one-off application of an illuminating *camera obscura* metaphor is applied to the speed-up effected by print and television media;

(5) an important qualifier mediates medium and message: "[T]he medium itself is the *ultimate* message;"[18]

(6) a new teaching method required by electric hegemony is evoked: "Reading . . . will have to be taught as if it is heraldry or some quaint codification of reality."[19]

All such comments are incidental (in the best sense of the word) to the blueprint McLuhan sets out for the educational equivalent of a unified field theory in physics.

He begins with the observation that "languages old and new would seem to be for participation rather than for contemplation or for reference and classification."[20]

With the tacit imprimatur of specialists in the field, or, at least, apparently without needing to advance his ideas in the face of opposition from their quarter ("My suggestion that we might regard languages on one hand as mass media and on the other hand as macromyths seems obvious to the point of triteness to the structural linguists to whom I have mentioned these approaches"),[21] McLuhan virtually weds his definition of myth to the definition of the word as sign, as formulated by the father of modern linguistics, Ferdinand de Saussure: "As a word uttered is an auditory arrest of mental motion, and the phonetic translation of that sound into visual equivalence is a frozen image of the same, is not a myth a means of static abstraction from live process?"[22]

From this starting point, McLuhan moves toward his conclusion with its clarion call to media ecology via linguistic means.

McLuhan believes that myth is typically defined in too literary a way; consequently, he characterizes it variously as the reduction of a complex process to a single inclusive image, a means of static abstraction from live process, and the means of access to collective postures in the past. The meaning of myth is stretched by McLuhan till it becomes macromyth and synonymous with language in the familiar sense (verbal language) and his new sense (*any* medium or technology). It is this expansive impulse that then allows McLuhan to declare that the medium is the message. "And in the long run, for such media or macromyths as the phonetic alphabet, printing, photography, the movie, telegraph, the telephone, radio, and television, the social action of these forms is also, in the fullest sense, their message or meaning."[23]

It is clear at this point that McLuhan has come a long way from *The Mechanical Bride*, and he candidly speaks of the incapacity of a literary bias for coping with images of the postliterate age: "My book, *The Mechanical Bride: Folklore of Industrial Man*, is a case in point. Turning literary guns on the new iconology of the Madison Avenue world is easy. But I failed at that time to see that we had already passed out of the mechanistic age into the electronic, and that it was this fact that made mechanism both obtrusive and repugnant."[24] McLuhan, it seems, was the first to take advantage of his own redefinition of myth and media.

Though it focuses mainly on the effects of printing, "Printing and Social Change," from *Printing Progress* (1959), pp. 89–112, anticipates themes from McLuhan's *Gutenberg Galaxy* and *Understanding Media*. The observation that "the printed word is an arrested moment of mental activity,"[25] recalling the discussion of myth and mass media from the essay discussed immediately above, brackets a medium and the "pure process" of thought exempt from the typical action of media in pairs, as elaborated in *Understanding Media*. A similar comment reveals the extent to which McLuhan is both analyst and historian of media: "[P]rinting was not an accident but the focal point of a great cluster of technological skills, each of which had a long social history."[26]

References to the Gutenberg era are, of course, frequent and explicit: "For some years now I have been concerned with the Gutenberg era as a period in which the vitality of new forms spread into all phases of life and consciousness."[27]

It is also clear that McLuhan is moving inexorably toward the formulation of his laws of media: "From one point of view the scanning finger of the TV screen is at once the transcending mechanism and a throwback to the world of the scribe. Any history of technology is filled with such unexpected reversals of form resulting from new advances."[28]

In borrowing from linguistics to develop his laws of media, McLuhan also suggests an agenda for linguists: "To detail the effects of phonetic linguistic culture on earlier language structure would be a worthy task."[29]

More central to McLuhan's own program and to the mindset he wishes to engender, in order to launch the educational reform required by the post-Gutenberg era, is a radical commitment to cast off the shackles of *visual* orientation and embrace "the *visionary* quality of scientific discovery."[30]

Among the social changes that McLuhan attributes to the ascendancy of print technology are (1) the power of applied science for social purposes; (2) a sense of individual identity; (3) the displacement of oral culture's complex and precise modes of language in favor of simplified forms—let us recall that McLuhan made this observation decades before text messaging; (4) the idea of words having fixed, alphabetized meanings; (5) awareness of visual perspective; (6) representational and realistic aims in poetry as well as in painting; (7) the displacement of the cyclic and simultaneous stage of the medieval theater by the proscenium arch favoring a perspective comparable to a succession of pages; (8) a preoccupation with the chain of efficient causation; (9) the restoration of the classical project for encyclopedism in both the arts and science; (10) schism and religious anarchy fostered by private reading of Scripture; (11) the transformation of music into new forms, because it gained its independence from poetry; (12) the isolation of a single trait to characterize the personae of literature and drama.

But McLuhan realizes that such changes, for all their pervasiveness, could be swept away as surely as the manuscript culture that they swept away. "The question remains whether our age has entered upon post-literacy via the electronic media and technology in a fashion which questions the entire validity of print and literacy."[31]

Regrettably, some critics of McLuhan took this as an implicit indictment of literary culture rather than a warning about the challenge that literary culture faced, a challenge to which Joyce had risen, a challenge that McLuhan would stress in *Understanding Media*.

. . . THE GALAXY

The Gutenberg Galaxy (1962), designed to look as if the text is struggling to burst the shackles of print, had the tidiest beginning of any McLuhan book. The original manuscript, written in neat longhand, flowed from McLuhan's Waterman in three months of uninterrupted work. When he had completed 399 carefully numbered pages, he stopped; numbers divisible by three being of particular significance and importance to him. Despite the short gestation period for the manuscript, the origins of the book can be traced back more than twenty years, to the period during which McLuhan was teaching at St. Louis University. In addition to compiling material that would find its way into *The Mechanical Bride*, he was discussing ideas about print as a medium and its effect on readers.

The cover of *The Gutenberg Galaxy*, promising by its title to be a science-fiction thriller, carried two huge "G"s. (Fifty years later the book remains in print with the same cover.) The letters are locked in a silent mirror-image echo, hinting at both a static maze and a churning vortex. The latter mocks the maelstrom of the media with a paralyzed, stylized parody of print technology impoverishing human perception by the gift of a bias in the guise of new power. But the interlocking design is also a labyrinth with easy access to its center, a medium within a medium, the lost but recoverable world of acoustic space.

The contract for the book McLuhan signed with the University of Toronto Press referred to it as "The Gutenberg Era," a phrase found in its pages. McLuhan settled on "Gutenberg Galaxy" for the title, not only for its alliterative value but to emphasize that a configuration of events had been spawned by the invention of the printing press. "Galaxy" allowed McLuhan to focus on those events as effects and to evoke his theme of effects as a cluster of environmental changes.

McLuhan cites dozens of writers and thinkers in his opening pages, mentioning Harold Innis only briefly, at first, but soon after paying him full homage with the remark that the entire book can be taken as a footnote of explanation to the economic historian's works. It is also very much a footnote to *Report on Project in Understanding the New*

Media that McLuhan had written as a sabbatical project two years earlier and a prelude to *Understanding Media*, to be published two years later.

Though the mosaic format of *The Gutenberg Galaxy* with its multiple points of view creates an intellectual energy that surges into a hundred different channels, the book focuses on one question: What sort of changes did the media of the printing press and movable type bring about? It meant the end of manuscript culture, to be sure, but the consequences were much more far-reaching than the loss of jobs for scribes and monks. Printing was the mechanization of writing. It promoted nationalism and national languages, because international Latin did not have enough scope to provide markets for the printers. Print also fostered a sense of private identity (by making copies available to individual readers in such large numbers) and imposed a level of standardization in language that had not prevailed until then, thus making "correct" spelling and grammar a measure of literacy.

Print culture intensified the effects of the older technology of writing. Before writing, mankind lived in acoustic space, the space of the spoken word, which is boundless, directionless, horizonless, and charged with emotion. Writing transformed space into something bounded, linear, ordered, structured, and rational. The written page, with its edges, margins, and sharply defined letters in row after row, brought in a new way of thinking about space.

Media effects did not end when Gutenberg's invention transformed writing into print. Whereas print had mechanized writing, four centuries later the telegraph electrified it. But McLuhan teaches that new media do not so much replace each other as complicate each other. It is this interaction that obscures their effects. The technology of mankind in the age of acoustic space, the technology from which writing, print, and telegraph developed, was speech. Transformed into writing, speech lost the quality that made it part of the culture of acoustic space. It acquired a powerful visual bias, producing carryover effects in social and cultural organization that endure to the present. But there was also a loss, in that writing separated speech from the other physical senses. The powerful extension of speech permitted by the development of radio produced a similar loss, for this medium reduced speech to one sense—the auditory-aural. Radio is not speech (because we only listen), but it creates the illusion, like writing, of containing speech.

The all-at-onceness of the stories on a newspaper page contrasts with the one-at-a-timeness of ideas developed in a book. The significance of this contrast for McLuhan is the effect it produced: artists like Joyce and Picasso saw beyond the superficial chaos of the newspaper page to a higher order of harmony. The apparent dislocations that mark the work of these artists are paralleled by the discontinuities that form the basis of quantum physics and relativity theory. In the social sciences, McLuhan detects further parallels in the approaches to history and culture to be found in the writings of Arnold Toynbee and Margaret Mead, where again all-at-onceness replaces one-at-a-timeness.

Such reorganization of perception bewilders those who cling to the comfort of the older, linear order of things and a (single) "practical" point of view. In *The Mechanical Bride* McLuhan had issued a challenge to readers to become as aware of new environments as they are of getting into a bath. Stepping into a newspaper is inevitable; perceiving it as an environment is indispensable to understanding its power and its effect.

The phonetic alphabet is medium par excellence—medium as extension *and* in the basic sense of in-between or go-between. As a result, it has subtle but powerful consequences. What does the alphabet mediate? Meaning and sound. Compare Chinese characters, where there is no representation of sound in the visual symbols, no component parts used in different combinations to show how those combinations are pronounced. Here the symbol is a whole, a unit. It carries its meaning as a whole, not as a sequence of elements. In alphabetic writing, there *is* a sequence, but its parts (letters) *and* the sounds they stand for are meaningless in themselves. Meaning only attaches to complete sequences.

Before the invention of the alphabet, communication among humans involved all the senses simultaneously, speaking being accompanied by gestures and requiring both listening and looking. The immediacy and rich complexity of this type of communication was reduced by the alphabet to an abstract visual code. This is part of McLuhan's teaching on the transition from the culture of acoustic space to that of rational space brought about by the invention of the alphabet. To this he adds two points: (1) the transition involves a shift away from tribal society to a society composed of individuals with private identities and capable of pursuing private goals; (2) the transition is a one-way process. This last point means that, since alphabetization is a reductive process, a nonalphabetic culture cannot assimilate it; it can only be assimilated by it.

Promising *Understanding Media* on its final page, *The Gutenberg Galaxy* was, in the words of McLuhan's sometime mentor and confidant, Harry Skornia, "not really a book in the usual organizational or formal sense. It only looks like a book. And since Marshall has to try to use the print medium, the book, to try to convey and illustrate non-print revelations, he is bound to be trapped into several approximations, exaggerations, and oversimplifications and apparent contradictions. The flashing lights, which GALAXY is, cannot be expected to have the characteristics of a steadily glowing headlight that can be traced back to its source, crossed and recrossed, sampled and analysed."[32]

Skornia understood that McLuhan's objective was to transform the hot medium of print into the cool medium of dialogue. Recalling his encounters with McLuhan as they consulted on the latter's sabbatical project, written for the National Association of Educational Broadcasters, Skornia said: "When I used to preside at meetings at which he spoke, I used to say, there should be a switch on him so I could turn him off, translate and discuss, and then turn him back on after we slow pokes had gotten the point."[33]

He was prepared to take *The Gutenberg Galaxy* and its author on their own terms: "In any criticism or analysis of Marshall, we miss the point if we quibble over whether he means 'the mosaic is THE ONLY way to reveal . . . etc. . . . ' or whether, on reflection, he may not mean that the mosaic analogy is a convenient and useful one. He can't be bothered with details like that."[34]

Other critics were not so magnanimous. Conceding the validity of McLuhan's view of media as shapers of mankind, Arthur Efron charged that his mosaic approach had not achieved its objective of abolishing point of view: "He instead introduces it in his spoken and unspoken assumptions . . ."[35]

Efron buttressed *his* point of view by invoking misconceptions about the Renaissance that McLuhan had outlined twenty years earlier in his dissertation on Thomas Nashe. Efron concluded: "In my mind *The Mechanical Bride* is a great work of cultural illumination, but *The Gutenberg Galaxy* is finally a reversion to a neoclassical or neoscholastic daydream."[36]

Such views did not disturb McLuhan, who wrote to Walter Ong: "My theory is only acceptable to Thomists, for whom consciousness as analogical proportion among the senses from moment to moment, is quite easy to grasp. But print technology actually smashes that analogical awareness in society and the individual . . . A *sensus communis* for external senses is what I'm trying to build."[37]

MCLUHAN AND THE BOOK

"Escape into understanding" was a phrase that McLuhan used in his public lectures and in his correspondence. It is an injunction, the injunction at the center of all his teaching and teasing, an invitation to join him on a voyage of discovery. Applied to McLuhan himself, to his life and his legacy, the phrase also summons the careful reader to escape from the misunderstandings that surrounded and still surround McLuhan's teachings.

A *Saturday Evening Post* advertisement for itself proclaimed that "McLuhan's argument has little application to our own sophisticated media-saturated society."[38] The magazine first misrepresented McLuhan as saying that television is a hot medium, print a cool one, and then took exception to this view as it hit its punch line: "The *Post* invites the active involvement of reading." Here already is a second distortion of McLuhan, for it implies that he discouraged the active involvement of reading. The *Post* ad refers to intellectual involvement, and has nothing to do with pronouncements about how the eye functions as it skims the printed page, pronouncements that came from a man who loved few things more than sitting by a fire with a book.

Though McLuhan likened television to bacteria and poison and prescribed the antidote of reading, journalists could confidently report that he excoriated print. Some commentators were confident enough in their misreadings of McLuhan to publish them amid absurd flourishes: "You tolled the knell a bit early sir. The book isn't dead. You see it as a pile of dry leaves on an otherwise tidy lawn, an organic embarrassment in this transistorized age. Put down your rake, Marshall."[39]

If we look carefully at what McLuhan taught, we find him saying that as new media develop they do not so much replace older ones as complicate them. Today, in an age of on-line encyclopedias and dictionaries and the ubiquitous CD as a vehicle for books, we may take this for granted; in 1964 it was obvious to few but McLuhan, and just as few reported his percepts with much accuracy.

Among the most appalling opinions ever voiced of McLuhan was that he took all his ideas from Norbert Wiener, the American mathematical logician and founder of cybernetics. Even casual inspection of McLuhan's writings makes it apparent that the rich variety of his sources includes fields as diverse as anthropology, economic theory, psychology, philosophy from antiquity to the twentieth century, literary criticism, English and European literatures spanning four centuries. What is less apparent, of course, unless one studies McLuhan's work in detail or delves into research on his formative years, is how those sources of influence came together to shape his thinking. What also becomes apparent is that McLuhan did not always have his head down poring over books; he spent just as much time looking very carefully at everything around him—like Poe's sailor.

What was the received view of McLuhan's stance on literary culture and on the book as technology? Some indication comes from the two preceding quotations. It is remarkable how widely the notion spread that McLuhan was "anti-book." Bumper stickers appeared, emblazoned with McLUHAN READS BOOKS, ostensibly deconstructing his self-contradictory message about media. Urban ecologist Lewis Mumford viewed McLuhan's work as a denigration of the book, and more than one reviewer of *Understanding Media* charged that it was a book against books. McLuhan received a proposal for an article titled "The Doom of the Book" by an author anxious to have his opinion on the inspiration he had drawn from McLuhan, who was already planning to write a book to be called The Future of the Book. No less an intellectual giant than French Catholic philosopher Jacques Maritain managed to read McLuhan as predicting the total disappearance of book culture. In the Soviet Union, McLuhan was despised for the widespread belief that he was anti-Gutenberg.

What *did* McLuhan say about book culture? He must have said something with the potential to make so many readers misconstrue his meaning. At least two passages from *Understanding Media* shed some light on this question:

> The printed book had encouraged artists to reduce all forms of expression as much as possible to the single descriptive and narrative plane of the printed word. The advent of electric media released art from this straitjacket at once, creating the world of Paul Klee, Picasso, Eisenstein, the Marx Brothers, and James Joyce.[40]

Had the Schoolmen with their complex oral culture understood the Gutenberg technology, they could have created a new synthesis of written and oral education, instead of bowing out of the picture and allowing the merely visual page to take over the educational enterprise. The oral Schoolmen did not meet the new visual challenge of print, and the resulting expansion or explosion of Gutenberg technology was in many respects an impoverishment of the culture . . . [41]

Nearly a decade after the appearance of *Understanding Media*, McLuhan co-authored *Take Today* with Barrington Nevitt. Unknown to McLuhan, the version of their collaborative effort that made its way to press contained a phrase that had been smuggled in by Nevitt: *print oriented bastards*. But the McLuhan-is-anti-book cliché was well established before *Take Today* was published and more likely to have arisen from unwarranted inferences relative to the two passages just cited.

Nevertheless, some of McLuhan's readers and reviewers were fully attuned to his thrust. Among them was Sam Neill, whose review of *Take Today* was explicitly intended to relate the book to areas of interest for librarians. In his abstract Neill wrote:

> Marshall McLuhan, who has gained a reputation as an enemy of books because he has called them obsolete . . . is, in fact, a man of the book as much as any librarian.[42]

McLuhan saw the review and wrote to Neill:

> I am very grateful for your review of *Take Today*. The book was begun four years ago at a time when I set aside two months to write a ninety page essay on the subject of the executive. Little did I know what sort of a vortex I was getting into with Nevitt. It was not wasted time by any means, but no matter what I produced, nor how much Nevitt agreed with it, he always managed to put it into a pattern that was his own. The result is an opaque tapestry with some very weird features. That bit about P[rint] O[riented] B[astards], by the way, was sneaked in against my express wishes. The phrase was invented by John Culkin and has never been used by me in conversation. The feeling of animus in it is not characteristic of me.[43]

In interviews and in private correspondence, McLuhan showed himself unequivocally to be a bookman. In reply to Jacques Maritain's fear that McLuhan had predicted book culture would vanish, the latter wrote:

> Each medium is unique in its properties and its effects upon our sensorium. That is why the book, aided by scriptural study, will survive even the electric age.[44]

Well before the age of personal computers, McLuhan realized that the page would survive not only on paper but on the screen. Writing to one of his publishers, he delved into precisely what was at stake in that survival and tied it implicitly to an implicit program of educational reform:

> One way of looking at the future of the book might be as follows: as print ceases to be the ordinary and pervasive environment, the book can be prescribed as a specific therapy for cultures where there is little or no "alpha-thinking" and a great excess of "beta-thinking". That is, to use the language of Owen Barfield in his *Saving the Appearances*, we can approach the book as a cultural therapy, an indispensable ingredient in cultural diet, necessary for the maintenance of civilized values as opposed to tribal values.[45]

It is clear from these comments that McLuhan's call was not for hybridizing book culture and electronic culture or inculcating the values of print culture through the electronic media. This becomes even clearer from an examination of his original evaluation of the teaching effectiveness of various media in relation to each other—the study from which *Understanding Media* grew. It appears as an appendix to *Understanding Media* (2003) and fairly cries to be updated for the electronic media that have proliferated in the nearly half-century since the original appeared.

Because McLuhan's primary interest was never in a technology of itself but in scrutinizing any technology's inevitable impact on society, he spoke not of the disappearance of print culture but the disappearance of the habits it had fostered:

> When the globe becomes a single electronic computer, with all its languages and cultures recorded on a single tribal drum, the fixed

point of view of print culture becomes irrelevant and impossible, *no matter how precious.*[46]

To some of his correspondents, McLuhan stated plainly that he was neither anti-book nor an opponent of the linear thinking that book culture had engendered:

> If I have any normal and natural preferences, they are for the values of the literate world. In so far as print bias renders us helpless and ineffectual in the new electronic age, I am strongly inclined to cultivate the kinds of perception that are relevant to our state. If I had the world's ten best books on a desert island, I should be strongly tempted to spend my time in shipbuilding rather than browsing the printed page.[47]
>
> As a person who has spent his life teaching people how to read and enjoy books, it always seemed to me that by describing in detail the enemies of the book, I was performing the highest possible service in the defense of literacy. Had I mounted a vehement, moralistic campaign against electric technology, I would have involved myself in countless absurdities of misunderstanding. Meantime the matter is relatively simple. I turned in the fire alarm and am charged with arson! In antiquity the messenger who brought bad news was slaughtered on the spot. In my case, I brought the bad news with aches and pain, and am branded as a Utopian.[48]
>
> I take it that you understand that I have never expressed any preferences or values since *The Mechanical Bride.* Value judgments create smog in our culture and distract attention from process. My personal bias is entirely pro-print and all of its effects.[49]

More than a decade after the appearance of *Understanding Media*, a decade during which misunderstandings surrounding McLuhan's teaching persisted among readers and commentators at large, he was asked if the situation was any better in university circles. His reply was emphatic:

> Oh no, no, no. They thought that everything I had to say was an absolute attack on their values. I said that electric technology was going to destroy all of our Western values. They thought,

therefore, that McLuhan believes it is a good thing that we're going to destroy all our Western values, including printing. It is true that electricity is taking over and is retribalizing the human character and getting rid of civilization. I explained that you would automatically liquidate civilization when you had TV and radio because these are tribal acoustic forms.[50]

What was his personal reaction to the situation?

In so far as print bias renders us helpless and ineffectual in the new electronic age, I am strongly inclined to cultivate the kinds of perception that are relevant to our state.[51]

Cultivating that kind of perception depended for McLuhan on situating the book within an overall view of media. This led him at first to the classification of media on the basis of the sense or senses they extend and ultimately to the laws of media formulated on the basis of each law's operation in relation to each of the other laws. Such was the big picture that began to take shape for McLuhan well before *Understanding Media* broke into print, culminating in the posthumously published *Laws of Media*.

In the same year that *Understanding Media* appeared, McLuhan wrote to his old friend Bernie Muller-Thym as follows:

Manuscript is low definition for the visual part of writing and the speech within the code, as it were, is in relatively high definition. So that a manuscript is read aloud and in depth. The same materials put in print have the visual code in high definition and the speech goes into very low definition and print is read silently and on a single plane.[52]

But even four years earlier, amid the discoveries that McLuhan was making in writing up his sabbatical project report for the National Association of Educational Broadcasters, he was edging his way toward the articulation of the interlocking laws of media.

"I wanted to draw your attention to the strange dynamic whereby the overall structure of any medium reverses many of its characteristics depending on whether the sensory input is of high or low definition . . . To high speed change no adjustment is possible. We become spectators only, and must escape into understanding."[53] The echoes of Poe's "A Descent into the Maelstrom" are unmistakable.

As McLuhan's media laws began to emerge, he was at pains to make a distinction between *obsolete* and *obsolescent*. The mistaken notion that he was anti-book likely arose in part at least from failing to make such a distinction—the negative connotations of *obsolete* being inevitable. To the editor of *Life* he wrote:

> Not "obsolete" but "obsolescent" is the term that applies to my analysis of the present status of the printed book. Obsolescence often precedes an extraordinary development in technology. The arrival of electric xerography certainly does not mean the end of the book, but rather a great enlargement of its scope and function. Earlier, photo-engraving and also photography had transformed the world of typography and of book production.[54]

More than a decade later, McLuhan was still tirelessly teaching the distinction between *obsolete* and *obsolescent*. Writing to another editor at that time, he underscored the contrast by way of an old cliché and his own percept:

> [Y]ou may have noticed that "If it works, it's obsolete. (Traditional business adage) Obsolescence is obsolete and innovation too."[55]

This is precisely why obsolescence would figure into the dynamics of the tetrad of *Laws of Media*. The *is* in *obsolescence is obsolete* is not the *isness* of essence but the fizz of effervescence. Obsolescence is not to be equated with extinction, in the McLuhan view. He pointed out repeatedly that photocopying had increased the circulation of print as much as Gutenberg's invention of the printing press had increased the circulation of manuscripts.

As for the impact of television on book culture, McLuhan noted that the new medium was no friend of literacy with one notable exception: it encouraged depth involvement in language as a complex structure, just as Joyce had done in *Finnegans Wake*. In his own writings too, McLuhan sought to give the hot medium of the book the cool dimension of dialogue format, encouraging readers thereby to escape into understanding. Likewise, more than a decade before *Understanding Media*, the preface of *The Mechanical Bride* had encouraged readers to read its chapters in any order they wished. As for *The Gutenberg Galaxy*, as one perceptive reviewer noted:

> *Galaxy* is not really a book in the usual organizational or formal sense. It only looks like a book. And since Marshall has to try to use the print medium, the book, to try to convey and illustrate non-print revelations, he is bound to be trapped into several approximations, exaggerations, and over-simplifications ands apparent contradictions.[56]

McLuhan bridled less at these latter charges than at the enduring misprision of his stance on book culture:

> When I published GG I was entirely mystified about the response which assumed it to be an attack on the printed word.[57]

UNDERSTANDING MEDIA

With a Canadian Governor-General's Award in hand for *The Gutenberg Galaxy* and projects at the Centre for Culture and Technology taking shape to his satisfaction, McLuhan was ready to stir what he called "Vat 69"—all the material he had assembled in preparing his sabbatical project report on media for the National Association of Educational Broadcasters. He had been ready since the day he finished *The Gutenberg Galaxy.* "By all means call [the new] book 'EXTENSIONS OF MAN,'" his colleague Ted Carpenter advised him, "UNDERSTANDING MEDIA title classifies it with all the old and current crap."[58]

The phrase "extensions of man," from Emerson's *Works and Days,* fit McLuhan's definition of technology perfectly, but he settled on *Understanding Media* to echo Cleanth Brooks and Robert Penn Warren's *Understanding Poetry*, retaining Emerson's expression as a subtitle.

McLuhan's collaborator on *Understanding Media* was to have been Harry Skornia, who read the draft and the proofs of *The Gutenberg Galaxy* and wrote the publicity, but their collaboration never progressed beyond a fond wish on the part of both men. To Skornia, McLuhan had spoken of his terror at the disaster civilization faced if mankind could not learn to use new media wisely, adding that this required understanding them in order to control their consequences.

McLuhan transformed his NAEB *Report on Project in Understanding the New Media* into the manuscript of *Understanding Media* by raiding his library. References to scores of authors sprang up throughout the new text, though some of these were eventually obscured by editorial cutting. McLuhan had sent a proposal and a sketchy first draft to McGraw-Hill in New York in June 1961. By the time associate editor Leon Wilson responded with an evaluation, McLuhan had sent him an expanded second draft. With it came a second proposal, for a project titled "Child of the Mechanical Bride," a study of advertising intended to update *The Mechanical Bride*. Wilson thought the *Understanding New Media* manuscript was brilliant but found the writing sloppy, so he gave McLuhan criticisms by the standard editorial guidebook. Changes would be needed "if your message is to be intelligible between covers."[59]

Wilson wrote to McLuhan in October 1962, without understanding or admitting McLuhan's definition of "message" as effect on the reader. The manuscript seemed "at heart a plug for *Finnegans Wake*" to the wary editor.[60]

He acknowledged some pleasure in reading McLuhan's "racy, gaudy, slashing style—when it works."[61]

But apparently that was not often enough, and though McGraw-Hill committed themselves to publishing the work, Wilson was determined not to have any of it. He wrote: "One of your friends and well-wishers . . . warned us . . . that we were probably in for a very difficult editorial task, citing your 'often incomprehensible tidal wave of ideas.' It was his feeling that you could not, even if you want to, make your material 'accessible and persuasive.' Marshall, get to work and prove him wrong!"[62]

McLuhan was incensed. Wilson told him he was overreacting.[63]

McLuhan feared prompting the "moral point of view" criticism that had greeted *The Mechanical Bride* if Wilson forced *Understanding Media* into a conventional mold.[64]

After publicity for the book had begun, Wilson wrote again to say "[We] would be anxious to avoid what you so casually announce as 'rewriting' it."[65]

McLuhan had already rewritten parts of his manuscript many times in anything but casual fashion, keeping at it with a concern for provoking his readers, satisfied only when he could find fresh twists bold enough to make himself exclaim "Ha! this will really get them!"[66]

And not "*they'll* get *this*." Here is Eliot's notion of dislocating language into its meanings, together with the lessons from the symbolist poets, Poe, Joyce, and Pound—the collective credo of early modernism—distilled into essential McLuhan. Apparently it never occurred to him to relent in this approach, even when it became clear that the world was not getting his message. But then how could he, without sacrificing part of the truth he had revealed in saying the medium is the message?

With the departure of Leon Wilson from McGraw-Hill in the summer of 1963, the *Understanding Media* file fell to David Segal. Having read all the correspondence about the work, he told McLuhan his curiosity was "wildly aroused."[67]

McLuhan seemed by now—midsummer—to have formed the misconception that *Understanding Media* was scheduled as a release for the fall of 1963. Segal quickly straightened him out on this matter (indicating that the likely publication date would be the spring of 1964), but he despaired of straightening out the manuscript: "I have rarely read anything that required so many unprepared mental leaps on the part of the reader."[68]

After a month in a state of shock, Segal felt an odd combination of elation and despair; he recognized that McLuhan's prose was crammed with insights, but had taken an accurate measure of the author, grasping at once that it was pointless to rehearse the standard editorial litany of clarity, brevity, unity for McLuhan's benefit. "All of which leads me to think that this is as coherent a book as you are going to write, that any massive effort at editorial assistance would be wasted. Also, I have a funny feeling that this manuscript, as you have written it, is, in a funny way, true to your intentions."[69]

This was the only indication Segal gave of coming close to understanding the purpose of *Understanding Media*, but he had no more of an advantage than future readers for grappling with a book whose theme was not announced till page 436: "It is the theme of this book that not even the most lucid understanding of the peculiar force of a medium can head off the ordinary 'closure' of the senses that causes us to conform to the pattern of experience presented."[70]

McLuhan exhausted Segal, who finally said: "If you are absolutely set on your mosaic style, I will back down entirely."[71]

By comparison with both earlier work, such as *The Gutenberg Galaxy*, and later work, such as *From Cliche to Archetype*, *Understanding Media* would give the appearance of a conventional book, and it was McLuhan who believed he had been obliged to back down on using mosaic style. When questioned on the reason for the stylistic transition between *The Gutenberg Galaxy* and *Understanding Media*, McLuhan replied: "I abandoned the mosaic approach in *Understanding Media* for a very simple reason. The McGraw-Hill editors wouldn't have it. One of their house rules is 'don't quote anybody at all unless you disagree with him.'"[72]

As for "Child of the Mechanical Bride," the project was stillborn, apparently dropped in a mutual conspiracy of silence between McLuhan and McGraw-Hill.

In the third and final draft of *Understanding Media*, submitted in the late fall of 1963, "The Medium is the Message," previously chapter two, became chapter one. However, it no longer opened with "The 'content' of any medium is always another medium," though this idea remained the focus of the chapter. The metaphor of a cloak of invisibility cast over any medium *from within*, that is, by its content, was dropped from the second draft, along with the original statement of media effects: "Yet the effect of any medium is overwhelmingly from the unnoticed medium itself, and the effect is always the greater when its source is ignored."[73]

Where the editors found the manuscript intolerably repetitive, they directed McLuhan to cut the limper versions of the offending passages, such as "The electric light is, perhaps, the only medium that does not 'contain' a message, or what is the same thing, another medium. The medium is the message and the only message of the electric light. Nevertheless, it is a medium that changes time and place and architecture."[74]

McLuhan made revisions principally in the early part of the book, with fewer in part two, tinkering there with chapter headings. "Clocks: Time with an American Accent" became "Clocks: The Scent of Time." "The Credit Card: The Tinkling Symbol" became "Money: The Poor Man's Credit Card" (with the tinkling symbol moving to the telephone chapter). And the long section on advertising, planned originally with illustrations in the style of *The Mechanical Bride*, went ahead in a drastically shortened final form without a single visual (this would form the basis of one reviewer's complaint), becoming "Ads: Keeping Upset with the Joneses."[75]

Where McLuhan discussed the wheel as an obsolete form in the twentieth century, his weary editor, unable or unwilling to follow him in one of his less daring leaps, even though a safety net of logic was clearly visible, wailed in the margin, "Why talk about clocks here?"[76]

Elsewhere, in his second draft, McLuhan had written: "All manner of utensils are a yielding to this bodily pressure [to extend storage, mobility functions, and portability] . . . as in vases, jars, and 'slow matches' (stored fire). The cave or the hole in the ground precedes the house as storage place, because it is not enclosed space but an extension of the body."[77]

The editor protested that "because it is not enclosed space" was a baffling statement. McLuhan scratched it out. The final typescript of *Understanding Media*, much revised and expanded, was shortened when the book went into production. But the chapters on "Hybrid Energy" and "Media as Translators," added by McLuhan to his final draft, were retained.

The book was released in the spring of 1964; by January of 1965 McLuhan had decided to begin work on a second edition. By late summer, perhaps recalling his offer to rewrite *Understanding Media* in C. K.Ogden's 850-word system of Basic English, he was proposing a children's edition to McGraw-Hill. This fresh burst of enthusiasm was inspired by the breakthrough McLuhan had achieved and announced to David Segal less than four months after *Understanding Media* first appeared: "Major insight on 'medium is the message' is this: each new technology, be it house, or wheel, or radio, creates a new human environment."[78]

Even without this insight, *Understanding Media* was on its way to sales of over 100,000 copies.

The richness of the book defies summary. That was the whole idea. Faced with information overload, the mind must resort to pattern recognition to achieve understanding. The ideas in *Understanding Media* are for seizing each time they whirl past. Here is the notion of electric light escaping attention as a medium of communication in the chapter on the medium as message. Here is the explanation for that inattention in the chapter on hybrid energy. Here is a discussion of the work of Hans Selye and Adolphe Jonas introducing McLuhan's notion of closure as equilibrium-seeking, as displacement of perception, as completion of image . . . Here is Narcissus, a regular Halley's comet in *Understanding Media* and McLuhan's

dual-purpose metaphor for the failure to understand media as extensions of the human body and the failure to perceive the message (new
environments) created by media (technology). Here is McLuhan
explaining that the response to the increased power and speed of
bodily extensions creates new extensions. So *that's* what he meant by
mankind becoming the sex organs of the machine world. Here are
Chaplin, Joyce, Chopin, Pavlova, Eliot, and Charles Boyer in the
same paragraph. When the maelstrom subsides, a serviceable raft for
passage to other waters may be constructed by the reader prepared to
lash together the ideas that have surfaced. They are ten.

(1) We think of media mainly as those that bring us the news:
press, radio, and television. McLuhan thought of a medium as an
extension of our bodies or minds: clothing is an extension of skin,
housing is an extension of the body's heat-control mechanism. The
stirrup, the bicycle, and the car extend the human foot. The computer extends our central nervous system. A medium, or a technology,
can be *any* extension of the human being.

(2) Media work in pairs; one medium proves to "contain" another
one. The telegraph, for example, contains the printed word, which
contains writing, which contains speech. In this sense, the contained
medium is the message of the containing one. Because this interaction of media is always obscured, and because its effects are so powerful, any message, in the ordinary sense of "content" or "information,"
is far less important than the medium itself. This is the fundamental
sense of "the medium is the message."

(3) There are exceptions to media working in pairs. McLuhan finds
two. In the example given above, speech is the content of writing,
but one may ask what the content of speech is. His answer is that
speech contains thought. Here the chain of media ends. Thought is
nonverbal and pure process. A second pure process, or message-free
medium, is the electric light. It permits activities that could not be
conducted in the dark, and McLuhan concedes that in this sense the
activities might be thought of as the "content" of the light. But this
simply reinforces his point that a medium changes the form of human
relations and activities.

(4) Media are powerful agents of change in how we experience
the world, how we interact with each other, how we use our physical
senses—the same senses that media extend. They must be studied for
their *effects*, because their interaction obscures those effects and
deprives us of the control required to use media effectively.

(5) McLuhan teaches that new media do not so much replace each other as complicate each other. It is this interaction that obscures their effects. The technology of mankind in the age of acoustic space—the technology from which writing, print, and telegraph developed—was speech. Transformed into writing, speech lost the quality that made it part of the culture of acoustic space. It acquired a powerful visual bias, producing carryover effects in social and cultural organization that endure to the present. But there was also a loss, in that writing separated speech from the other physical senses. The powerful extension of speech permitted by the development of radio produced a similar loss, for this medium reduced speech to one sense—the auditory-aural. Radio is not speech (because we only listen), but it creates the illusion, like writing, of containing speech.

(6) Many commentators thought McLuhan was penetrating in his observations when he published *The Mechanical Bride*; just as many thought he was wrong. When he published *Understanding Media*, some disagreed even with his basic classification of media as hot or cool. It is a classification that hinges on special senses of the words "definition" and "information"—and on our physical senses more than word-senses. McLuhan borrowed the phrase "high definition" from the technical language of television. It means well-defined, sharp, solid, detailed, etc., in reference to anything visual. Letters of the alphabet, numbers, photographs, and maps, for example, are comparatively high definition. Forms and shapes and images that are not so distinct as these are low definition. For these, our eyes scan what is visible and fill in what is missing to "get the full picture," as in the case of sketches, cartoons, etc. Here is a contrast with the examples of high-definition visuals such as maps of the world, where no guesswork is involved in determining where South America ends, no doubt as to whether Spain is connected to Africa.

When McLuhan speaks of the information that a medium transmits he does not refer to facts or knowledge but to how our physical senses respond to the medium. Our examples so far have been only of the visual, but the principle applies to sounds as well. A high-definition medium gives a lot of information and gives the user little to do; a low-definition medium gives little information and makes the user work to fill in what is missing. This is the basis of the contrast between hot and cool media: high definition is hot; low definition is cool.

The lecture/seminar contrast shows that hot media are low in participation, whereas cool media are high in participation. Looking at the other examples, we have a reminder that participation does not refer primarily to intellectual involvement but, like "definition" and "information," to how a medium engages our physical senses.

(7) In discussing the myth of Narcissus, McLuhan begins by pointing out the common misrepresentation in which Narcissus is said to have fallen in love with *himself.* In fact, it was his inability to recognize his image that brought him to grief. He succumbed to the same numbing effect that all technologies produce, if the user does not scrutinize their operation. Technologies create new environments, the new environments create pain, and the body's nervous system shuts down to block the pain. The name Narcissus comes from the Greek word *narcosis*, meaning numbness.

The story of Narcissus illustrates mankind's obsessive fascination with new extensions of the body, but it also shows how these extensions are inseparable from what McLuhan calls "amputations." Take the wheel. As a new technology, it took the pressure of carrying loads off the human foot, which it extends. But it also created new pressure by separating or isolating the function of the foot from other body movements. Whether you are pedaling a bicycle or speeding down the freeway in your car, your foot is performing such a specialized task that you cannot, at that moment, allow it to perform its basic function of walking. So, although the medium has given you the power to move much more quickly, you are immobilized, paralyzed. In this way, our technologies both extend and amputate. Amplification becomes amputation. The central nervous system reacts to the pressure and disorientation of the amputation by blocking perception. Narcissus, *narcosis*.

McLuhan finds a lesson on the power of media once again in Greek mythology. It was the king Cadmus who sowed dragon teeth from which an army sprang up. It was also Cadmus who introduced the phonetic alphabet (from Phoenicia) to Greece. The dragon's teeth may, therefore, represent an older form of hieroglyphic writing from which the much more powerful alphabet grew.

(8) In the case of Narcissus, a new medium both extends and amputates the human body; McLuhan finds another dimension of opposing effects accompanying the transition from mechanical to electronic technologies. This transition has involved a relentless acceleration of all human activity, so extensive that the expansionist

pattern associated with the older technology now conflicts with the contracting energies of the new one. Explosion (whether of population or knowledge) has reversed into implosion, because electronic technology has created a global village where knowledge must be synthesized instead of being splintered into isolated specialties.

In *Understanding Media*, McLuhan offers examples of overheated technologies and overextended cultures, and the reversals that they cause. The overextended road turns cities into highways and highways into cities; in the industrial society of the nineteenth century, with its extreme emphasis on fragmented procedures in the workplace, both the commercial and social world began to put new emphasis on unified and unifying forms of organization (corporations, monopolies, clubs, societies). McLuhan characterizes Samuel Beckett's play *Waiting for Godot* as dealing with the destructive aspects of the vast creative potential unleashed by the electronic age. This type of reversal is crucial in the integrated laws of media formulated late in McLuhan's career.

(9) McLuhan's analysis identifies the effects of media in all areas of society and culture, but the starting point is always the individual, since media are defined as technological extensions of the body. As a result, McLuhan often puts his questions and conclusions in terms of the ratio between our physical senses (the extent to which we depend on them relative to each other) and what happens when that ratio is modified. Any such modifications inevitably involve a psychological dimension. In this respect, they point to the inadvisability of a rigid separation of the physical from the psychological, perhaps in all analysis, but especially for an understanding of McLuhan's teachings. When the alphabet was invented and brought about the intensification of the visual sense in the communication process, sight swamped hearing so forcefully that the effect spilled over from language and communication to reshape literate society's conception of space.

McLuhan stresses sense ratios and the effects of altering them: in Africa, the introduction of radio, a hot medium distorting the sensory balance of oral culture, produced the inevitable disorienting effect and rekindled tribal warfare; in dentistry, a device called an *audiac* consists of headphones bombarding the patient with enough noise to block pain from the dentist's drill; in Hollywood, the addition of sound to silent pictures impoverished and gradually eliminated the role of mime, with its tactility and kinesthesis.

The examples involve the relationships among the five physical senses. These senses may be ranked in order of how fragmented the perceptions are that we get through them. Sight comes first, because the eye is such a specialized organ. Then come hearing, touch, smell, and taste. Reading down the list, we move to less specialized senses. By contrast with the enormous power of the eye and the distances from which it can receive a stimulus, the tongue is thought capable of distinguishing only sweet, sour, bitter, and salt, and only in direct contact with the substance providing the stimulus.

(10) Western culture, with its phonetic literacy, when transplanted to oral, nonliterate cultures, fragments their tribal organization and produces the prime example of media hybridization and its potent transforming effects. At the same time, electricity has transformed Western culture, dislocating its visual, specialist, fragmented orientation in favor of oral and tribal patterns. McLuhan retains the metaphors of violent energy in speculating on the final outcome of these changes—the fission of the atomic bomb and the fusion of the hydrogen bomb.

The hybridization of cultures occupies McLuhan most fully, but he offers other examples, such as electric light restructuring existing patterns of social and cultural organization by liberating the activities of that organization from dependence on daylight.

McLuhan emphasizes that media as extensions of the body not only alter the ratios among our physical senses, but that when the media combine they establish new ratios among themselves. This happened when radio came along to change the way news stories were presented and the way film images were presented in the talkies. Then television came along and brought big changes to radio.

When media combine, both their form and use change. So do the scale, speed, and intensity of the human endeavors affected. And so do the environments surrounding the media and their users. The hovercraft is a hybrid of the boat and the airplane. As such it eliminates not only the need for the stabilizing devices of wings and keels but the interfacing environments of landing strips and docks.

Neil Harris, a Harvard history professor, wrote to McLuhan to say what a great impression *Understanding Media* was making. As reviews began to appear, *The New Statesman* proclaimed that "Marshall McLuhan is now a power in more than one land."[79]

It was not intended as a compliment. Reviewer Christopher Ricks alluded to "Mr. McLuhan's clutch of crystal balls" and found that the book's themes of electric speed, media as extensions, and media effects "cohabit not very fruitfully." Acknowledging the importance of these themes, he remarked that "they are altogether drowned by the style." (One can hear Leon Wilson and David Segal saying "I told you *so*.") The probes of *Understanding Media*, intended to irritate readers into thinking, proved so abrasive as to prevent Ricks from seeing that McLuhan *redefines* content in terms of media. Reviewers had identified a moral stance in *The Mechanical Bride*, though McLuhan had anticipated readers would think his detached amusement was indifference; *The New Statesman* review likening in the deferral of moral judgment in the opening pa standing Media*, to cast McLuhan somewhere bet showman.[80]

Commonweal Review called it an infuriating b insights and turgid incoherences, dismissing as quate" McLuhan's discovery of the rise of national At home, *The Tamarack Review* detected "an a knowingness."[82] The *Toronto Star* reviewer found book, but saw McLuhan as guilty of the same s that marked Pasteur, Freud, Darwin, and Marx.[8]

Reviewers began taking aim at each other: er Sinclair fumed in *The Globe Magazine* that *Under* as full of words about pictures but contained not a n, dismissing the book outright.[84] Alan Thomas the ir for his "fit of pique," noting that he had ch th McLuhan's work by the easiest method ever ki n't understand something, but can't afford to ignore "[85] Thomas offered the public advice on how to read McLuhan. ou have any skill at reading poetry, use it."[86]

A reader responding to *Time's* review pointed out that it had said not one word about the theme *Understanding Media* announced by its title.[87] And a popular misreading of McLuhan's thought was not long in taking hold. In a review obscurely titled "Reverse Canadian," the *Riverside Press-Enterprise* of Riverside, California, branded *Understanding Media* "a book against books."[88]

The reaction in Riverside must have made McLuhan wonder if the malice and stupidity he had come to count on in Canada would await him in sunny California, where he would soon be arriving. A converted fire hall in San Francisco was the headquarters of Generalists Incorporated, a consulting firm run by adman Howard

Luck Gossage and proctologist/ventriloquist Gerald (Gerry) Feigen. It was Gossage who would later produce fifty thousand bumper stickers reading "WATCHA DOIN MARSHALL McLUHAN?"

The firm catered to clients in the business world whose requirements could not be met by the fragmented knowledge offered by traditional, academic specialists. Gossage and Feigen needed a resource like McLuhan. A friend had sent Feigen *Understanding Media* in the belief that it was about advertising. Feigen spent long hours trying to figure out what it was about, all the while reciting "the medium is the message" like a mantra. He soon realized that "What is it about?" is the wrong question for McLuhan (though it contains the answer to the right question, where "about" means *around* or *surround*, putting the focus on medium as environment and message as effect). All the pieces of the medium-message-senses-television-effects mosaic fell into place for Feigen. He shared this with Gossage, and by the time they had gone through the whole book together, both men suspected McLuhan was a genius. They telephoned him in Toronto and invited themselves for a visit.

McLuhan was waiting for them when they arrived at the Royal York Hotel on a balmy spring evening. Feigen later described the intense look McLuhan reserved for first encounters as "a marvellous moment of inquiry."[89] It was the start of a long evening over dinner, with McLuhan's scrutiny reciprocated by the visitors. They learned that "one talks only about McLuhan's subject, and during an ordinary conversation one remark would spark multiple responses from him."[90] But there was also "a satisfying lack of conceit or egotism in his approach to discussion."[91]

And it was fun for McLuhan and Feigen, who quickly discovered their mutual love of jokes and puns. Feigen had indexed over two thousand of them, and McLuhan was prepared to hear them all before he left. McLuhan also delivered many of his favorites; though his sense of timing, in Feigen's opinion, was sorely lacking, they were all lead-ins to rich observations on literature and technology. Gossage had little taste for humor, at least in the huge dollops his tablemates were serving each other, and sat through it all with a long face. When McLuhan left, after midnight, Gossage and Feigen then turned to the serious business of reviewing their impressions.

McLuhan had been in top form, answering their questions, setting out the projects underway at the Center for Culture and Technology, soaring from topic to topic. Both Gossage and Feigen felt as if he had given them heavy reading assignments for their next meeting, less than twelve hours away. If they had any doubts at all that night, it was very clear to them before they left Toronto two days later that they wanted to make a commodity of McLuhan in the United States. It is a moot point whether Gossage, who said of *The Mechanical Bride* only that it was "bizarre,"[92] ever penetrated McLuhan's teachings well enough to understand why the man could not be packaged.

First it was to be New York. McLuhan was hesitant, because he had final exams to mark. But after Gossage and Feigen pointed out that they were opening a door leading away from such drudgery, McLuhan finished his marking and met them in Manhattan, regaling his first select audience of business types with the message that they knew nothing about media. The executives were dumbfounded; Gossage and Feigen were delighted and began making plans to bring their find to the San Francisco fire hall for the first McLuhan Festival.

Feigen recalls the event as a string of lunches and dinners at San Francisco's Off Broadway restaurant, McLuhan recognized the environment as a virtual tactorium and needed to explain to his table-mates their hopelessly visual reaction to the topless waitresses.[93]

McLuhan paid the food as little attention as the girls, but displayed his usual healthy appetite for endless talk. In six days of nine-to-five sessions he explained many wonders, and then the event closed with a party, where Gossage had a twelve-piece mariachi band to herald in his Canadian discovery/discoverer. There was some question as to whether McLuhan, with his hypersensitive hearing, found the blaring trumpet stunt all that amusing. When Feigen spoke of what the future could hold, McLuhan asked: "Do you mean it can be all fun?"[94] That question too remained open.

At the 1965 meeting of the American Association for Public Opinion Research, Dr. Herbert E. Krugman, then manager of corporate public opinion research at General Electric, advanced the idea of television as a medium of low involvement by comparison with print. The researcher defined involvement by the number of spontaneous thoughts that subjects made while viewing television— thoughts linking the content of their viewing to something in their own lives. Such a definition contrasts with what McLuhan meant by a "cool medium" in *Understanding Media*. Krugman was examining subjects registering mental reaction; McLuhan was describing a physical process where a medium provides little information and requires highly active involvement of the eye or the ear to fill in what is missing. Once they became aware of each other's work, McLuhan picked up Krugman's description of the contrast between the active responses to print and passive responses to television in terms of fast versus slow brain waves. For some observers, this might have signalled that McLuhan was moving from physical to mental criteria for describing the contrast between cool and hot media, or a tacit recognition that the contrast was blurred by the neurophysiological realities underpinning it. Krugman believed the world should be moving toward McLuhan. He did not regard the differences he had uncovered as controversial, but he thought that few people had fully appreciated them, and he added: "We need now to spell out, if we can, the meanings of these differences, and to catch up, if we can, with Marshall McLuhan . . . In a sense he could not really be understood by a world raised on print and print theory about communication."[95]

McLuhan eschewed *transportation* in favor of *transformation* as a model for describing the process of communication, and Krugman grasped the contrast well: "It seems to me that McLuhan might characterize our field of communication theory as horse-and-buggy, or at best a 'Pony Express' type of theory. That is, we are wedded to a view of someone preparing a message, the message carried across a distance . . . and a receiver reading or decoding the message at the other end."[96]

Krugman also understood that it was the technology of television broadcasting that had led McLuhan to scrap the old model. In fact, television could not even be called mass communication in the old sense. The transportation model was no longer valid, because viewers were not decoding anything on their screens. Even when a primed message is shown on the screen, the letters must first be processed by the eye in a manner which is not required of letters in ink on paper. Krugman captured the essence of McLuhan's lesson on television's effect on the human sensorium, and the paradox of television, when he said of viewers that "their eyes and ears have been 'extended' into the situation portrayed on the screen. *They are participating in an experience*—even if it is passive participation."[97]

The EEG data emerging from Krugman's experiments confirmed McLuhan's observations on the television medium, including the paradox that it is and is not a medium of communication.[98]

The only way to salvage the transportation model of the communication process was to think of the television viewer as transported. But that would reduce the model to a metaphor, and McLuhan's sensitivity to the power of metaphor would not allow him to debase it. In their correspondence, McLuhan reminded Krugman of a principle articulated in *Understanding Media*: "There is a sense in which the 'content' of any medium is another medium. This is a natural fact of figure-ground relationships."[99]

McLuhan alluded to a source for the work of his own mentors and peers: "The work of I. A. Richards and Empson and F. R. Leavis in part stems from the psychological explorations of F. C. Bartlett in his *Remembering*. His discovery that all perception is in effect the restructuring of any situation whatever led Richards and others to test this on the printed page. They discovered at once that people rearrange whatever is presented to them in patterns that do not remain unchanged. From week to week and year to year the same experiences are, according to Bartlett's recorded observations, undergoing perpetual change. The objects on a table seen twenty years earlier are given new patterns, etc. Hence his title *Re-membering*."[100]

As for television, he pointed out that "TV is not merely rear projection. There is also the entire electric mesh—what Joyce calls 'the charge of the light barricade.'"[101]

Was it his ideas or McLuhan himself and his provocative way? The question defies an answer, because McLuhan never separated his ideas from his style, his percepts from the provocative probes that embodied them. These probes, beginning with *the medium is the message*, remained his preferred tool for intellectual inquiry and remind us still that he never sought to *isolate the concepts* behind words but rather to *integrate them as percepts*.

If we ask what was McLuhan's unique and enduring contribution to twentieth-century thought, it is important to go beyond the facile reply that he foresaw videocassettes (he called them "television platters"), the Internet, and, by implication, much else in our electronic age. The question is best answered in terms of the objectives that McLuhan set for his own vast and integrated program of intellectual inquiry. He said repeatedly that he was concerned about the world moving into the twenty-first century with nineteenth-century perceptions. The clear implication, given the scope of *Understanding Media*, is that the *impact* of twentieth-century technology was not understood, as it evolved in its increasing complexity, and that the prospect of achieving any such understanding depends on viewing media in their relation to each other. In providing a basis for such a perspective, McLuhan established his place among twentieth-century thinkers and became, at the same time, the first educator to issue a challenge for wholesale educational reform, based on a unique definition of media as extensions of our physical bodies and sensory lives.

Because of this focus, McLuhan often puts his inquiry *and* his conclusions in terms of the ratio between the physical senses (the extent to which we depend on them relative to each other) and the consequences of modifications to that ratio. This invariably entails a psychological dimension. Thus, the invention of the alphabet and the resulting intensification of the visual sense in the communication process gave sight priority over hearing, but the effect was so powerful that it went beyond communication through language to reshape literate society's conception and use of space.

McLuhan stresses the effects of altering sense ratios. In Africa, for example, the introduction of radio distorted the existing sensory balance of oral culture, produced a disorienting effect, and rekindled tribal warfare. In Hollywood, the addition of sound to silent movies impoverished and gradually eliminated the role of mime, with its emphasis on the sense of touch.

Such examples involve the relationships among our five physical senses, which may be ranked in order of the degree of fragmentation of perceptions received through them.

These are some of the basic lessons of *Understanding Media*. The book brought McLuhan to prominence in the same decade that celebrated flower power. It was San Francisco, the home of the summer of love, that hosted the first McLuhan Festival, featuring the man himself. The saying "God is dead" was much in vogue in the counterculture that quickly adopted McLuhan but missed the irony of giving a man of deep faith the status of an icon.

Spectacular sales of *Understanding Media*, in hardback and then in paperback editions, and the San Francisco symposium brought him a steady stream of invitations for speaking engagements. He addressed countless groups from the American Marketing Association and the Container Corporation of America to AT&T and IBM. In March 1967, NBC aired "This is Marshall McLuhan" in its *Experiment in TV* series. He played on his own famous saying, publishing *The Medium is the Massage* (coproduced with Quentin Fiore and

Jerome Agel), even as he was signing contracts for *Culture Is Our Business* and *From Cliché to Archetype* (with Canadian poet Wilfred Watson) with publishers in New York. Dozens of universities awarded McLuhan honorary degrees and he secured a Schweitzer Chair in the Humanities at Fordham University. At the University of Toronto's Center for Culture and Technology, where McLuhan was director, a steady stream of visitors arrived from around the world to absorb his lessons on media, or just to see him and be seen with him. Andy Warhol was scheduled to visit but did not show (when McLuhan finally met him some time later, he pronounced him a "rube"); John Lennon and Yoko Ono arrived unannounced. *Understanding Media*, which was eventually translated into more than twenty languages, overshadowed the only McLuhan book-length publication from the 1960s that took him back squarely to his roots as a professor of English literature, the two-volume *Voices of Literature* (edited in collaboration with Richard J. Schoeck). By the time the decade ended, he had collaborated with Canadian artist Harley Parker on *Through the Vanishing Point: Space in Poetry and Painting* and once more with Quentin Fiore and Jerome Agel on *War and Peace in the Global Village*. This popular paperback, exploding at every page with McLuhan's observations juxtaposed to a visual chronicle of twentieth-century happenings, bore the improbable title *an inventory of some of the current spastic situations that could be eliminated by more feedforward*. The book looks and feels light years away from the Cambridge University of the 1930s where McLuhan trained, but that was just where McLuhan had picked up the idea of *feedforward* from his teacher I. A. Richards.

CHAPTER FIVE

MCLUHAN'S TOOL BOX: FROM *THROUGH THE VANISHING POINT* TO *LAWS OF MEDIA*

Through the Vanishing Point (Marshall McLuhan and Harley Parker, 1968) is a short book. But the introduction alone crams in:

***HOW deodorants have created the bland, undifferentiated spaces typical of American culture.

***WHAT those same deodorants have done to our memories (McLuhan is always interested in how our perceptions relate to each other; it turns out that perception itself is an act of remembering.)

***WHY the people of the beautiful Indonesian island of Bali say "we have no art."

***WHAT seventeenth-century French philosopher and mathematician René Descartes and Shakespeare's Hamlet have in common: they both experienced alienation; they were the victims of the bias of visual culture.

***WHY the newspaper is a Romantic art form.

All this to help readers through the maze (and the haze) of technologies—new *and* old—and to explain why primitive times and the world of the Middle Ages share much with our electronic age.

The guided tour of the centuries in *Through the Vanishing Point* teaches about the effect that Isaac Newton's great work *Optics* had on eighteenth- and nineteenth-century painting and poetry. It encouraged great emphasis on visual and uniform space, and that uniformity "neutralized" the way artists showed nature.

But then came a reaction by the Romantic artists who began taking an interest in such things as the effect of light on natural colors. These artists also started turning away from showing things in themselves and put a new emphasis on *process* (another McLuhan favorite). The English artist Joseph Turner with his paintings featuring storms, steam, mist, water, and light is a good example.

With French artist Georges Seurat, a whole new technique came into painting—divisionism—where every dot of paint on a canvas became a light source. All of a sudden, traditional perspective was reversed—

THE VIEWER BECAME THE VANISHING POINT

All this is a clue for McLuhan to the link between the sensory life of Paleolithic Man and Electronic Man. We are back to McLuhan's idea of the retribalization of the Western world.

There is more—much more—in *Through the Vanishing Point*. It has to do with sonnets and haiku (Japanese verse form in three lines of five, seven and five syllables respectively), Oscar Wilde's butterflies, and McLuhan's key themes explored anew.

FROM CLICHÉ TO ARCHETYPE

In sharp contrast to the mosaic form of organization of *Through the Vanishing Point* is the encyclopedia format of *From Cliché to Archetype* (1970). The ten years of cooperation between McLuhan and poet-playwright Wilfred Watson that the book would require was more sporadic than cooperative. Watson had wanted to do a play based on *The Mechanical Bride*, because he found it to be less of a book than a superb piece of idiosyncratic satire. The play did not materialize, but Watson accepted McLuhan's offer to collaborate.

The husband-and-wife team of the Watsons, Wilfred and Sheila, held appointments as visiting professors at the Center for Culture and Technology during 1968–1969, when McLuhan and Watson were to make the final push on their joint effort. Watson, who had begun to feel overwhelmed in his solo runs at the work, looked forward to the year in Toronto as the solution for bringing the project to completion, but it brought only conflict. Seeing that he and McLuhan were at a serious impasse, Watson suggested that he write his portion for the left-hand pages, and that McLuhan make his contribution on the right. Of course, it was a jest—and perhaps a reminder to McLuhan of his own observation that jests are based on grievances. Looking back long after *From Cliché to Archetype* was finished, Watson put their troubles down to McLuhan's preferred method of writing by dialoguing with his collaborator and getting a secretary to record the outcome. The terms *cliché* and *archetype* appear as separate entries in the book, but the reader soon learns that they are inseparable in their operation. McLuhan and Watson explore the various meanings of *archetype*, including the basic one linking it to *type*, referring to a pattern or model. In literary analysis, an archetype is a symbol or image, recognizable because it is met repeatedly. But clichés are also repeated. It is repetition that makes them clichés. For this reason, McLuhan and Watson emphasize the connection between the two terms.

An archetype is an expandable category; a cliché is neither a category nor expandable. But it can be modified, and McLuhan and Watson have much to say about how this is done in the hands of artists. Just as McLuhan stretched the sense of "medium," he and Watson stretch the sense of "cliché," defining it at different times as an extension, a probe, and a means of retrieving the past. The resonance among these notions demonstrates how fundamental the study of cliché is in the McLuhan canon.

McLuhan and Watson call perceptions clichés, since the physical senses form a closed system. They regard all communications media as clichés, insofar as they extend our physical senses. And even art is cliché, because it retrieves older clichés.

The simplest definition of cliché for McLuhan and Watson is that of a probe. Here is an apparent paradox, as the authors freely acknowledge. But art is the sharpening of clichés into probes, into new forms that stimulate new awareness. What is familiar, even worn out, becomes new. McLuhan's favorite example to illustrate this process comes from James Joyce, whose writing wakes up language (creates new clichés) by putting it to sleep (destroying old clichés). Or, as McLuhan put it in commenting on the treatment of this theme: "All cliché is always being put back on the compost heap, as it were, whence it emerges as a shining new form."[1]

Between archetypes and clichés there is both contrast and interaction. A cliché is incompatible with another, even when they are of similar meaning. One may choose between the expressions "getting down to the nitty-gritty" and "getting down to brass tacks" but not combine them into "getting down to brass nitty-gritty" or "getting down to nitty-gritty tacks." But an archetype is an open set or group to which members (clichés) can be added.

McLuhan and Watson define the archetype as a retrieved awareness or new consciousness. Such awareness is created when the artist probes an archetype with an old cliché. Eventually, the probe itself turns into a cliché. *From Cliché to Archetype* views all form—whether in language, visual arts, music, or other domains—as reversal of archetype into cliché. But cliché also reverses into archetype. Beyond language, cliché occurs in past times, fixed and unalterable, because they are irretrievable. These become the archetype of pastimes—an open category the hobbyist may modify endlessly.

McLuhan and Watson emphasize that clichés are not confined to the verbal; they also note parallels between the verbal and the nonverbal type. They find strong similarity between phrases like "green as grass" or "white as snow" and the internal combustion engine. These similarities relate to both the form of the clichés involved and the key McLuhan teaching on new environments created by technology.

The banal phrases in question and the engine operate without any control over their *form* by the user. This is ultimately less important than their environmental impact. Both the clichés and the engine create new environments in three distinct ways: (1) meaningless communication and endless commuting, respectively; (2) invisible/visible junkyards of speech/writing—the vehicles of thought and visible junkyards of the road vehicles of yesterday, respectively; (3) disfigured mindscape and landscape, respectively.

McLuhan and Watson probe the connection between verbal and nonverbal clichés and archetypes. They observe that language provides extensions of all the physical senses at once, reminding us that these are integrated when language is spoken, whereas the visual sense becomes highly specialized with written language. Because McLuhan and Watson take clichés as extensions or media or technologies, they can discover not only similarities but direct links between the effect of past technologies and the accumulation of clichés in language. So, hunting with dogs gave English the phrases *to turn tail, top dog, underdog, bone of contention, to give the slip to, to run to earth, to throw off the scent, to be on the track of,* etc.

Inspired by W. B. Yeats's poem "The Circus Animals' Desertion," McLuhan and Watson develop the idea that the interaction of clichés and archetypes in language has counterparts beyond language.

Examples include that of a flagpole flying a flag. The flag by itself is a cliché—a fixed and unalterable symbol of the country it represents. Citizens don't have the option to modify it at will. But a flag on a flagpole is an archetype, since any flag can be hoisted in place of another.

Any cliché can interchange with another in the archetype. McLuhan and Watson challenge readers to discover the full meaning of their thought throughout *From Cliché to Archetype*. The book's table of contents appears neither at the beginning nor at the end but alphabetically under "T." Since all the material in the book is arranged in alphabetical order, the table of contents is useless, except as a reminder that archetypes can reverse into clichés. This careful order was botched by the publisher, who insisted on printing the footnotes ("Notes on Sources") at the end of the book instead of alphabetically under "N."

The interplay of cliché and archetype, and the close connection of both to McLuhan's most fundamental preoccupations, are perhaps best seen in the following passage: "The archetype is a retrieved awareness or consciousness. It is consequently a retrieved cliché— an old cliché retrieved by a new cliché. Since a cliché is a unit extension of man, an archetype is a quoted extension, medium, technology, or environment."[2]

McLuhan had looked forward with optimism to the appearance of *From Cliché to Archetype*, but if he was in any measure satisfied with the book at first, he became ambivalent afterward. And he found the French translation superior to the original, ascribing the credit for this to his personal collaboration with the translator. Even so, the work could irritate him when he returned to it. "A stupid book," he fumed, on one occasion, because he could find nothing to learn from it on rereading.[3]

Yet it led him to the discovery that the interplay of cliché and archetype is the interplay of figure and ground. The concept of archetypes also gave McLuhan a take on structuralism, in which he identified the paradigms of European structuralists as a set of archetypes. His decision to develop a complete book around the term *archetype* might have been motivated in the first place by a desire to appropriate it from his rival, Northrop Frye. There are five references to Frye in the book, including a "Frigean Anatomy of a Metamorphosis" for Eugene Ionesco's *The Bald Soprano* and an extensive quotation from a commentary by William Wimsatt criticizing Frye for failing to maintain his own distinction between *value* and *criticism* in *Anatomy of Criticism*. McLuhan wrote to Cleanth Brooks with some satisfaction of his discovery in Jean Piaget's writings that archetypes, as defined in Frye's approach, were unnecessary.[4]

The archetype was nevertheless a useful enough tool to have appeared eight years earlier in the closing pages of *The Gutenberg Galaxy*. As for cliché, McLuhan linked it even to his personal experience in the aftermath of brain surgery: "*Cliché* appears in many modes. All media whatever are environmental clichés. The effect of such surrounds is narcosis or numbing. This is a kind of *arrest* which, mysteriously, results in metamorphosis. Even anaesthesia has this effect. I was told after my long operation that many recent memories would disappear and many older ones would re-appear. This indeed happened. It also happens with the environmental clichés that are media."[5]

McLuhan's preference for percepts over concepts was a strategy for avoiding clichés by recourse to pure process. In his correspondence with Herbert Krugman, he linked this process to his original probe, pointing out that any medium surrounds both its users and earlier media. The result is resonance and metamorphosis between media and their users. This nonstop process was the subject of *From Cliché to Archetype*.

Within the body of McLuhan's work, *From Cliché to Archetype* marks the emergence of the notion of *retrieval*—the fourth of the media laws he would integrate with those of *extension, obsolescence,* and *reversal.* "Retrieval" is the only entry in the book under "R." McLuhan's correspondence following the appearance of the book indicates the central place *retrieval* occupied there and in his evolving thought: "I had asked the publisher to put on the flap of the jacket this formulation of the process that is cliché to archetype: Print scrapped scribe and Schoolmen and retrieved pagan antiquity. Revival of the ancient world created the modern world. Electricity scrapped hardware and industrialism and retrieved the occult."[6]

When the reviews of *From Cliché to Archetype* appeared, Hugh Kenner, then teaching at Harvard University, wrote: "No art can step up the voltage of boiled spinach."[7]

This was a phantom blow for McLuhan, an echo from one of his own favorite sayings, attributed to the Balinese: "We have no art; we do everything as well as possible."[8]

Now his old student and friend was telling him that he had neither done everything as well as possible nor been artful enough to cover it up. Other reviewers also spoke of a rehash and raised the usual charge of obscurity, reactions prompting a *Toronto Daily Star* editorial by Peter Newman entitled "McLuhan, hurrah!" calling him "the most influential prophet of our age."[9]

PROBES

Without an anti-environment, all environments are invisible.
Today man has no physical body. He is translated into information, or an image.
Each new technology is reprogramming of sensory life.
                    —*Marshall McLuhan & David Carson*
            The Book of Probes, *pp. 32–33, 92–93, 162–163*

McLuhan the media analyst sought to make his audiences ask: "How can we escape the inevitable changes that new technologies bring?" This he did with his probes. Like the speculative instruments of I. A. Richards—the words Richards used to expand his own understanding and that of his students—McLuhan's probes were drills. McLuhan's death brought tributes and retrospective appreciations. And though interest in his thought never waned entirely in the 1980s, it was a period marked principally by works following directly from his own, while it is particularly since the 1990s that critical reassessments have appeared.

Though the story of McLuhan's life is an intellectual odyssey, the hero is no wandering Ulysses. In retrospect, the coherence of his work becomes apparent; it stems from his genius for returning constantly, not to a single point, but to a single strategy: probing and testing the forms and limits of an idea, forging links among ideas, developing a method for escape into understanding. This he did by using the prison walls of language as ramparts.

McLuhan's thoughts on language are linked to his reflections on spiritual questions as early as his undergraduate days at the University of Manitoba. His meditations on Pentecost at that time, written more than thirty years before *Understanding Media* put the name of Marshall McLuhan in the public eye, are closely tied to one of the least-quoted passages in the book, closing chapter eight,

"The Spoken Word." It is a speculation on the potential of electronic technology for recreating the Pentecostal experience in the global village.

Tongues of fire empowering believers on the day of Pentecost is not simply part of the imagery that McLuhan carried with him both before and after his conversion to Roman Catholicism. Fire is the ancient symbol of becoming, of the process of transformation, of transcendence, and so of the power of the Holy Spirit and the power of a medium, combined at Pentecost in language.

Understanding Media refers to language as mankind's first technology for extending consciousness.[10]

It is the technology that has both translated (thought into speech) and been translated by a succession of other technologies throughout the course of civilization (hieroglyphics, phonetic alphabet, printing press, telegraph, phonograph, radio, telephone, and television).

Language is central to McLuhan's teaching on media, their transformations and interactions. It was central in the work of those artists who first understood the upheavals that accompanied the transition from literate to retribalized culture in the Western world. Among these artists were the French symbolist poets who perceived language as decayed past the point of allowing a new Pentecost. But McLuhan, realizing that electronic technology does not depend on words, sees further. The computer is the extension of the central nervous system. It offers the possibility of extending consciousness without verbalization, of getting past the fragmentation and the numbing effect that makes the Tower of Babel the counterpart to Pentecost, of providing a way to universal understanding and unity.

The intellectual ferment of the Cambridge years, with their emphasis on the training of perception, prepared the way for the innovations that marked McLuhan's thought till the end of his career, but also produced early results in his thesis on Thomas Nashe. The McLuhan who detected coherence in the multiple traditions represented in Nashe's writings is the McLuhan who challenges readers to detect coherence in his own writings. The McLuhan who admonished earlier commentators for refusing to take Nashe on his own terms is the McLuhan whom few commentators took on his own terms. Above all, the McLuhan who discovered that the illumination of Nashe's work demanded nothing less than a study of the classical trivium was the McLuhan who took from that study the analogical method of the ancient grammarians as the unifying element of his own life's work. Though the study of Nashe might have become the focus of a lifetime of scholarship for McLuhan, Nashe remained in the background once McLuhan gave priority in his published work to the training of perception.

This was the focus of McLuhan's teaching, writing, public lecturing, and the intellectual investigations that informed them. A summary account of these investigations is given below, with McLuhan's probes serving as headings. As such, the probes should remind us that McLuhan sought not to isolate the concepts behind the words but to integrate them as percepts. Viewing the McLuhan probes in this way is a first step toward recognizing unity in the rich variety of thought he left as his legacy.

Acoustic Space

Acoustic space was a key topic for McLuhan. The idea was developed at the University of Toronto by Professor E. A. Bott of the department of Psychology, and news of it came to the interdisciplinary seminar through Carl Williams. Though McLuhan never met Bott, he acknowledged his work as a stimulus for his own "study of olfactory space, tactile space, and the rest."[11]

Writing to Jacques Maritain, McLuhan brought faith, physics, philosophy, and language through the vanishing point by way of acoustic space: "The ear creates acoustic space whose centre is everywhere and whose margins are nowhere. This has often been mistaken for God by tribal societies as well as by neo-Platonists and the Oriental world."[12]

As for modern physicists, incapable of recognizing acoustic space or its features, McLuhan saw their idea of quantum mechanics as bedeviled by the misguided effort to reduce Linus Pauling's rich metaphor of *resonance* for the chemical bond to visual terms. With or without the snare of metaphors, philosophers and psychologists had fallen into equally serious error, in McLuhan's view, by treating the human sensorium as "passive receptors of experience," by preferring "to study the mechanisms of the senses" (an insidious metaphor) "rather than the worlds created by them."[13]

A promising alternative came from the approach of anthropologist Edward T. Hall, who "directed attention to the amazing variety of social spaces created by different cultures of the world."[14]

Hall's study appealed to McLuhan because it left room for the dynamics of cognition and avoided any hint of technological determinism.

Less than a month before his devastating stroke of September 1979, McLuhan was wedding his latest interest, as intellectual historian, to one of his teachings on media effects from the earliest days of the interdisciplinary seminar: "I have begun to work on the relation between Kant and Hegel and their followers to the coming of the electric age and the return of acoustic space."[15]

A rare challenge to McLuhan to change one of his key probes came from his former student Richard Berg: "[Buckminster Fuller] gets his ideas of discontinuity and decentralization from atomic structure and from modern transport and communications. It is not necessary to think always in terms of acoustic space to understand discontinuous structures and properties. The drift now in communication theory, as you are aware, is toward the study of how the whole range of the electromagnetic spectrum affects human beings."[16]

This appeal by way of the transformation theory of communication came well after McLuhan had championed it himself, and the reference to Fuller provided little incentive to scrap the idea of acoustic space. Though he had enjoyed many meetings with Fuller, McLuhan found him incurably linear in his thinking. Besides, there was enough evidence for acoustic space to give it more status than that of an expendable probe.

Figure and Ground

In the early pages of *Understanding Media*, McLuhan refers to "the unified 'field' character of our new electromagnetism."[17]

Only his quotation marks around *field* hint that the familiar word has a special meaning. Much later in the book, he discusses the automobile and how it "has quite refashioned all of the spaces that unite and separate men."[18]

The first passage invites a reference to the "field theory" shared by linguistics, physics, and gestalt psychology, while the second fairly cries for a McLuhan twist on the figure/ground analysis provided by the gestalt approach. But only in the year following the publication of *Understanding Media* did McLuhan add figure/ground to his intellectual toolbox. It eventually became his favored probe. The automobile could now be described as a figure against the ground of highways, service stations, motels, billboards, drive-in theaters, and suburbs.

In April 1965, McLuhan circulated a draft of a paper emerging from the research and discussions conducted at the Center for Culture and Technology during its first year of operation. By then he had fully realized that the great potential of figure/ground analysis lay in its application to media ("radio service is ground, whereas radio program is figure"),[19] to the unnoticed environments they create (the restructuring of cityscape and landscape alike under the effect of the automobile), and to the equilibrium of the human senses altered by technology (mankind given an eye for an ear with the advent of television).

McLuhan applied figure/ground analysis at first to advertising and journalism: "Any connection medium is useful to the ad or, 'good news industry,' only so long as [the ad] has the character of a 'figure' in relation to some larger 'ground.' As circulation expands, the figure tends to become a ground and its relation to both the reader and ad client is finished. (This is complementary to the basic fact that advertising as 'good news' is a threat to everybody's way of life, whereas 'hard news' or 'bad news' has the opposite effect of releasing survivor emotion and general euphoria.)"[20]

Returning to his literary studies, McLuhan saw the part figure/ground had played in the perceptions of his favorite authors: "Perhaps it was Flaubert who first hit upon the procedure of taking the social *ground* itself as *figure* for structural study. It is to this that Pound alludes in *Mauberley* when he says: 'his true Penelope was Flaubert.' A mob of aesthetes had been trying to make the art figure an object for their quest while ignoring the hidden social *ground* which was the true *figure* for their pursuit."[21]

McLuhan applied the same principle to his analysis of the work of Wyndham Lewis: "In figure ground terms I think it is easy to see that Lewis saw the artist *figure* as enemy of the social ground. The artists, apropos, instead of attacking the enemy, merely befriend one another, as it were. Put that way, I think Lewis's work becomes a great deal clearer."[22]

McLuhan recast Harold Innis in the gestalt mold: "More and more I see the Innis approach as a gestalt *figure-ground* approach. Innis was one of the very few people to recognize the *ground* or environment created by technologies as the area of change."[23]

Aquinas could be seen in the same way: "By the way, the word *medium* in Aquinas refers to the gap or interval, the emptiness between matter and form as such, i.e., the *hidden* ground of Being, and in every sense, it is the message. The work I am doing with Bob Logan on the alphabet and ancient science will provide a beach-head for exploring the effects of the alphabet in giving priority to efficient cause over others. Formal causality or total surround returns with the acoustic and simultaneous electric environment, i.e., we move into the pre-Socratic position once more."[24]

Figure and ground offered an explanation for the mechanism of dreams: "In dreams the symbol is minus the *ground* of effects and ergo more bearable as abstract, but the *figure* is the area of causation and direct responsibility."[25]

And communication theory could be profitably reworked through the figure/ground approach: "Communication is not transportation. Communication is change. It is change in both the maker and the user—the user being the public. Communication is the study of ground rather than of figure. In the case of Plato, it is not a study of his thought but of the people he worked for, and the people he tried to help."[26]

The discovery of figure/ground was one of breakthrough proportions for McLuhan, a key to liberation from the shackles of visual bias: "Visual man is unaware that visual space is figure minus ground. The symbolists were precisely the ones who broke through this visual structure into the acoustic structures of figure/ground. Ezra Pound is always figure/ground, always concerned with the public and the effects and changes to be introduced into that public."[27]

McLuhan sensed that an approach through figure/ground could hold the answer to very large questions: "For reasons I have not yet grasped adequately, alphabetic or visual man has constantly blanketed or suppressed *ground* in all his studies of the arts and technologies."[28]

Figure/ground also provided a means of describing the contrast between film and television, confirming and giving cogency to McLuhan's earlier pronouncements on these media: "Movie is a figure/ground pictorial form, TV is iconic in the full sense that iconic merges figure and ground . . . The Platonist, with his specialized and merely visual archetypes (figures without ground rather than merged with ground), gets a sense of divinity from his abstraction of figure from ground. The Aristotelian, with his hylo-morphic figure and ground interplay, seems more earthy and rooted. In the same way, the movie would seem to many to be Platonic and visual compared to TV with its mingling of the senses in an iconic merger."[29]

By the time he made these observations, McLuhan considered the figure/ground probe indispensable: "The inability to play with *figure* and *ground* is like trying to get along with a wheel without an axle or vice versa."[30]

Figure/ground analysis became a cornerstone of McLuhan's media analysis because it dealt with perceptions, whether of the whole panoply of electronic extensions of the body and nervous system or of mankind's first technology—language. The ground for poetry, on this view, is the entire language. The poet's experimental figures both stand out against this ground and interact with it.[31]

With figure/ground analysis came an insight for McLuhan into learning strategies and media effects: "A child can see the ground or environment as easily as figure. Is not this a clue to the ability of kids C-M [center without margin] learning of language? Having no bias for figure such as comes with literacy, they can accept the ground itself as figure . . . An example of 'rip-off' would be the effect of phonetic literacy in substituting eye for ear, thereby switching figure and ground."[32]

Figure/ground was irresistible for McLuhan, but his audiences resisted it. He met with much skeptical reaction and was even accused of having either invented figure/ground analysis or being an agent for spreading such a nefarious notion.[33]

McLuhan had greatly enjoyed meeting Yousuf Karsh, who had done his portrait. Karsh professed trouble in understanding McLuhan, who sought to enlighten him with the teaching tool of figure/ground: "I want to 'pick a bone' with you about your supposed difficulties in understanding McLuhan. Let us simply use your own medium, the camera. What I study is not the content but the *effects* of the instrument itself on whole situations. The camera obviously turns the user into a hunter . . . In your case, the camera turns you into a 'lion' hunter, a big game hunter. What does it do to the game or the people involved? Obviously, it turns them into extremely self-conscious and sensitive beings. The camera represents an enormous increase in self-consciousness. Do you find anything difficult about what I've said so far? Notice that what I say requires that the reader pay precise attention to the *figure/ground*, or the total situation . . . The pretense that McLuhan is incomprehensible is surely a way of protecting people's laziness and impercipience."[34]

Undeterred by audience reaction, McLuhan was well on his way to integrating figure/ground with his other probes:

(1) It coalesced for him with the study of causes, in that causes could be viewed as ground while effects corresponded to figure: "The peculiarity of ground, however, is invisibility . . . The satellite as ground transforms planet Earth into figure."[35]

(2) The figure/ground distinction aligned, in turn, with efficient and formal cause. "Ignorance is hidden *ground,* i.e., formal cause. A man's knowledge would be *figure*, i.e., efficient cause, while his ignorance is *ground.* It is worth thinking about the ways in which the ignorance is the predominant shaping factor . . . The enclosed sheet from *The Listener* ['Does TV keep us in the dark?'] [11 November 1976] states the amazing proposition that we should not talk about the effects of the media lest it put weapons in the hands of the *hoi polloi.* Explains a lot about their attitude to me."[36]

(3) In so saying, he had already discovered hot media as figure and cool media as ground.[37]

(4) When searching for equivalent terms for figure/ground in French, McLuhan realized that his distinction between cliché and archetype constituted a parallel to figure/ground.[38]

(5) There was even a link to the original McLuhan probe: "Apropos 'the medium is the message,' I now point out that the medium is not the *figure* but the *ground* . . . Also I point out that in all media the user is the content, and the effects come before the invention."[39]

McLuhan also made a connection between figure/ground and . . .

(1) linguistics:

Saussure explains that a sign is an *effect* of a hidden process, whether it be a word or a finger-post. From this point of view . . . it is possible, I think, to say that any technology whatever is a *figure* in a hidden ground or vortex of complex processes.[40]

(2) his emerging tetrad of media laws:

Figure/ground yielded an explanation for the law of obsolescence: "It is, of course, the change in the *ground* that obsolesces the *figure* and draws attention to the interplay between *figure* and *ground* as the means by which relevance is achieved."[41] But McLuhan could also see uses for figure/ground outside media analysis in relation to . . .

(1) pornography:

> Pornography and obscenity, in the same way, work by specialism and fragmentation. They deal with figure without ground—situations in which the human factor is suppressed in favor of sensations and kicks.[42]

(2) politics:

> I have just been doing a piece on inflation as a new form of crowd behavior . . . Our present inflation has nothing to do with supply and demand . . . What has happened is that the old economics and the old commodity markets are now old figures embedded in a new subliminal ground of instant and worldwide information. The new ground of electronic information is a "software" information world of instant promises and instant delivery in which the old markets are used as mere *pastimes.*[43]

Among McLuhan's devoted and thorough students, Kamala Bhatia declared that his use of *figure* and *ground* was "a cornerstone of Hindu logic. What appears to be true of a thing in one of its aspects may at the same time be false in another."[44]

Roger Poole, a visiting Commonwealth Fellow at Toronto's York University during 1976–1977, questioned McLuhan carefully on the matter of figure/ground:[45]

> I find myself blocked and frustrated [in trying to answer McLuhan's questions] by never being quite sure whether you are operating your figure/ground distinction as (1) a media-technological affair only or as (2) a philosophical affair as well or whether in fact you aren't really hinting at (3) a theological level, which you never state but only assume . . . Whereas linguistics and logic generally are sophisticated toys (intellectual substitutes for children's red and blue bricks, books) there is no reality, no certainty whatever, except in the theologically conceived Logos. In the opposition

linguistics-logic/logos you surely have the major fundamental opposition figure/ground do you not? Am I entirely wrong in intuiting that the basic model in your mind, the unstated ground of all your own figures, is the Bible? [Commenting on McLuhan's own comment in his letter of 24 November 1977 that when he says medium is message medium is always ground and not figure:] What you really seem to me to be indicating is the lack of a Logos in which the Hegelian Logic can be "grounded" . . . It does not seem to me that you open the possibility anywhere in your thinking (or rather in your published work) to what one might call "theological space."[46]

McLuhan replied: "It was while reading Newton's *Optics* . . . that I came across his observation about the occult qualities which underlay *[sic]* any phenomenon. Somehow this enabled me to recognize phenomenology as that which I have been presenting for many years in non-technical terms. It does not seem to matter whether it is Hegel, or Husserl, or Heidegger, phenomenology is the light coming through a *figure* from a hidden *ground* and this leads to all the techniques and doubts and 'bracketing.' I think that the obfuscation via jargon which has been going on under the name of philosophy during these centuries is a professional racket."[47]

To this McLuhan added: "*Finally* discovered what happened to the Greeks via the alphabet—it developed the acoustic world of Homer into the visual world of Plato and Parmenides."[48]

Did he really not know this before? Of course he did. It is in *The Gutenberg Galaxy* sixteen years earlier, but here it is a new discovery because it can be—described in terms of figure/ground, allowing the fact to be integrated with every other one that is covered by figure/ground. What is discovered is thus a new relation, and the validity of the figure/ground analysis is confirmed by the discovery.

After twelve years of working with figure/ground McLuhan could say: "It is only recently that I realized that 'understanding media' means study of their subliminal *ground.*"[49]

The final transformation and integration of the figure/ground probe was still ahead.

Effects

The study of effects is the thread running through all of McLuhan's media analysis—if not its entire rationale. It takes its roots in his training in Practical Criticism, where McLuhan learned to heed I. A. Richards's call to "give a fuller and more entire response to the words" of poetry and to develop "the fullest realization of their varied powers upon us."[50]

Examining and revealing effects remains a constant objective, even as the McLuhan probes change. Unarticulated, left to the reader to discover, and obscured by the sheer good fun of *The Mechanical Bride*, McLuhan's focus on "effect" surfaces amid the chapter glosses of *The Gutenberg Galaxy*, then becomes a key word from the opening paragraphs of *Understanding Media*. As he wrote his report for the NAEB project in 1960, McLuhan realized how closely the discovery of effects was linked to his other interests, particularly the classification of media in relation to how the physical senses process input: "The break-through in media study has come at last, and it can be stated as the principle of complementarity. This is the principle that the structural impact of any situation is subjectively completed as to the cycle of the senses. That the effect of a medium is in what it omits and what we supply, but the factors of high or low definition image may qualify this radically. That in telephoning, for example, we are dealing with such a low definition auditory image that we are engaged in completing that rather than filling in the visual, etc. Low definition, on the other hand is the basic principle of organized ignorance, and of the technique of invention."[51]

McLuhan found even more compelling reasons to study the effects of media. In an unfinished manuscript he was preparing on the work of American author and critic Lewis Mumford, he explains: "Personally, having found the utmost ambiguity in all human technologies, and having never discovered a fixed position from which to view or measure them, I have settled for studying their on-going effects on the users."[52]

Writing to Frank Kermode, McLuhan went further, speaking of the *impossibility* of studying media from a fixed point of view.[53]

Like Poe's sailor, McLuhan found himself obliged to observe the maelstrom of the media from multiple points of view and to observe effects.

Shortly after *Understanding Media* appeared, Harry Skornia published *TV in the Court Room*. It gave McLuhan fresh insights into the scope needed to fully treat the question of media effects as the sum total of their impact on the human psyche and on society. Such a treatment required history to serve as the laboratory in which to observe change, and Skornia's article offered McLuhan a model of this approach. McLuhan wrote to Skornia, noting that "it is contemporary history, of course, but history for all that. By showing the effect of a medium upon a diversity of institutions, you gain the historical dimension in the present."[54]

Here McLuhan is already working his way toward the notion of transcending the synchronic/diachronic distinction—a topic to which he attached considerable importance when he discovered the work of Swiss linguist Ferdinand de Saussure.

McLuhan's notion of electronic technology as an externalization of the human subconscious on a global scale (made possible because such extension requires no connections of a linear nature) brought an even greater prominence to the question of effects: "The new responsibility is to develop awareness of *process* and the effects of specific processes."[55]

To this McLuhan added a comment relating to the moral viewpoint he so often claimed to abjure, and which his critics just as often persisted in attributing to him: "Awareness of process tends to push value judgments into abeyance."[56]

Those who could not, like McLuhan, work *backward* from effects to causes doggedly advanced a moral point of view they assumed or expected him to share. McLuhan later attributed this tendency to left-hemisphere dominance. McLuhan found himself in distinguished intellectual company as a student of effects:[57] Ovid, Darwin, Joyce, and Harold Innis.[58]

Like Innis, McLuhan became absorbed with causality. "I have been forced to observe that most of the effects of any innovation occur before the actual innovation itself. In a word, a vortex of effects tends, in time, to become the innovation. It is because human affairs have been pushed into pure process by electronic technology that effects can precede causes."[59]

To James W. Carey, director of the Institute of Communications Research at the University of Illinois, McLuhan wrote: "In a simultaneous world which structures information at the speed of light, effects are simultaneous with their causes, or in a sense 'precede' their causes."[60] *In a sense.* Quotation marks. Rare qualifiers to find in McLuhan's writing.

The effect of electronic technology that most troubled McLuhan personally, because of its implications for Christianity, was the loss of the physical body: "One of the effects of instant speed is that the *sender is sent . . .* That is, man has become essentially discarnate in the electric age. Much of his own sense of unreality may stem from this. Certainly it robs people of any sense of goals or direction."[61]

McLuhan was puzzled by the willful somnambulism that made audiences react with hostility to his teachings on media effects: "It is almost like the anger of a householder whose dinner is interrupted by a neighbor telling him his house is on fire. This irritation about dealing with the effects of anything whatever, seems to be a specialty of Western man."[62]

But he came to an understanding of this reaction: "Bob Logan mentioned that many people resent me because I have made so many discoveries and from the point of view of subliminal life this may well be a clue. People feel angry when something they had 'known' all along surfaces. It happened with Freud. The point is, we create our subconscious ourselves and resent anybody fooling around with it. When I study media *effects*, I am really studying the subliminal life of a whole population, since they go to great pains to hide these effects from themselves!"[63]

Eventually, McLuhan merged his observations on media effects not only with the question of causality but with his preoccupation with the notion of the figure/ground relationship. In one of his last extensive letters on media effects, McLuhan sets the topic in a much larger context, providing incidentally one his most illuminating examples of the merging of effect and cause. He tells Sister St. John O'Malley of his push to revise his Ph.D. thesis (referring to it not as "the Nashe" but identifying it as "my history of the trivium"), noting that the effort paid off by unexpectedly revealing odd and arresting features in the history of logic and dialectic: "We have discovered the reasons for the streamlining tradition which leads to the omission of *grammatica* in dialectics."[64]

Here "discovered" means extending one of his observations from *Understanding Media* to a wider field of application. "[The streamlining tradition] began with the phonetic alphabet itself, which was business man's (Phoenician's) invention for expediting his transactions. The Alphabet is the supreme streamlining which gets rid of the spoken word, and all manner of corporate paraphernalia. Once launched on this pattern of getting to goals with expedition, the appetite has grown to include the computer and the moon-landing. Logic itself is a technique for omitting the *ground* in favor of dealing only with figures, a process which the Schoolmen and Descartes handed on to the mathematical logicians of our time. There is a single appetite to reduce all situations to more and more ethereal quality."[65]

Causes

Long before illness took McLuhan from public view, he had become an iconic figure, in a world that knew little of his percept that the iconic merges figure and ground. But the popular consciousness of McLuhan the icon had earned him a limerick for his pronouncements on the merging of effect and cause:

> Runs one of McLuhan's mad laws,
> The effect always precedes the cause.
> Thus the baby's produced,
> Ere the maid is seduced;
> Is it impertinent to ask who the pa is?

If the question does not invite a serious answer, McLuhan nevertheless supplied one, naming a hardy reincarnation of efficient causality as the offspring of print. And he pointed a finger at print for obscuring the offspring's cousin—and child of earlier media—formal causality: "Print gave great stress and access to all phases of efficient causality."[66]

To this McLuhan added a rare, plain statement of definition: "But I refer to formal cause not in the sense of classification of forms, but to their operation upon us and upon one another."[67]

Aristotle might have protested such a wholesale revision of formal causality, but he might also have been assuaged when McLuhan later linked it to figure/ground. McLuhan had "gravitated toward the center of formal causality," finding his media studies "forcing me to re-invent it."[68]

For two years, he buttonholed colleagues steeped in the traditions of the medieval Schoolmen on the subject of formal cause, "only to discover they had no use for it whatever," because the danger of relativism lurked there.[69] They found the static universals of Platonism safer. McLuhan replied in the words of Joyce, "how cudious an epiphany."[70]

McLuhan's method remained linked, in his own accounts, for many years to formal causality and *increasingly* to media effects. Responding to an article about his work in *The Listener,* he noted:

"My own writing has been entirely in the world of formal causality, the study of *effects*, rather than the assertion of values. This approach I owe to Harold Innis and his *Bias of Communication*."[71]

If McLuhan had followed at first in Innis's footsteps, few could keep up with him once he began to beat his own path. In correspondence, he looked to Etienne Gilson for help in understanding "the causes for the non-interest in causes."[72] The question eluded Gilson. McLuhan's attempt to engage Jacques Maritain met with no success: "At no point does Maritain understand formal causality in art and philosophy."[73]

At St. Michael's, in 1974, McLuhan tried to reopen the causality dialogue nearly twenty years after his first efforts had been in vain. (He had by now revised his definition of formal cause and was also exploring efficient cause.) The results were only slightly more encouraging: "[Father Joseph Owens] conceded entirely, and at my insistence, that the formal cause of any philosophy is the public (either conscious or subliminal) amidst which the philosopher works. The implications of this he blithely ignores. I asked him especially which is the efficient cause in any writing or thinking, and he conceded at once that it was the user or reader, i.e., the cognitive agent."[74]

McLuhan was not about to concede the battle to articulate a large new percept, even if he was the only soldier.[75] In fact, he opened new fronts, summoning allies from Aquinas to Joyce, including that wheezy old colonel, Chesterton.[76] Casualties were registered on the other side and a glimpse of the final victory foreshadowed when McLuhan detected the inability of structuralists such as Claude Levi-Strauss and Roman Jakobson to accommodate the distinction between acoustic and visual space.[77]

Cause and effect, efficient cause/formal cause . . . now came the tie-in to gestalt psychology and its foundational duality: "In gestalt terms, formal causality is *ground* as opposed to *figure*, and it is the interplay between these that releases insights. In Joyce this is partly accomplished by the use of a sub-plot. Since the phenomenologists have taken an increasing interest in language, they have also begun to pay more attention to the hidden *ground* in all structures, as witness Levi-Strauss. Without knowing it, they are phasing themselves out of the Hegelian tradition."[78]

The subject could be broached in terms of environments, too: "Mass media in all their forms are necessarily environmental and therefore have the character of formal causality. In that sense all myth is the report of the operation of formal causality. Since environments change constantly, the formal causes of all the arts and sciences change too."[79]

For good measure, McLuhan added the linguistic perspective[80] (by now coming more and more to the forefront of his thought) and an implicit *ricorso* or return to media, via effects. This allowed him to equate formal cause, in linguistic terms, with a synchronic as opposed to a diachronic approach.[81] The new equations here brought with them a turning point in the ideas now being worked out by the father-and-son team of Marshall and Eric McLuhan.[82]

Laws of Media

When the nucleus of McLuhan's posthumously published *Laws of Media* (1988), appeared in essay form in *et cetera / ETC.: A Review of General Semantics* (San Francisco, New York: International Society for General Semantics) Vol. 34, No. 2 June 1977, pp. 173–179, it may have seemed an unlikely forum. But general semantics, in the vision of its founder, Alfred Korzybski (1879–1950), was essentially a form of applied philosophy, organized loosely around the basic objective of training the human animal to recognize pitfalls of language and thereby make more efficient use of the central nervous system. In this respect, there is more than a tenuous link between Korzybski's vision and McLuhan's call for educational reform based on understanding the operation of new media *as languages* and their effect on the interplay of our physical senses. In fact, as Korzybski continued his work during the 1940s, McLuhan took notice of it and made prominent mention of it in the introduction to his doctoral thesis. There are oblique references to Korzybski in various McLuhan publications and specific references to his concept of time-binding (man is the only animal to control time as a dimension of his environment). In *Understanding Media*, McLuhan had already developed three of the four laws of media without naming them as such; here all four are established in relation to each other as the two figures and two grounds of metaphor, and their ratios "extend to the four irreducible relations in [all] technology."[83] What Korzybski might have thought of McLuhan's laws of media, given that their source is traced here to Aristotle, must remain a matter of speculation with substantial prospect for revealing principled opposition between the two thinkers, for Korzybski referred to his general semantics as based on non-Aristotelian, infinite-valued orientation. But there can be little doubt that he would have appreciated the spirit in which McLuhan asserts that all media are fundamentally linguistic.

McLuhan credits his reading of Karl Popper's definition of a scientific hypothesis as one that is capable of falsification for moving him toward hypothesizing the laws of media. He ascribes a second impetus to the suggestion by Hans Hass, in *The Human Animal*, that the human power to create additional "organs" adds incalculable consequences to evolution, although Hass's observation scarcely seems to do more than consolidate the link between McLuhan's longstanding interest in causality and his characterization of technologies as extensions of the human body. He also cites a theme found in the writings of Sir Peter Medawar: that of developing technology as a defining feature of humans. The unified formulation of the laws of media and their wide application consolidated for McLuhan the awareness that all human artifacts, referred to in the *et cetera* piece as "sensory and motor accessories,"[84] are words. In *Understanding Media*, he had called the spoken word mankind's first technology;[85] now he was equating all technologies with words. It was a move that liberated phrases such as *the "grammar" of games* or the *"syntax" of the steam engine* from their quotation marks. And on close reading, one discovers that the move had already been made in tentative and exploratory fashion in *Understanding Media*.[86]

The laws of media are not statements but questions that constitute a discovery procedure for inquiring into the operation of any medium and its effects upon other media (typically older ones that it has eclipsed), upon the environment, upon individual users, and on users collectively, that is society as a whole. There are always and only four questions to be asked, four features of the medium to be determined, and they exist in analogical proportion to each other.

(1) What does it enhance?
(2) What does it obsolesce?
(3) What does it retrieve that had been obsolesced earlier?
(4) What does it flip into when pushed to the limits of its potential?

In diagrammatic form, the application of the laws of media produce what McLuhan dubbed a *tetrad* structure. With or without the benefit of a diagram, the four laws reveal that "all the extensions of man, verbal or non-verbal, hardware or software, are *essentially* metaphoric in structure, and that they are in the plenary sense linguistic . . ."[87]

That is, they all reflect mankind's first technology for letting go of the environment in order to grasp it in new ways. Thus, the structure of the tetrad applicable to all technologies reflects the dynamics of verbal metaphors with their characteristic four terms that are discontinuous but in ratio to one another:

Retrieval is to Obsolescence as Amplification is to Reversal
—and—
Retrieval is to Amplification as Obsolescence is to Reversal.

The structure also converges with McLuhan's figure/ground probe by consistently offering double figure and double ground within the four-term ratio. It is also at this point that the laws of media link up with Aristotle's views on analogy in the *De Anima* (Book *III*, chapter *VIII*) *and* his application of four-part analogy to psychological as well as verbal operations.

Applied to verbal metaphors *and* to themselves, the laws of media yield:

Metaphor
(1) enhances awareness of relations;
(2) obsolesces simile, metonymy, connected logic;
(3) retrieves understanding through semantic field properties of a word;
(4) reverses into allegory.

Tetrad
(1) enhances awareness of inclusive structural process;
(2) obsolesces the logic of efficient causality in favor of formal causality;
(3) retrieves metaphor;
(4) flips hardware technology into the software of the spoken word.

As for the application of the tetrad of media laws to technologies that bridge the software of language and the hardware that transmits language, McLuhan offers this example:

Radio

(A) Enhances simultaneous access to the entire planet: "On the air you're everywhere!"; (B) Obsolesces wires and cables and physical bodies; end of rational and lineal; end of Euclidean space; end of Western Time and Space; (C) Retrieves tribal ecological environments—trauma, paranoia, and the primacy of the right hemisphere of the brain; (radio was the hidden ground to the figure of the retrieved prohibition of drug abuse in the television age); (D) World reverses into "talking picture"—audience as actor participating in its own actor-experience.[88]

In elaborating the final version of *Laws of Media*, the McLuhans realized that nature has only two parts and works as ground with no figures at all, there being no formal or final cause within nature. This had been a tentative line of inquiry in the essay in *et cetera*: "Whether these ratios are also present in the structure of the 'natural' world raises an entirely separate question. It is perhaps relevant to point out that the Greeks made no entelechies or studies of the effects of man-made technology, but only of what they considered the objects of the natural world."[89]

This put a clear contrast in place between the two-part structure of natural phenomena and the four-part tetrads emerging as the new corner stone of media analysis. The McLuhans now identified the tetrads completely with formal causality and had a large new perspective: "Have discovered that every single artefact, verbal *and* nonverbal, has this four part structure, two figures and two grounds in interface, *which constitute metaphor*."[90]

This was the justification for assimilating nonverbal artefacts to verbal ones and calling all human technologies, all extensions of the human body, linguistic *in structure*. To characterize the spectrum between "things of a tangible 'hardware' nature such as bowls and . . . computers" to "things of a 'software' nature such as theories or laws of science"[91] as *linguistic* is to add another ring to the statement in *Understanding Media* that "the spoken word was the first technology by which man was able to let go of his environment in order to grasp it in a new way."[92]

Structuralism

McLuhan's thinking in the 1970s, particularly in the middle years of the decade, was dominated by his own unique brand of structuralism.

At first, it had little direct link to the complex and ramified school of thought deriving from the work of the Swiss linguistic genius Ferdinand de Saussure. In the early pages of *Understanding Media,* McLuhan had already outlined structuralism in the broadest terms: the trend of modern thought, in areas as diverse as physics, painting, and poetry, whereby "specialized segments of attention have shifted to total field."[93]

It was a trend that supported his notion that the medium is the message; gave the phrase its full meaning; and illustrated effect preceding cause in twentieth-century intellectual history, and in the development of his own thought. It was also a trend that could accommodate the probes that he was still developing.

Shortly before *Understanding Media* appeared, McLuhan declared that structuralism was fundamental to his method of intellectual inquiry, linking it to "modern depth criticism," meaning Practical Criticism in the manner of I. A. Richards.[94]

In McLuhan's own account, more than a decade later, when his overview of the subject had been reconfigured, he continued to acknowledge Richards as the principal source among those who had nourished his structuralist approach: "My structural approach began with I. A. Richards but developed very much through Sigfried Giedion, the Swiss art historian, and especially through my studies in classical rhetoric."[95]

McLuhan also put Poe,[96] Lewis,[97] Innis, Joyce, Pound, and Eliot[98] under the heading of structuralists. Structuralism appealed to McLuhan for its own merits *and* because it invited the type of interdisciplinary inquiry to which he spontaneously gravitated.[99] When McLuhan said he had "reached the structuralist stage where content is indifferent,"[100] he tied this directly to his media studies. He had learned structuralism as part of his literary apprenticeship at Cambridge, but it had also opened the way to him for media analysis, carrying him permanently beyond the precinct(s) of literary scholarship.

The flow of mail in response to *Understanding Media* brought McLuhan a letter from Montreal: "[Raymonde Dallaire of Montreal] claims there is a great affinity between linguistics and my sort of structural approach to media. She became interested in *Understanding Media* because she regards it as a suburb of linguistic study."[101]

Though Dallaire's take on McLuhan's work sprang from the interdisciplinary impulse he never resisted, he paid little attention to it.

It took a few more years, and a pointed suggestion to look to Saussure, to begin moving McLuhan toward a structuralism that was much less familiar to him than the legacy of Richards. It was a potent suggestion, combining the appeal of free play between media analysis and linguistics (itself a discipline at the crossroads of anthropology, psychology, and philosophy) with the prospect of sharpening the original McLuhan probe. Wrote Max Nanny: "By the way, I have found out that the difficulties concerning your insight 'The Medium is the Message' can elegantly be solved by a recourse to de Saussure's distinction between 'langue' and 'parole': the medium as 'langue' is the message; the medium as 'parole' is rather content oriented, or as you said, the user!"[102]

After Nanny made this suggestion, James M. Curtis published an article on McLuhan in relation to French structuralism to which McLuhan reacted favorably: "Your piece on me and French Structuralism pleased me a good deal . . . The most controversial area of my structural approach concerns the factor known only to James Joyce, the greatest of all structuralists, namely the conflict and complementarity of audible and visible space."[103]

To Curtis, McLuhan revealed his apprehensions and reservations about European structuralism: "So far as I can discover, the European structuralists work with a set of archetypes as paradigms. This ensures that there be a minimum of exploration and a maximum of mere matching in their activities."[104]

The situation was no better in North America, as far as McLuhan was concerned: "Apropos [D. E.] Berlyne, I agree that he is using the old visual systems approach but I think by pushing it as far as he does he has flipped into the non-visual world via structuralism. The same seems to me to be true of C. E. Osgood, with his semantic differential. By pushing the yes-no approach into the structural world, they get into territories which they don't understand for what they are."[105]

The territories in question are those of linguistics and anthropology, already alluded to by McLuhan in writing to Curtis and repeated frequently in his correspondence, beginning in 1972.[106]

But there was a paradox in structuralism that appealed to McLuhan: "Paradoxically, what is called 'structuralism' in linguistics and in the arts is characterized by the disappearance of merely visual lay-out in favour of iconic and multi-sensuous structures."[107]

And there was a further appeal. Not only could structuralism "solve the problem" of "the medium is the message," as Max Nanny had suggested, but it did so by fostering the integration of other McLuhan probes: "This approach is basically concerned with the *effects* of human artifacts, be they words or other signs or things . . . What I have used as an approach to the media was gathered from the symbolists. The structural linguists came out of the same symbolist world. Recall that Edgar Allen *[sic]* Poe started it all with his insistence that in order to make a poem, one must start with the effect and then look around for the means to such an effect."[108]

With respect to figure and ground, McLuhan wrote: "In Piaget's *Structuralism* he explains that with *figure-ground* there is no need for archetypes. They can be seen as existential results of the interplay of *figure* and *ground*. This was the work of Descartes in throwing aside rhetorical decorum and the public in favor of the pure ideas minus any *ground*."[109]

As McLuhan delved into Saussure and Piaget, a new brand of structuralism reconciling acoustic space and linear space became part of his working apparatus. "This matter is the theme of *Through the Vanishing Point* . . . But I push the matter a good deal further in *Take Today*, and this has been possible since discovering the nature of tactile space in quantum mechanics and modern physics."[110]

McLuhan was now citing Saussure and James A. Boon (*From Symbolism to Structuralism*) as supporting his own notion of media, inasmuch as "Saussure explains that a sign is an effect of a hidden process."[111] though Saussure needed help that McLuhan was ready to give him: "[Saussure] regards all language as central to such hidden processes [ground for figures] and studies all language patterns as *effects*. He divides all structures into the *diachronic* or visual, and *synchronic* or acoustic. He doesn't happen to understand the difference between the visual and the acoustic, and so uses these terms only as classifications without fully understanding their structures" . . .[112]

In so saying, McLuhan was also on his way to elaborating the interlocking laws of media and tetrads, and here too structuralism was exerting its influence. By 1976 he could say: "All of man's artifacts are *structurally* linguistic and metaphoric."[113]

A year before the stroke that ended his research and writing, he could call the galaxy of ideas forming structuralism "the perfect fulfillment of my research."[114]

In elaborating this idea, he reverted once more to his concern for the discarnate state of mankind under electronic technology.

Linguistics is often said to be the most human of the sciences and the most scientific of the humanities. It is a saying that surely would have appealed to McLuhan, though it appears to be little help in answering the criticisms brought against him. What are the criteria of scientific theory that Jonathan Miller found lacking in McLuhan's work? It must be formal (i.e., formulated independently of language), testable, and have the power to predict, or show itself to be universally applicable. In *Laws of Media* the McLuhans follow the method implicit in this definition of scientific theory, but their discoveries ultimately challenge the first part of it, in that the laws of media prove not to require formulation independently of language: "Utterings are outering (extensions), so media are not *as* words, they actually *are* words."[115]

Laws of Media (2)

There are four laws of media, and all four apply to all media. The McLuhan challenge to find a medium to which fewer than the four laws apply, or to find a fifth law, remains open. The laws are not given as statements but as questions, so as to invite their application to as wide a variety of humankind's endeavors as possible: "They apply to all human artefacts, whether hardware or software, whether bulldozers or buttons, or poetic styles or philosophical systems."[116]

Here, once again, are the four questions that the McLuhans invite us to ask about any medium:

What does it extend (amplify or enlarge)?
What does it make obsolete?
What does it retrieve?
What does it reverse into?

For "extend," in the phrasing of the first law, we may also substitute "enhance," "intensify," "make possible," or "accelerate," depending on the case. A refrigerator enhances the availability of a wide range of foods. Perspective in painting intensifies a single point of view. A photocopier makes possible the reproduction of texts at the speed of the printing press. The computer accelerates the speed of calculations and retrieval of information.

Obsolescence is a consequence of extension. When a medium fulfills its function of extending the body, or replacing another medium, parts of the environment of whatever was extended become obsolete. When the car replaced the horse, it did away with stables, blacksmiths, saddle makers, harness-menders, hitching posts, horse troughs, carts, stagecoaches, etc.

Under the law of retrieval, older structures and environments, older forms of action, human organization, and thought are brought back by a new medium. They were part of the human environment that became obsolete at least two technologies ago. Feminism, in extremist form, retrieves the corporate identity of matriarchal society. A dinner table retrieves the picking and choosing options surrendered by early humans, who discovered in the lap a site for isolating, manipulating, and defending their food.

The principle of reversal comes into operation in cases when a technology is pushed to its limit: it will take on the complement of its original features or of its intended function. A dinner table, if very large, no longer offers the ease of reach for which tables were originally designed. If overcrowded, the dinner table can reverse from a place for sharing food into a site where table mates aggressively intrude on each other's space.

The laws of media interact. They reveal a dynamic pattern of interlocking effects typical of any technology or human construction. Extension and obsolescence are linked as action to reaction, which is not the case for retrieval and reversal. A medium does not reverse into its opposite because some older form has been retrieved; it reverses because it is pushed to its limit.

There are complementary qualities among the laws taken in pairs, *either horizontally or vertically*, if the components of a given tetrad are arranged in diagrammatic form:

AMPLIFICATION	REVERSAL
RETRIEVAL	OBSOLESCENCE

This is clear from the effects noted in the following examples:

(1) Alcohol enhances energy but reverses into depression.
(2) The car enhances individual privacy but reverses into the corporate privacy of traffic jams.
(3) Earth-orbiting satellites extend the planet and retrieve ecology.
(4) Cubism makes visual space obsolete and reverses into the nonvisual.

(5) The microphone makes private space obsolete and reverses into-collective space.

In the realm of language itself, *Laws of Media* offers, among others, tetrads for semiotics, written language, slang, cliché, the spoken word, symbolist poetry, hyperbole, rhetoric, dialectic, metaphor, irony, metonymy, and the word "is" as a copula. This profusion of tetrads may suggest that language is too complex to be described by a single tetrad, but both McLuhan's definition of language as mankind's first technology and the tetrad structure itself appear to be respected if it formulated as:

SELF-EXPRESSION THROUGH SPEECH

EXTENDS thought   RETRIEVES feeling
REVERSE INTO gesture   OBSOLESCES grunts and groans

Given the consistently central place of language in McLuhan's work throughout his career, one is tempted to ask if McLuhan is a linguist. The question would have made him laugh. It needs to be unasked, because it invites an answer that accepts assumptions, divisions, and categories. It was McLuhan's business to tear these down, not build them up, much less put himself within their confines. Those who taught McLuhan to think about language (F. R. Leavis, Mansfield Forbes, I. A. Richards) did not call themselves linguists, nor did McLuhan develop approaches to language along any lines that present-day linguists would claim as their own. And yet, if we are prepared to grant that psychoanalyst Jacques Lacan is a linguist because of his reconstruction of Saussure's concept of the sign, or that philosopher Jacques Derrida is a linguist because of his deconstruction of Saussure's analytical framework, then we must accord McLuhan the same honor. But Lacan, Derrida, and McLuhan all appropriate Saussure's notions to their own purposes outside linguistics. How far outside? In McLuhan's case, perhaps no further than the context that Saussure himself envisaged for linguistics, namely semiotics. In this respect McLuhan comes closer to realizing Saussure's ultimate objective than Lacan or Derrida or any other appropriator of Saussure's thought. It is interesting to note that whereas Saussure imports metaphors (planets in the solar system, the chemistry of water, chess, music, natural species, patched cloth, plant life, photographs, tapestry, and life-belts) to describe language, McLuhan uses language itself as a metaphor for all media (all extension of our physical senses), all human artifacts. This suggests that McLuhan's approach offers the prospect of integrating linguistics and semiotics in a fashion bolder than any hinted at by Saussure himself and yet compatible with the foundations he laid. Moreover, McLuhan's metaphor *of* language *for* media is no metaphor at all, just as the body of Christ in the Roman Catholic faith, so important to McLuhan, is no metaphor but a real presence created by the mystery of transubstantiation in the Eucharist.

CHAPTER SIX

USING MCLUHAN'S TOOLS

If McLuhan's ideas are better understood today than they were when supporting evidence for them was less apparent, it is still possible to come across the occasional newspaper item emblazoned with a heading such as "McLuhan wrong about TV"! (see below). It is also possible to open that newspaper as McLuhan did, as he counsels his readers to do, perceiving it as an environment that creates effects on its user. The same approach to any technology, including the many that had not yet been invented in his day, allows us to evaluate critical reactions to McLuhan, to test the validity of his media laws in new applications, and to evaluate the usefulness of his framework for studying the interaction of culture and technology. This chapter is intended to consolidate the whole core of McLuhan's thoughtscape and help readers put it to new uses.

(1) *How does McLuhan's third media law (the law of retrieval) apply to e-mail?*
Answer: E-mail retrieves the telegram—brings it back into use in a new (wireless, paperless) and intensified form.

(2) *How does the same law apply to the Blackberry?*
Answer: The Blackberry retrieves the fax—brings it into use in a new (wireless, paperless) and intensified form.

(3) *Darren Wershler-Henry (see References) states: "Masses of technical details can imply a sense of importance by their sheer volume and density, but they are often mute as to why we should care about them." What reason does McLuhan give as to why we should care about them?*

Answer: Because any technology has a far-reaching effect on the speed and scale of the human activity that it facilitates and on the pattern of human relations that it introduces or modifies. The author of the quotation above makes the same point when he states: "It's the cultural factor [of the book under review] that makes for compelling reading, because it links our technologies to the processes that groomed us into the forms we currently hold. The cultural history of an artefact, in other words, is what explains its relevance to us." (The book under review is Henry Petroski's *The Toothpick: Technology and Culture*.)

(4) *The South Western Ontario Software Quality Group tetrad for the car states that it reverses into buses and suburbs. Is this consistent with how McLuhan himself applied his media laws?*

Answer: Absolutely. It might seem odd to lump buses and suburbs together, but here are some key points to remember: (i) *Reverses into* here has nothing to do with a careless car driver backing into a bus; it means the flip into a new form that occurs when a technology is pushed to its limit. Make a car big enough to hold 50 people and you have flipped it into a bus. (ii) Don't forget that the media laws apply both to technologies themselves and to the human environments they affect. (This point was already brought home in the quotation in (3) above.) Hence, the reference here to suburbs. (iii) The four media laws interact in complementary ways, including *extends* is to *reverses into* as *retrieves* is to *obsolesces*. For the present example one complementarity in the full tetrad for the car is *car extends city (urban sprawl)/car flips city into non-city (suburb)*.

(5) *An interviewer, exasperated with McLuhan's way of thinking, once asked him how a book could be a technology, exploding then with "It's too small!" What's the answer?*

Answer: Apparently the besotted interviewer had never heard of microchips, which are all substantially smaller than even real small books but definitely qualify as technology. How could the size of whatever be the crucial factor for qualifying it as a *technology?* (The interviewer in question must have been thinking of those first-generation computers that were the size of rooms.) A technology, any technology, any medium, for McLuhan, is something that extends one or more of our five physical senses. The book is a form of print, is a form of writing, is a visual form of the voice giving expression to ideas, which is where the chain of media working in pairs ends.

Ideas don't hang around by themselves. Unless they are uttered (outered, or ushered of our brains and into our mouths with the help of lungs and teeth and other human body sound equipment) they are unknown to anyone but ourselves and unknown even to ourselves, unless we have learned their outerings through the conventional signs of a language. Here we are back to media working in pairs, and technology in the McLuhan sense, and size does *not* matter.

(6) *What is the subliminal message in this line?*
Answer: Because the medium is the message, the medium of print "sends a message" that it is to be read from left to right, from top to bottom, one unit, one letter at a time. Print is linear, rational, uniform. Because it dominated the way we received information for hundreds of years (that is until electronic technologies displaced it), it has a spill over effect—the arbitrary privileging of one-at-a-timeness, the linear, rational, uniform use of space. For McLuhan, it is no accident that students typically sat around their teacher before the invention of print, but sitting in neat rows became the school room norm once print technology came into the ascendancy. Print also fostered the mechanical hegemony of the Industrial Revolution: assembly lines, etc.

(7) *What do a hammer, a house, and a hydrofoil have in common?*
Answer: They are all technologies, all extensions of the body. The hammer extends the fist (for giving blows), the house extends our skin (for giving warmth), and the hydrofoil, a hybrid of the boat and the airplane, extends our feet.

(8) *What do a hammer, a language, and electric light have in common?*
Answer: They are all technologies, all extensions of the body. A hammer extends the fist (for giving blows), a language is a technology for letting go of the environment in order to grasp it in new ways (*Understanding Media*, p. 85), and electric light extends our eyesight.

(9) *McLuhan often comments on popular language in relation to media and media effects. What do you think he would say about the expression "to split the scene" (meaning "to leave")?*
Answer: Split is *tactile* and scene is visual. The expression suggests a desire for in-depth participation in an environment that does not offer that possibility. The solution is to react against the environment, to split the scene.

(10) *What is the role of environment in the street gang activity known as "swarming"' (a group of attackers surrounding a victim)?*
Answer: The activity articulates a reaction to an invisible, hostile environment by creating a visible, hostile environment.

(11) *One of the signs of the Holy Spirit at Pentecost was the wind. How does wind relate to our physical senses?*
Answer: Wind is primarily audio-tactile, but it also has an olfactory (sense of smell) dimension, capable of wrapping us in the environment of elsewhere. It is presence and absence together, coming to and intensifying all our senses except sight. Visually it reveals only its effects.

(12) *A cartoon shows a mother with her infant son looking at a text message saying "C-U-L8R." She says "Sound it out." What point is she missing?*
Answer: The alphabet (C, U, L, R) is phonetic, showing us how to "sound it out," but 8 is not. The shape of 8 does not tell us how to pronounce it, any more than & shows us the three sounds of *and* or % represents those of *per cent*. Text messaging is a hybrid of phonetic and nonphonetic forms, so it can't be consistently sounded out in the same way as a message represented completely in the standard phonetic alphabet.

(13) *Look at the cover of Wired magazine. What is the graphic design doing with the hot medium of the alphabet?*
Answer: Everything is working to turn it into a cool medium. Figure and ground are in constant play: where the color of the ground for a figure (letter) is different from that of the full page, the color of the alternate ground shades the figure (letter), and there is an interplay of back-lit ground and back-lit figures.

(14) *McLuhan said that a medium is an environment and that a message is an effect. Since he also said that the medium is the message and the user is the content, what is the logical consequence of the four statements?*
Answer: The environment is the effect it has on its user. With message as effect differentiated from content but user identified with content, *the medium is the message* becomes totally uncontroversial. Would a hay fever sufferer dispute that the environment (pollen) is the effect (sneezing)?

(15) *What is the effect of the fad for mounting fluorescent lighting on the underside of a car?*

Answer: The car becomes iconic and sculptural, intensified as figure by a new intermediate ground of light. The illusion is created that the car is floating rather than rolling. Flashing or sequential lighting for license plate frames is acceptable in conjunction with the hot medium of the letters and numbers so framed, but would not be for the cool medium of the car.

(16) Wired *magazine's Jargon Watch for March 2009 (useful at this point to review McLuhan's lesson on cliché/archetype and his reminder that a cliché can only identify what is already passé) identifies self-embedding disorder as a "disturbing trend among teenagers involving the insertion of small objects under the skin for self-injury. Radiologists have found needles, paper clips, and glass embedded in the fingers and necks of patients" (p. 033). How would McLuhan explain this trend?*
Answer: Since electronic technology constitutes a metaphorical ripping off of the flesh, an effect which is felt without its cause being recognized, a natural reaction manifests itself in an attempt to pre-empt the effect by self-mutilation.

(17) *Glue, cement, nails, scotch tape, paper clips, and rubber bands are technologies for extending what?*
Answer: All of them hold things together, making them extensions of fingers, hands, and arms.

(18) *What have been the effects of the car and the computer on police forces?*
Answer: The car took the policeman off the beat and put him in his cruiser. The computer keeps him in the cruiser.

(19) *What is the tetrad for the car?*
Answer: You will find it below in #68.

(20) *A media illiterate wrote "the invigorating effect of TV that was predicted by McLuhan has failed to materialize?" (*Globe and Mail, *3 February 1988, p. A7). What exactly did McLuhan say about the "invigorating effect of TV?"*
Answer: Nothing. In fact, in *Understanding Media*, he stresses the opposite, stating that he examines "the never-explained numbness that each extension brings about in the individual and society" (*Understanding Media*, p. 8).

(21) *What changes would Rush Limbaugh have to make in his appearance if he were a spokesman for the left wing?*

Answer: He would need to be slimmer, with longer hair and a beard. These are iconic features of left-wing spokespersons.

(22) *"Something utterly divine/about a friend of mine/making a mixed tape/flipping through discs, vinyl fits/ of brilliance, phasing in, rewinding, finding,/bleedin' Costello into cream, Prince into/pixies, playing with pace/the space between./ Playing with pace/the space/between./ It was collage and tribute/of timing and artful leaps/but mostly it was awkward. Digital has/made us/impatient."* "New Year's Resolution: All Things Awkward" by Nanci Lee (The Coast, *Halifax, Nova Scotia, 27 December 2007, p, 20). Impatient for what?*
Answer: For digital itself. Yes or no, plus or minus, one or zero. It lends an ironical sense to the phrase *digitally remastered*, both in this context and in the context of text messaging with our opposable thumbs. Compare McLuhan's comments on dialectics in the context of the classical trivium.

(23) *What is made obsolete by the twinning of illustrated books and interactive CDs?*
Answer: The integrity of the book. Unless the author has intended her work to be twinned, the interruptions created by the computer result in the loss of structure and effects of style intended by the author.

(24) *What effect would the computer have had on Shakespeare's writings?*
Answer: It would depend on whether or not he used his style-checker. When Hamlet's "to be or not to be" speech was run through a style-checker, it detected thirty-four errors and commented that the language was obsolete and overwritten, suggesting that the whole speech be concisely rephrased as "Is it better to live with bad luck or end it all and have nightmares?"

(25) *What is the tetrad for e-cigarettes?*
Answer: They *extend* independence from tobacco, *obsolesce* tobacco combustion and smoke, *retrieve* the hookah in a new form, and *reverse into* nicotine addiction.

(26) *When it was discovered during the shooting of a movie that the real name of the actor playing John Lennon (up till then the filmmakers had known only his stage name) was the same as the real-life killer of Lennon, the actor was fired. Is there a lesson about technology here?*

Answer: Yes, about what McLuhan called mankind's first technology: language. When language first emerged, mankind did not distinguish between word and thing. The word *was* the thing. It was dangerous to name a god or savage beast by its true name, because it might appear, so taboos and euphemisms came into use. In the late twentieth century, this effect, known as *word magic*, still retains its power, because we remain unaware of media effects. The moviemakers acknowledged that it was just an extraordinary coincidence but felt that it was in the best interests of the project for another actor to be cast as John Lennon.

(27) *What is the tetrad for word magic?*
Answer: You will find it below in #68.

(28) *Remembering that McLuhan says that media contain or extend other media, what are the primary media contained by television?*
Answer: Light (which contains no other medium) and speech (which extends thought).

(29) *The deciphering in the early 1980s of what was believed to be the earliest writing system indicated that the Sumerians kept extensive records relating to taxation, business contracts, agricultural and industrial output, bureaucratic titles, etc. Does this confirm any of McLuhan's observations?*
Answer: It confirms his view that the effect of writing is to create fragmentation and specialization.

(30) *The technology has been in place since the early 1990s to put credit cards on line with electronic lotteries. What process does this intensify?*
Answer: Annual global sales of lottery tickets already exceeded $25 billion before the development of this technology that makes money more than ever a metaphor. In *Understanding Media*, McLuhan called money the poor man's credit card.

(31) *What are some consequences of computer commuting (working from home via computer)?*
Answer: Environmental damage from overuse of cars is reduced, traffic accidents are reduced, child-care costs can be eliminated, expenses for dressing for the workplace and for eating away from home can be reduced, illness transmitted in the workplace can be reduced, relief from the aggravation of daily commuting is provided, time cost as

well as monetary cost of commuting is eliminated, prejudicial practices are eliminated by the computer environment.

(32) *DNA testing of goatskin parchment may allow fragments from the Dead Sea Scrolls to be assembled and deciphered. Scholars will also be able to determine locations of goatherds relative to scribes, where and when scrolls were written, and whether Essenes wrote or simply collated the scrolls. What would McLuhan have to say about this?*
Answer: The technology involved retrieves message as content in "the medium is the message."

(33) *What might explain the popularity of tattoos, body-piercing, etc., in the twenty-first century?*
Answer: The computer as an extension of the central nervous system and bioengineering have turned the body into a site for experimental art forms. (Compare #16 above.)

(34) *Among McLuhan's critics, a comment such as the following is typical: McLuhan was wrong when he described the TV as creating a global village. What is the inaccuracy in this statement?*
Answer: McLuhan did not say that TV created the global village, he said that electronic interdependence (all electronic media together) restructured the world in the form of a global village.

(35) *Canadian poet and novelist David Helwig has described sound as the most concrete and imposing of perceptions, noting that you can turn your eyes away from an objectionable sight, but that you cannot turn your ears away. Is this related to a McLuhan percept?*
Answer: Yes, the percept of acoustic space, which interested McLuhan because it is a sort of wraparound space, boundless and without horizon, unlike visual space, which is rational, linear, and sequential. One of McLuhan's observations, similar to Helwig's, is that you cannot see around a corner but you can hear around it.

(36) *Do pen-based computers, like the Apple Newton, that recognize the letters you print turn the alphabet into a cool medium?*
Answer: No, these computers instantly translate what you write into high-definition typed text for transmission or printing. The *principle* of the alphabet is not affected by this technology, but the *future* of the alphabet is uncertain, because it is a high-definition medium now in constant use on low-definition computer screens.

(37) *What is the human reflex that goes with McLuhan's notion of closure as completing an image?*
Answer: Squinting.

(38) *What is the human reflex that goes with McLuhan's notion of closure as the closing down of one of our physical senses?*
Answer: The closing down *is* a reflex.

(39) *An advertisement promoting retirement savings plans for a bank gives a top-down view of stacks of coins arranged to spell out RSP. What lesson does this recall from McLuhan's teachings?*
Answer: Money is a medium as much as the alphabet. In the advertisement, the coins are an iconic form of money, as is the abbreviation RSP.

(40) *Does the advent of cable television with hundreds of channels support McLuhan's description of the global village?*
Answer: Yes, he described the global village as "fission and fusion," "discontinuity, division and diversity."

(41) *David Helwig has said that the Holocaust has been cheapened by being turned into a general phrase for evil. Is this related to a McLuhan concept?*
Answer: Yes, it is an example of an archetype turning into a cliché.

(42) *"Morphing" is a film industry technique in which transformations of a primary image are computer-generated. It has been used in such films as* Terminator II, *where the evil humanoid turns to liquid, passes through iron bars, transforms body parts to weapons, etc. What is gained and lost in this process?*
Answer: Speed and technical efficiency are gained. Without the technique, illustrators must draw incremental changes in an image one by one. Morphing ensures uniformity of imagery, but pushed to the limit, it removes the illustrator from the craft altogether.

(43) *A beer ad reads: "we take the time to brew it light." Is this a cliché?*
Answer: No, the cliché "take the time to do it right" is reworked here as a probe. This is what McLuhan means when he says that Madison Avenue has turned ads into art.

(44) *Canadian artist Alan Flint shapes words out of wood, brick, cardboard, plastic, plaster, etc. In a field he dug out the word "WOUND"*

in giant letters to symbolize the effect of human systems on the earth. Is this an example of the medium being the message?
Answer: Yes. Language is technology for McLuhan and words are artefacts. Flint's "WOUND" is part of the technology of language executed in a way that reminds us that the technology of digging wounds the earth. Flint weds his words to different technologies but in every case reminds us of the link between the word's meaning and the technology used in spelling it out. He also reminds us that words are artefacts and forces us to reflect on the medium and the message by forcing them together in new ways. (This is also another example of an artist making probes out of clichés.)

(45) *What has been the effect of the wireless microphone on musical theater?*
Answer: Voices are mediated by backstage sound boards, the sound engineer's decisions as to appropriate volume level superseding performers' modulations and breaking the unity of the projected voice and the stage presence.

(46) *What techniques have newspapers like* USA Today *borrowed from television?*
Answer: Heavy use of color, eye-catching graphics, news stories presented in concise texts. Compared to the page layouts of more traditional newspapers, those of *USA Today* approach what McLuhan called the tactility of the television screen. It is very much the newspaper of the TV generation.

(47) *Galvanic skin response (GSR) technology amplifies changes in the electrical conductivity of skin and transforms them into signals that can control a computer. What media does this technology potentially eliminate?*
Answer: The skin responses are modulated forms of thought. All technologies from numbers to fingers that mediate between a user's thought and the operation of the computer are potentially eliminated by GSR.

(48) *One of the most memorable photographs taken when the Berlin Wall fell in 1989 showed East Germans and West Germans holding hands and dancing atop the Wall, with the Brandenburg Gate in the background. What made this image so compelling?*
Answer: It is a powerful mix of iconic clichés for separation, union, celebration, and empire, never possible until that moment and never

repeatable. (It was quickly appropriated by a telephone company as part of a reach-out-and-touch-someone advertising campaign.)

(49) *Is the international money market like a light bulb?*
Answer: McLuhan calls the light bulb "pure information"—all medium and no message. On the money markets, media of exchange are exchanged for each other—not for commodities or services or anything else.

(50) *Illiteracy is inability to read and write; postliteracy is an environment where reading habits (especially attention to detail from the age dominated by print) no longer prevail. What are some technological factors, other than the pervasiveness of TV, contributing to postliterate culture?*
Answer: Word-processing at electric speed, the "authority" of style-checking software, books on tape and CD, low-density printing on PC screens (designed for cursory rather than careful reading), formula books.

(51) *Is it correct to say that clichés are hot and archetypes are cool?*
Answer: Yes, clichés are fixed, high-definition, and require no participation; archetypes are open-ended and invite participation.

(52) *In his philosophical novel* Lila, *Robert Pirsig says that "Dynamic Quality is not structured and yet is not chaotic. It is value that cannot be contained by static patterns" (p. 142). How does this relate to McLuhan's work?*
Answer: It is a description of the media effects that McLuhan studies (and, incidentally, a description of his own style of writing).

(53) *Is Wii an example of the McLuhan principle of the user as content?*
Answer: Wii is an interactive technology that integrates the user's movements with images on a screen, but McLuhan articulated his principle long before any such technology existed. He identified the user of a medium as its content *because* any medium is an extension of the human body.

(54) *High-tech contact lenses capable of beaming video programming directly into the eyeball may become available. They would be powered by body heat. In the context of the standard McLuhan tetrad, what does this as-yet undeveloped technology have the potential for reversing into?*

Answer: Metaphorical blindness.

(55) *The British supermarket Sainsbury's announced in the spring of 2009 an initiative to spare seafood shoppers the embarrassment of buying pollock (sounds like "bollocks—British slang for testicles). The new name for the fish is "colin." As a visual reminder of the old name, prepackaged portions come in bright, splashy wrap suggestive of a Jackson Pollock painting. Is this another example of word magic, as in #25 above?*
Answer: Yes.

(56) *Is the pollock-Pollock connection an example of the medium being the message?*
Answer: Yes and no. Media that pervade some aspect of social inter-action, as the book and television pervade communication, put their unique imprint on that interaction and in that sense *carry their own message*, independently of the information that they transmit. Likewise, the Jackson Pollock-inspired fish wrapper carries a pack-aging message that it shares with all other packaging *and* a second message specific to itself: "Hey, I look like a Pollock, and I'm wrapped around a pollock." But a shopper has to get the connection for the latter to become its own message; a television viewer does not need to understand the effect of the medium on her eye for that effect to take place. McLuhan wrote *Understanding Media* to wake the world up to such effects.

(57) *McLuhan opens the Introduction to the second edition of* Understanding Media *with "[Television host] Jack Paar mentioned that he once had said to a young friend, 'Why do you kids use <cool> to mean <hot>?'" More recently,* The Toronto Star (24.01.04) *fea-tured an article headed, "Why 'cool' will always remain hot." Does the McLuhan tetrad of media laws offer any insight into the apparent paradox here?*
Answer: Yes, in the tetrad structure the interrelated processes of amplification, obsolescence, and retrieval are completed by reversal, or flip, such as documented for *hot* and *cool* in the two quotations here. Long before completing his media research with the develop-ment of the tetrad, McLuhan devoted a chapter of *Understanding Media* to the reversal of an overheated medium. With respect to the hot medium of the book and the cool medium of television, it is pertinent to note that a talking head on television is an overheating

of a cool medium but a one-word sentence occupying a full page of print is not an overcooling of a hot medium.

(58) *Erik Davis (*Techgnosis, *New York: Harmony Books, 1998), speaks of "technology, in both the metaphoric sense of techniques and the literal sense of tools" (p. 128). Does McLuhan also distinguish between the metaphoric and literal senses of technology?*
Answer: No. He sees all technologies, including all forms of hardware, as having the four-part structure of metaphor, which ties in with the tetrad of media laws and double figure/double ground analysis. Davis would not agree. In another context, he states that "McLuhan often went overboard with his rhetorical bravura . . ." (p. 175).

(59) *Erik Davis (*Techgnosis, *New York: Harmony Books, 1998), recounts a portion of one of the Gnostic gospels as follows: "Christ (a.k.a. the Logos) secretly enters the garden [Eden] disguised as the serpent, and thus manages to unload some redemptive knowledge . . ." (p. 99). This notion of Christ/serpent is typical of symbolism's union of opposites. Is it compatible with the reversal principle in McLuhan's tetrad of media laws?*
Answer: Yes, but Gnosticism was repugnant to McLuhan, a devout Roman Catholic.

(60) *An ad for text messaging says "Let your thumbs do the talking." Is the "thumb" bit like the "numb" bit from James Joyce's "Who gave you that numb?" Is it "allforabit" all over again?*
Answer: It's more like "dumb" (silent) for "numb" in the sense that mute letters substitute for the voice in text messaging. And it's more like two bits for all (two digits only functioning instead of all ten)— opposable thumbs opposing nothing.

(61) *AFP News Service reported in March 2009 that one in five U.S. teens has had 'tech sex,'—that is, sent nude or partially nude images of themselves to someone by e-mail or mobile phone. Is this what McLuhan meant in saying that man is the sex-organ of the machine?*
Answer: No. In the first place, McLuhan always distinguished between machine technology and electronic technology, computers and mobile phones do not qualify as machines in his overview, because they function essentially by electronic circuitry and not by moving parts. He was simply referring to mankind's urge to constantly create new technology.

(62) *Ron Burnett*, How Images Think *(Cambridge: MIT Press, 2004)*, states: *"Clearly information transmission depends on the medium in use, and in that narrow sense, the medium is the message. In all of this the issues of content and semantics seem to disappear. McLuhan's popularization of the medium is the message has had a negative impact and overdetermined impact on the cultural understanding of communications technologies" (p. 163). What points from McLuhan's ideas has Burnett missed?*

Answer: McLuhan never said the medium is the message *in the narrow sense.* On the contrary, he was always stretching meanings. Content and semantics do not disappear in McLuhan's perspective, but there is a fundamental distinction to be made, in his view, between a simple, uncontroversial, and unproblematic sense of *content* (information in the conventional sense of data and its transmission) and the sense of *message,* as social impact of a medium.

(63) *An ad for Blackberry carries the heading "Clickalicious," stating that the first-ever touch screen Blackberry smart phone feels better than any previous product because the screen clicks like a button when the user presses it. What is going on here from McLuhan's perspective?*

Answer: In the first instance, the touch screen simulated buttons but eliminated both the conventional tactility and the sound of high-definition buttons being pressed. The new Blackberry restores the latter, giving the new model an intensity that brings it back one step toward the integration of the five physical senses.

(64) *The Wall Street debacle of 2008 can be imputed to the use of the Gaussian formula $P=\Phi$ (A, B, γ) for calculating risk management and valuations. It failed because its final element (γ) is a correlation parameter that was assigned a constant value. Is there a lesson from McLuhan's work that predicts this failure?*

Answer: McLuhan predicted the complete disappearance of the stock market by the year 2000 (and spaceships with edible interior parts for astronauts), not a crash. On the other hand, the outcome of Poe's story of the Maelstrom warns, in its own way, about assigning a constant value to a correlation parameter. The brother who drowned did this by clinging to the ring-bolt aboard the ship. The other understood that long objects such as planks and tree trunks were sucked down by the Maelstrom, as were spherical objects, so he assigned them both a correlation value of x. When he saw that barrels did not go down, he assigned them a correlation value of y, clung to one, and survived. (He would have avoided ring-bolt futures in the market of '08.)

(65) *Consult confickerworkinggroup.org/infection_test/cfeyechart.html. How does the Conficker Eye Chart relate to McLuhan's work?*
Answer: The Conficker Eye Chart is a diagnostic test. The link between how the chart appears on your screen and your PC being infected by the Conficker worm works backward from effect to cause, as McLuhan did in all of his analysis of media effects. But more than one screen display is possible, so not all effects unequivocally indicate the presence of the Conficker worm as their cause. This makes the screen display a weak diagnostic sign and takes the whole discussion here to a level of semiotics that McLuhan did not investigate.

(66) *Remembering that McLuhan called language mankind's first technology, his tetrad of media laws must apply to all forms and uses of language. What is the tetrad for puns?*
Answer: The pun multiplies (*extends*) meaning, scraps (*obsolesces*) single meaning, retrieves an archetype, and flips into (*reverses into*) cliché. Joyce's pun *allforabit* extends the meaning of *alphabet* to include the lesson on semiotic reduction that McLuhan privileged, obsolesces the literal meaning (no pun intended) of *alphabet*, retrieves the archetype of the concept of reduction, adding *allforabit* to it, but becomes a cliché itself by being cited and repeated.

(67) *McLuhan called language a corporate mask worn by all the speakers of a language. What is the tetrad for a mask?*
Answer: You will find it below in #68.

(68) *Read the following extract from the script of a multi-media piece and proceed to the questions at the end.*

NOW IS:
The Life and Work of Marshall McLuhan
(libretto for multi-media)

Section 3: From Fire to Spire

Cast: Mansfield Forbes, Cambridge/Wisconsin McLuhan, Wisconsin Student (1936), pre-Socratic philosopher, Gerard Manley Hopkins, Ferdinand de Saussure, The Nymph Echo, Narcissus, James Joyce, Pablo Picasso, An Aspiring Artist, The TV McLuhan, Corinne

McLuhan at age 25 (nonspeaking part), Ludwig Wittgenstein, Vittorio Gassman, Student (2009), 3 more Wisconsin students, An Irritated Parent, Henry Ford, Jonathan Miller, Thomas Nashe, e.e. cummings, Wyndham Lewis, Tom Wolfe, Sir William Gilbert, Sigmund Freud.

Offstage Voice: Cambridge, 1934.
Mansfield Forbes (*at lectern*): Your other professors have told you what ground they will cover with you. I will cover no ground; I will teach you to dig in the most fertile parts.
Offstage Voice: Madison, Wisconsin, 1936.
Cambridge/Wisconsin McLuhan (*turns 180 degrees away Forbes*): Your other professors have told you . . .
Wisconsin Student: Professor McLuhan, I just want to say that I've seen *every* movie with Frederick March, and I think you look just like him.
Offstage voices: Roar of laughter from rest of class.
Mansfield Forbes: I will cover no ground . . .
Pre-Socratic Philosopher: Fire, air, water, earth . . .
Gerard Manley Hopkins: That Nature is like the Heraclitean fire and of the power of the Resurrection . . .
Saussure: Fire, spire, figure, earth
    Syllables of built-in worth
    Echo power - - -
C/W McLuhan (*by himself, to himself*): Your other professors . . .
Mansfield Forbes: I will cover no ground . . .
C/W McLuhan: I will discover ground . . .
The Nymph Echo: Water's not what fishes see. Nor he (*pointing to Narcissus*).
Narcissus: I will discover no ground. (He goes down on one knee as to look at his image reflected in water and Echo looks over his shoulder.)
James Joyce: As for the viability of vicinals, when invisible they are invincible.
Picasso: I will recover ground.
Aspiring Artist: Ground is background, figure is foreground.
Picasso: But in cubism . . .
TV McLuhan: Ground cannot be dealt with conceptually or abstractly, it is ceaselessly changing, dynamic, discontinuous, and heterogeneous, a mosaic of intervals and contours. It is all

medium and no message . . . unless the medium *is* the message and the user is the content.
Pre-Socratic Philosopher: Fire . . .

Stage goes dark and then illuminated intermittently by stationary mirror ball before stage lights come up again.

Pre-Socratic Philosopher: Fire, air . . .

Stage goes dark and then illuminated by rotating mirror ball before stage lights come up again.

TV McLuhan: The student today lives mythically and in depth.
Wisconsin Student: Do you believe in God, Professor McLuhan?
James Joyce: In the name of the Farbung, the Scent, and the Holiodrops . . .
Gerard Manley Hopkins: I caught this morning/morning's min-ion/kingdom of daylight's dauphin/ dapple-dawn-drawn falcon/ in his riding over rolling level underneath him steady air . . .
C/W McLuhan: Your other professors have told you . . .

Bell sounds to end class and students stampede onto dance floor illuminated by mirror ball.

TV McLuhan: Visual space is the space of detachment; acoustic space is tactile. It is the space of involvement.

Dance sequence. Students only at first, then Cambridge/Wisconsin McLuhan in white tails and top hat and Corinne McLuhan enter dancing upstage left and exit dancing downstage right.

TV McLuhan (*looking after the dancing McLuhans*): The meaning of experience is typically one generation behind the experience. (*He pauses.*) All words at every level of prose and poetry and all devices of language and speech derive their meaning from figure/ground relation.
Saussure (looking up from the chessboard where he is playing against Wittgenstein):
>   Fire, spire, figure, earth

> Syllables of built-in worth
> Echo power - - -

TV McLuhan: The Bible belt is oral territory and therefore despised by the literati.

C/W McLuhan: Today we will look at Addison.

Student #1 (*robotic delivery*): Joseph Addison, English essayist, 1672–1719 . . .

C/W McLuhan: Did I say *look* at Addison?

Student #2 (*robotic delivery*): Joseph Addison was educated at Queen's College and Magdalen, Oxford . . .

C/W McLuhan: They're looking in books.

Student #1 (*robotic delivery*): Joseph Addison wrote *The Campaign*, 1704 . . .

C/W McLuhan: . . . looking *at* books.

Student #2 (*robotic delivery*): . . . the opera *Rosamund*, 1706.

C/W McLuhan: Bogged down in books.

Student #1 (*robotic delivery*): 274 numbers of the *Spectator* signed C or L or I or O . . .

TV McLuhan: Faced with information overload, we have no recourse but to pattern recognition.

Student #3 (to the tune of Harvest Moon: "January, February . . ."): Addison in Madison, C, L, O or I.

TV McLuhan: The reader is the content of any poem *and* of the language he employs to use *any* form of language. To use language is to put it on.

Vittorio Gassman: Non facciamo bella figura!

2009 Student: Go figure!

Wisconsin Student: Go figure? Scratches her head and walks offstage.

TV McLuhan: School is the advertising agency which makes you believe you need the society as it is.

C/W McLuhan (*thoughtful and excited*): Today (*long pause*) we will look at advertising.

TV McLuhan: Madison Avenue comes to Madison, Wisconsin.

C/W McLuhan: The modern artist, deluged with the art styles of all times and places, has been obliged just for self-preservation to seek not a style but to penetrate to the essence of the art function and process itself. Exactly the same program is forced upon political and social thought today. Either we penetrate to the essential or we continue as flotsam and jetsam on a flood of transient fads and ideas that will drown us with impartiality. Fads and ads . . .

Slide show of material from *The Mechanical Bride.*

The outlines of world order are already quite visible to the student of the swirling flood released by industrial technique. And they are to be discerned in the very way the flood operates. Edgar Allen Poe's sailor in "The Maelstrom" saved himself by cooperating with the action of the vortex itself. In the same way we can learn from the art of such moderns as Mallarmé and Joyce analogical techniques not only of survival but of advance. How often do you change your mind, your politics, your clothes? Are you properly impressed by what people are saying, seeing, doing, discarding? Are you in the groove? That is, moving in ever diminishing circles?

Song that will continue playing on car radio below begins here. Bell sounds to end class. Students encircle C/W McLuhan in ever diminishing circles. C/W McLuhan disappears into this vortex and reappears to displace the TV McLuhan.

C/W McLuhan: Tomorrow we will look at comics. Al Capp's Li'l Abner. Dogpatch is not in the South. It is not in the country. It's the country of the ordinary mind bamboozled by chaotic imagery from the outside and drugged by sentiment from the inside. Do you like Al Capp? Then you'll love *Finnegans Wake.*

Four seats arranged as for car in Module One. The car is parked at a drive-in restaurant and Narcissus is at the wheel. The car radio is blaring.

C/W McLuhan: What do you hear, Narcissus?
TV McLuhan: The subliminal depths of radio are charged with the resonating echoes of tribal horns and antique drums.
Irritated Parent: It's jungle music!
TV McLuhan: Print-dominated culture takes a dim view of scandalous affairs between the book page and electronic creatures from the other side of the linotype. But the same culture passively accepts its own affair with the mechanical creature of the assembly-line type. If Gutenberg made it possible to see the mother tongue in uniform dress, Henry Ford made it possible to possess a bride without seeing her as a technological extension of the self. What's that in the rear-view mirror, Narcissus?

MCLUHAN: A GUIDE FOR THE PERPLEXED

Henry Ford: What's that you are saying about my assembly line?
James Joyce: What's that in the ear-view mirror, me Johnny?

Strains of "The Miller of Dee."

Jonathan Miller: The millennium is the message.
TV McLuhan: I am concerned with society moving into the twenty-first century with nineteenth century perceptions. Phenomenology is dialectic in ear-mode . . . a massive and decentralized quest for roots, for ground . . .
C/W McLuhan: Is that Echo in the rear-view mirror, Narcissus?
TV McLuhan: What's that echo in the ear-view mirror, Narcissus?
James Joyce: Bless us and save us, said Mrs. O'Davis. In that european end meets Ind.

Thomas Nashe reminds audience via flip chart that the classical trivium consists of grammar, dialectic, and rhetoric.
C/W McLuhan alone at writing desk, completing manuscript; he ponders various titles he has been considering.

C/W McLuhan: What to call it? Typhon in America?
TV McLuhan: A giant whom Juno produced by striking the earth. Typhon was considered the source of all evils.
C/W McLuhan: 50 million Mama's boys?
TV McLuhan: Advertising and comics show us over and over how the North American male has become a shell. In one generation, Life with Father became Bringing Up Father. The newspapers document the decline of American manhood. Dagwood! *Putting* Up with Father.
C/W McLuhan: Guide to Chaos?
TV McLuhan: How did the sailor in the maelstrom save himself from his environment?
C/W McLuhan: The Mechanical Bride.
James Joyce: Do I hear a mouchical umsummable?
e.e.cummings: She sang her didn't, she danced her did.

The Dance of the Mechanical Bride. The dance is preceded by visual of the Marcel Duchamp painting on backdrop and followed by visual of Jeff Wall's "The Giant."

Loud blast. Stage lights go out. Spotlight comes up on Wyndham Lewis, center stage left. Spotlight circles to C/W McLuhan at center stage right as Lewis speaks. Lewis's speech ends when light reaches McLuhan. Light pauses on McLuhan as he begins to speak and then continues to circle back to Lewis. McLuhan's speech ends when light reaches Lewis. Circling light continues in this manner to the end of their alternating speeches. Nashe is not in their circle.

Wyndham Lewis: The art of advertisement, after the American manner, has introduced into all our life such a lavish use of superlatives, that no standard of value whatever is intact.

C/W McLuhan: So that the exhortation to think for yourself is, in these circumstances, a cause of discouragement only. It positively encourages a plunge into any collective myth that happens to have an appeal.

Thomas Nashe: The superlative absolute of advertising.

Wyndham Lewis: The artist is always engaged in writing a detailed history of the future, because he is the only person aware of the nature of the present.

Thomas Nashe: There is no present like the time.

C/W McLuhan (*to Nashe*): It was my turn, but I'll forgive you, since you illustrate beautifully . . .

TV McLuhan (*to C/W McLuhan*): It *is* your turn, but it's up to me to explain how that flip . . .

Thomas Nashe: There's no present like the time.

TV McLuhan: Thank you . . . how that flip illustrates the interplay of cliché and archetype. For example: Li'l Abner is a cluster of the swarming hero images; from them Al Capp extracts now one sample, now another. One day Li'l Abner's face resembles a Frankie Sinatra, the next it may have the somber cast of Gary Cooper or the determination of Dick Tracy. The hero image is the archetype, the cluster-symbol; from this collective, the clichés, the individual icons, emerge. And return. And reemerge.

Nymph Echo: Cycle, recycle; cycle, recycle.

James Joyce: Brings us by a commodius vicus of recirculation back . . .

TV McLuhan: All media of communications are clichés serving to enlarge man's scope of action, his patterns of association and awareness. These media create environments that numb our powers of attention by sheer pervasiveness.

Tom Wolfe and Thomas Nashe appear back to back. Wolfe in white, Nashe in black.

Tom Wolfe (pointing over his shoulder): Back to black.

Drum roll.

Thomas Nashe: Le tambour des Toms.
Tom Wolfe: From Tom to Tom.
The Ukrainian Apothecary: Tamtenetam.
Vittorio Gassman: Adesso, facciamo bella figura!
TV McLuhan: Figure/ground . . .
Thomas Nashe: Time is the daily ground.
Tom Wolfe: Back to black.
TV McLuhan: Background black.
Thomas Nashe: As Tom goes by.
James Joyce: Echoland!

The Nymph Echo jumps up and down with Joyce.

TV McLuhan: Back to the archetype.
Jonathan Miller: The miller's the messenger. Marshall McLuhan.
  Mushrooming meanings.
Thomas Nashe: Moskastrom! Loskascam!
Vittorio Gassman: Che figura è questa?
Wyndham Lewis: Momaco!
C/W McLuhan: Mimico!
Wyndham Lewis: Figure!
TV McLuhan: Ground!
Wyndham Lewis: Cliché!
TV McLuhan: Archetype!
Thomas Nashe: Mimicking the Momma's boys in Mimico!
Sir William Gilbert: Miminy, piminy! Rimini, Giminy!

All characters on stage freeze in their positions. From offstage comes the portion of the recording of *The Medium is the Mass*age concluding with McLuhan saying: "The trouble is, I keep thinking of better ways to say it." As the recording plays, only the TV McLuhan reacts, looking around for the source of the voice.

Thomas Nashe (*softly*): New clichés emerge from the archetype.

TV McLuhan: When I say the medium is the message I am merely stating the fact that meaning is a happening, the interplay of events. I have found sometimes that it helps to say the medium is the massage, because the medium is a complex set of events that roughly handles and works over entire populations.

Replay of "The trouble is I keep thinking of better ways to say it."

TV McLuhan: A propos the medium is the message, I now point out that the medium is not the figure but the ground. Also I point out that in all media, the user is the content, and the effects come before the invention.

Wittgenstein: McLuhan, I really don't understand what's going on with all these tools. You just take one and turn it into another one!

Strains of Elvis singing "Understanding solves all problems . . ."

James Joyce: Hark back to the harketype.

TV McLuhan (*to Wittgenstein*): I never stop translating, so I don't need to kick the ladder away—that's the difference between a ladder and a spire.

James Joyce: Let us get nearer to the spire, so that we can see what we are saying.

Henry Ford: Did somebody say tools?

Wittgenstein: Ja, McLuhan is monkeying with his wrenches.

Henry Ford: Get with it man! The age of mechanization is past. Drill is to spiral is to vortex as hardware is to myth is to nature.

Wittgenstein: Hardware? Mechanization is past? Somebody get me a ladder.

Henry Ford: You were so busy with your beetle box at the end of the last module that you missed the lesson about the tetrad.

TV McLuhan: Uh, we never actually called it that . . .

C/W McLuhan: Uh, actually, we did.

Henry Ford: OK, the box that isn't; the box that's outside in.

Thomas Nashe: Create no crate without; create without a crate.

Henry Ford: You are who, exactly?

Thomas Nashe: Thomas Nashe.

Henry Ford: Nash(e)!?! Not a name we use much around our house.

James Joyce: Naming is numbing.

Henry Ford: In more ways than one. Let's get Witters clear on the tetrad. (*To Wittgenstein*) Take my model T . . .

Wittgenstein: Was there a model S?

Henry Ford: Yes!

Wittgenstein: O?

Henry Ford: No!

Wittgenstein: Why not?

TV McLuhan: Why not follow up on word magic and number magic with a little letter magic? Understanding M.

James Joyce: Definitely not for the ABCED-minded.

Visual kaleidoscope of variations in the form of the letters of the alphabet as they evolved from Sumerian prototypes. M > MM > vortex

Henry Ford: I'd like to finish my bit here.

James Joyce: Allforabit.

TV McLuhan: We just did that bit, bit by bit, for the alphabet. You're on, Ford.

Henry Ford: My model T is linguistic in structure.

Saussure: What !?!

Wittgenstein: I get it, Model A, Model B, Model C, Model D . . . und so weiter . . . allforabit.

TV McLuhan: Not so, Ford's alphabet went A, B, C, F, K, N . . . You've still got the floor, Henry.

Henry Ford: Thanks, Mars. The four features of all media are exactly the same as the four features of all metaphors. In other words, *all* human technologies are linguistic outerings or utterings of man.

Thomas Nashe: Dialectic functions by converting everything it touches into figure. But metaphor is a means of perceiving one thing in terms of another.

Wittgenstein: This is just word magic!

Henry Ford: OK, let's do the tetrad for word magic.

Wittgenstein: You should stick to cars.

Henry Ford: OK, let's do the tetrad for the car. The car extends privacy . . .

TV McLuhan: Going out to be alone . . .

Henry Ford: It obsolesces the horse-and-buggy, retrieves the knight in shining armour . . .

TV McLuhan: And flips into the corporate privacy of traffic jams. Does that ring a bell? Bring on the tetrad for word magic.

Henry Ford: Extends feeling, obsolesces thought, retrieves being, flips into paralysis.

Thomas Nashe (holding a mask of James Joyce in front of his face): What about a mask?

Henry Ford: Extends the face, cancels individual identity, retrieves anonymity, flips into facial expression.

TV McLuhan: Face and anonymity are ground; facial expression and individual identity are figure.

Vittorio Gassman: Si fa bella figura!

Wittgenstein: Let's do the tetrad for the beetle box.

TV McLuhan: No, we're going to let the audience work on that . . . very soon.

TV McLuhan: I'm really enjoying this.

C/W McLuhan: I'm really learning a lot.

Visual of McLuhan from history of alphabet repeated with audio fragments added to create effect of the maelstrom of his ideas. When it subsides, TV McLuhan is at center stage with Sigmund Freud. They are seated in chairs with a pedestal ashtray between them, smoking cigars.

Tom Wolfe (*downstage right*): Suppose he is what he sounds like, the most important thinker since Newton, Darwin, Freud . . .

TV McLuhan: Nice to get a break from the maelstrom.

Sigmund Freud: Ja, for sure, but what was that you said about my couch and the ablative absolute of backside?

TV McLuhan: My method is vertical rather than horizontal, but that doesn't mean I have a point of view. The scenery does not change but the texture does. In your later work you became aware of the environment and conceived of it as a study of effects without causes. When I say the medium is the message I too am saying that it is the medium as an environment of services that produces effects.

Sigmund Freud (taking his cigar out of his mouth and wiping his brow): Oh, boy!

Stage goes dark to signal end of Module Three.

Questions

Why does the Nymph Echo say that neither fish nor Narcissus recognize water?
Answer: Fish do not recognize water as the environment that they live in any more than humans are normally conscious of air. As for Narcissus, he failed to recognize the low-tech medium of water providing an extension of himself (his reflected image) and drowned as a result.

Is this related to what TV McLuhan says about Henry Ford?
Answer: Yes: "Henry Ford made it possible to possess a bride without seeing her as an extension of the self." (The chapter on the car in *Understanding Media* is titled "The Mechanical Bride.")

Why does Ford call the tetrad of media laws "the box that's outside in?"
Answer: Because a tetrad is not a container. It relates four processes to each other in a way that is better represented visually by a single point with the four vectors for extension, obsolescence, retrieval, and reversal emanating from that point and away from each other. The tetrad turns clichés into complementarities forming a collective archetype, aligns two figures with two grounds, and prioritizes effects over causes.

Why does TV McLuhan say to Wittgenstein, "I don't need to kick the ladder away."
Answer: At the end of Wittgenstein's *Tractatus Logico-Philosophicus* he makes the comparison between his propositions and the steps on a ladder. Anyone using the ladder to climb beyond the propositions must, he says, "throw away the ladder after he has climbed up it" (6.54). McLuhan says that his exploratory probes, unlike the steps of Wittgenstein's ladder, can be retained, because they are integrated as in a spire.

Why is this section of the piece called "From Fire to Spire?"
Answer: These are two symbols of becoming, of pure process. Joyce links them by reworking an old cliché, substituting *spire* for *fire,* when he says "Let us get nearer to the spire, so that we can see what we are saying."

Why does Freud ask McLuhan what he said about Freud's couch and the "ablative absolute of backside?"

Answer: He is looking for clarification of the passage in *Understanding Media* where McLuhan says: "[O]urs is the century of the psychiatrist's couch. As extension of man the chair is a specialist ablation of the posterior, a sort of ablative absolute of backside, whereas the couch extends the integral being" (p. 7).

NOTES

CHAPTER ONE BACKGROUND, CONTEXT, DEFINITIONS, AND . . . STUMBLING BLOCKS

1. *The Mechanical Bride*, p. v.
2. Edgar Allan Poe, "A Descent into the Maelstrom," in *The Complete Tales and Poems of Edgar Allan Poe* (New York: The Modern Library, 1935), p. 135.
3. Matie Molinaro, Corinne McLuhan, and William Toye, eds., *Letters of Marshall McLuhan* (Toronto: Oxford University Press, 1987), pp. 82–83. (Henceforth *Letters*.)
4. Jan Gorak, ed., *Northrop Frye on Modern Culture* (Toronto: University of Toronto Press, 2003), pp. 20–21.
5. Mark Poster, ed., *Jean Baudrillard: Selected Writings* (Stanford, CA: Stanford University Press, 1988), pp. 207–208.
6. Malcolm Muggeridge, *Christ and the Media* (London: Hodder & Stoughton, 1977).
7. Umberto Eco, *Travels in Hyper Reality* (San Diego, CA: Harcourt Brace Jovanovich, 1983), p. 138.
8. Ibid.
9. Ibid., p. 139.
10. Ibid., pp. 233–234.
11. Ibid., p. 235.
12. Ibid., p. 111.
13. Ibid., p. 110.
14. *Understanding Media*, p. 418. References to *Understanding Media* throughout are to the critical edition of 2003.
15. Ibid., p. 442.
16. Marshall McLuhan with Bruce Powers, *The Global Village: Transformations in World Life and Media in the 21st Century* (New York: Oxford University Press, 1989), p. 7.
17. *Understanding Media*, p. 85.
18. *Letters*, p. 50.
19. Ibid.
20. John Paul Russo, *I. A. Richards: His Life and Work* (Baltimore, MD: The Johns Hopkins University Press, 1989), p. 295.
21. National Archives of Canada, McLuhan Archive, volume 3, file 6, McLuhan's notes on the lectures of I. A. Richards. (Henceforth NAC.)

22. *Vogue*, volume 123, August 1966, pp. 70–73, p. 111.
23. Ann Berthoff, *Richards on Rhetoric* (New York: Oxford University Press, 1991), p. 19.
24. Ibid., p. 50.
25. *Understanding Media*, p. 89.
26. *Letters*, p. 355.
27. John Fekete, *The Critical Twilight* (London: Routledge, 1977), p. 135.
28. In Gerald E. Stearn, ed., *McLuhan Hot and Cool*, p. 238.
29. Ibid., p. 285.
30. Fekete, p. 214.
31. *The Medium is the Massage*, p. 67.
32. In Gerald E. Stearn, p. 272.
33. *Laws of Media*, p. ix.
34. Douglas Parker, "Reverse Canadian," *Riverside [California] Press–Enterprise*, 24 May 1964.
35 NAC, volume 28, file 12.

CHAPTER TWO LITERARY LINKS

1. "G. K. Chesterton: A Practical Mystic," *The Dalhousie Review*, January 1936, p. 455.
2. Ibid.
3. Ibid.
4. Ibid.
5. Ibid., p. 456.
6. Ibid.
7. Ibid., p. 457.
8. Ibid.
9. Ibid.
10. Ibid., p. 458.
11. Ibid., p. 461.
12. Ibid.
13. Ibid., p. 462.
14. Ibid.
15. Ibid.
16. Ibid.
17. Ibid., p. 463.
18. Ibid., p. 464.
19. NAC, volume 166, file 23.
20. Eugene McNamara, *The Literary Criticism of Marshall McLuhan* (New York: McGraw-Hill, 1969), p. 83. Henceforth McNamara.
21. Ibid., p. 91.
22. Ibid.
23. Ibid., p. 92.
24. *Understanding Media*, p. 29.
25. Ibid., p. 96.
26. McNamara, pp. 75–76.
27. Ibid., p. 78.

28. Ibid., p. 79.
29. Ibid., pp. 80–81.
30. "Pound, Eliot, and the Rhetoric of *The Waste Land*," *New Literary History* 10, 3 (1979), p. 557. Henceforth *NLH*.
31. Ibid., p. 572.
32. Ibid., p. 572.
33. Ibid., p. 576.
34. McNamara, p. 23.
35. Ibid., pp. 23–24.
36. Ibid., p. 26.
37. Ibid.
38. Ibid., p. 27.
39. Ibid., p. 31.
40. Ibid., p. 30.
41. Ibid.
42. Ibid., p. 31.
43. Ibid., pp. 32–33.
44. Ibid., p. 37.
45. Ibid.
46. Ibid., p. 47.
47. Tyler, pp. 255–256.
48. "Inside Blake and Hollywood," *McLuhan Unbound* #10, p. 12.
49. Ibid., p. 6.
50. Ibid., p. 5.
51. Ibid., p. 6, quoting Frye.
52. Ibid.
53. Ibid., p. 8.
54. Ibid., p. 10.
55. Ibid., p. 9.
56. Ibid.
57. Ibid., p. 10, emphasis added.
58. Ibid., p. 12.
59. Ibid., p. 13.
60. Ibid.
61. p. 7.
62. p. 68.
63. p. 138.
64. p. 175.
65. p. 211.
66. p. 217.
67. p. 226.
68. p. 226.
69. p. 220.
70. p. 229.
71. p. 241.
72. p. 253.
73. p. 36.

74. pp. 5–6.
75. p. 4.
76. p. 5.
77. p. 17.
78. Ibid.
79. *Understanding Media*, p. 85.
80. p. 42.
81. p. 50.
82. p. 39.
83. pp. 63–64.
84. p. 81.
85. p. 99.
86. p. 86.
87. p. 104.
88. p. 103.
89. p. 105.
90. p. 105.
91. p. 112.
92. p. 119.
93. p. 123.
94. p. 132.
95. p. 132.
96. p. 133.
97. p. 134.
98. pp. 132–133.
99. p. 134.
100. p. 134.
101. p. 134.
102. p. 134.
103. p. 146.
104. p. 161.
105. p. 157.
106. p. 174.
107. p. 174.
108. p. 175.
109. p. 169.
110. p. 180.
111. p. 189.
112. p. 188.
113. p. 202.
114. p. 208.
115. pp. 213–214.
116. p. 213.
117. p. 219.
118. p. 241.
119. p. 253.
120. p. 238.

CHAPTER THREE FROM MADISON, WISCONSIN TO MADISON AVENUE: *THE MECHANICAL BRIDE* AND HER ELECTRICAL BROOD

1. *McLuhan Unbound* #7, "The Humanities in the Electronic Age," p. 14.
2. NAC, Marshall McLuhan to Felix Giovanelli.
3. NAC, Marshall McLuhan to Reynall & Hitchcock, Publishers.
4. NAC, volume 64, file 1.
5. Ibid.
6. Ibid.
7. Ibid.
8. Ibid.
9. Ibid.
10. *The Mechanical Bride*, p. 120.
11. Ibid.
12. Ibid., p. 156.
13. From an early draft of *The Mechanical Bride* (NAC).
14. "Commercials become villains at communications conference," *Globe and Mail*, 25 August 1973.
15. *Culture Is Our Business*, p. 7.
16. NAC, Marshall McLuhan to Bill Jovanovich, 23 July 1970.
17. NAC, Joe Keogh to Marshall McLuhan, 11 July 1970.
18. Ibid.
19. Ibid.
20. Ibid.
21. Ibid.
22. "Humanities in the Electronic Age," *The Humanities Association Bulletin* (1961), p. 14. (See endnote 1 above for reprint information.)
23. Ibid., p. 6.
24. Ibid., p. 8.
25. Ibid., p. 10.
26. Ibid.
27. Ibid., p. 11.
28. Ibid., p. 12.
29. Ibid., p. 16.
30. Ibid., p. 17.

CHAPTER FOUR FROM MEDIA AS POLITICAL FORMS TO *UNDERSTANDING MEDIA*

1. p. 5 (emphasis added). All references are to the reprint version in W. Terrence Gordon, ed., *McLuhan Unbound*, #14 (Corte Madera, CA: Gingko Press, 2005).
2. p. 7.
3. p. 8.
4. Ibid.
5. p. 12.
6. p. 14.

7. James Joyce, *On Ibsen* (Copenhagen: Green Integer, 1999), p. 73.
8. "Media as Art Forms," p. 6. (See note #1 above for publication information.)
9. Ibid., p. 6.
10. Ibid., p. 11.
11. Ibid., p. 11.
12. Ibid., p. 7.
13. Ibid., p. 8.
14. p. 9.
15. p. 15.
16. p. 10.
17. Ibid.
18. p. 14 (emphasis added).
19. p. 15.
20. p. 7.
21. pp. 11–12.
22. p. 8.
23. p. 7.
24. pp. 16–17.
25. p. 4. All references are to the reprint version (See note #1 above for publication information.)
26. p. 6.
27. p. 5.
28. p. 6.
29. p. 8.
30. p. 31 (emphasis added).
31. pp. 28–29.
32. NAC, Harry Skornia to Arthur Efron, 6 November 1962.
33. Ibid.
34. Ibid.
35. NAC, volume 8, file 52.
36. Ibid.
37. *Letters*, pp. 280–281.
38. NAC, volume 10, file 16.
39. Ibid.
40. *Understanding Media*, p. 79.
41. Ibid., p. 103.
42. "Books and Marshall McLuhan" *The Library Quarterly* 41, 4 (1971), 311–319.
43. NAC, McLuhan to Sam Neill, 12 September 1972.
44. NAC, McLuhan to Jacques Maritain, 28 May 1969.
45. NAC, McLuhan to Bill Jovanovich, 9 March 1966.
46. *Letters*, p. 261.
47. *Letters,* p. 302 (1964).
48. NAC, volume 169, file 33, McLuhan to Robert Manning.
49. *Letters*, p. 405.
50. NAC, volume 17, file 1.
51. *Letters*, p. 302.

52. *Letters*, p. 262.
53. NAC, MM to Claude Bissell, 8 March 1960.
54. *Letters*, p. 334.
55. NAC, MM to Robert Manning, Editor-in-Chief, *Atlantic Monthly*, 21 July 1971.
56. NAC, Harry Skornia to Arthur Efron, 6 November 1962.
57. *Letters*, p. 507.
58. NAC, volume 77, file 6. Ted Carpenter to MM, n.d.
59. NAC, Leon Wilson to MM, 25 October 1962.
60. Ibid.
61. Ibid.
62. Ibid.
63. Ibid., 30 October 1962.
64. NAC, MM to John Rowan, 17 December 1969.
65. NAC, Leon Wilson to MM, 28 June 1963.
66. Interview with Eric McLuhan.
67. NAC, David Segal to MM, 12 July 1963.
68. Ibid., 26 July 1963.
69. Ibid., 23 August 1963.
70. All references are to the critical edition of *Understanding Media*, Gingko Press, 2003.
71. NAC, David Segal to MM, 11 September 1963.
72. NAC, MM to Richard Berg, 16 November 1964.
73. NAC, volume 76, file 32.
74. Ibid.
75. Ibid.
76. Ibid.
77. Ibid.
78. NAC, MM to David Segal, 8 September 1964.
79. Christopher Ricks, "Electronic Man," *New Statesman*, 11 December 1964.
80. Ibid.
81. C. J. Fox, "Our Mass Communications," *Commonwealth Review*, 16 October 1964.
82. Ronald Bates, "The Medium is the Message," *The Tamarack Review* 33 (1964), pp. 79–80.
83. *Toronto Star*, 13 June 1964.
84. *The Globe Magazine*, 11 July 1964.
85. Alan Thomas, "Misunderstanding Media," *Toronto Telegram*, 22 August 1964.
86. Ibid.
87. Joseph Ford, "Letters to the Editor," *Time*, 10 July 1964.
88. Douglas Parker, "Reverse Canadian," *Riverside (California) Press-Enterprise*, 24 May 1964.
89. Gerald M. Feigen, "The McLuhan Festival," in George Sanderson and Frank Macdonald, eds., *Marshall McLuhan, The Man and His Message* (Golden, CO: Fulcrum, 1989) 65–69 (p. 66).
90. Ibid.

91. Ibid.
92. Howard Luck Gossage, "You Can See Why the Mighty Would Be Curious," in Gerald Emanuel Stearn, ed., *McLuhan Hot and Cool* (New York: Signet Books, 1969), 20–30 (p. 25).
93. Tom Wolfe, "Suppose he is what he sounds like . . ." ibid., 31–48 (p. 47).
94. Feigen in Sanderson and Macdonald, p. 69.
95. NAC, "Electroencephalographic Aspects of Low Involvement: Implications for the McLuhan Hypothesis," by Herbert E. Krugman, 21–23 May 1970. Krugman's report was published in *The Journal of Advertising Research*, volume 11, 1 February 1971.
96. Ibid.
97. Ibid.
98. NAC, MM to Frank Kermode, 4 March 1971.
99. NAC, MM to Herbert Krugman, 25 June 1970.
100. Ibid.
101. Ibid.

CHAPTER FIVE MCLUHAN'S TOOL BOX: FROM
THROUGH THE VANISHING POINT TO *LAWS OF MEDIA*

1. NAC, Marshall McLuhan (Henceforth MM) to Pete Buckner, 19 June 1974.
2. *From Cliché to Archetype*, p. 21.
3. Diary, 19 May 1974.
4. NAC, MM to Cleanth Brooks, 16 May 1977.
5. *Letters*, p. 417.
6. NAC, MM to David Sohn, 3 February 1971.
7. *New York Times Review of Books*, 13 December 1970.
8. *Understanding Media*, p. 98.
9. *Toronto Daily Star*, 30 December 1970.
10. *Understanding Media*, p. 85.
11. NAC, MM to Roger Broughton, 15 May 1968.
12. NAC, MM to Jacques Maritain, 30 May 1969.
13. NAC, MM to Robert J. Leuver.
14. Ibid.
15. NAC, MM to Neil Postman, 28 August 1979.
16. NAC, Richard Berg to MM, 21 November 1976.
17. *Understanding Media*, p. 44.
18. Ibid., p. 301.
19. NAC, MM to Charles Silberman, 23 August 1972.
20. NAC, MM to Jamie Shalleck, 27 February 1973.
21. NAC, MM to O. Rudzik, 23 November 1972.
22. NAC, MM to David Parsons, 11 February 1972.
23. NAC, MM to Joel Persky, 27 February 1973.
24. NAC, MM to Rev. Gerald Pocock, 7 May 1976.
25. NAC, MM to Bill Key, 26 September 1973.

26. NAC, MM to William Wimsatt, 17 April 1973.
27. NAC, MM to Max Nanny, 27 July 1973.
28. NAC, MM to Richard Berg, 9 March 1973.
29. NAC, MM to Jane Bret, *Letters*, pp. 459–460.
30. NAC, MM to Joe Foyle, 11 March 1974.
31. NAC, MM to Geoffrey Cannon (*Radio Times*), London, 22 September 1970.
32. NAC, volume 172, file 7.
33. NAC, MM to Hans Selye, 12 August 1974.
34. NAC, MM to Yousuf Karsh, 8 November 1976.
35. NAC, MM to Pete Buckner, 12 September 1972.
36. NAC, MM to Eric McLuhan, 9 February 1977.
37. Diary, 1 August 1973.
38. Diary, 26 May 1974.
39. NAC, MM to Jerome Agel, 27 March 1973.
40. NAC, MM to Fritz Wilhelmsen, 28 June 1974.
41. Ibid.
42. MM to Clare Westcott, *Letters*, p. 514.
43. NAC, MM to Bill Davis, 28 August 1973.
44. NAC, Kamala Bhatia to MM, 8 June 1978.
45. NAC, MM to Roger Poole, 24 November 1977.
46. Roger Poole to MM, 31 March 1978.
47. NAC, MM to Roger Poole, 24 July 1978.
48. Ibid., emphasis added.
49. NAC, MM to Lou Forsdale, 6 April 1977.
50. NAC, volume 3, file 6.
51. NAC, MM to Bernie Muller-Thym, 19 February 1960.
52. York University, CSWS Archive, file 287.
53. MM to Frank Kermode, *Letters*, p. 426.
54. MM to Harry Skornia, ibid., p. 305.
55. NAC, MM to Bonnie Brennan, 28 October 1966.
56. Ibid.
57. NAC, William Wimsatt to MM, 19 November 1971.
58. NAC, MM to Fritz Wilhelmsen, 18 January 1971.
59. NAC, MM to Muriel Bradbrook, 5 November 1971.
60. NAC, MM to Melvin Kranzberg, 10 July 1973.
61. NAC, MM to Bonnie Brennan, 12 September 1973.
62. NAC, MM to Pete Buckner, 19 June 1974.
63. NAC, MM to Barbara Rowes, 14 April 1976.
64. NAC, MM to Sister St. John O'Malley, 9 February 1978.
65. Ibid.
66. MM to Peter Drucker, *Letters*, p. 259.
67. Ibid.
68. Ibid.
69. Ibid.
70. Ibid.
71. NAC, volume 166, file 25.

72. *Letters*, p. 421.
73. NAC, MM to Fritz Wilhelmsen, 17 June 1975.
74. Ibid., 19 September 1975.
75. NAC, volume 127, file 19.
76. NAC, volume 166, file 25.
77. Diary, 16 August 1974.
78. NAC, volume 166, file 25.
79. NAC, MM to Ruth Nanda Ashen, 2 July 1975.
80. NAC, MM to Joe Keogh, 24 July 1970.
81. NAC, MM to Barbara Rowes, 29 April 1976.
82. NAC, MM to Eric McLuhan, 24 September 1975.
83. *McLuhan Unbound*, #19, p. 9.
84. Ibid., p. 6.
85. *Understanding Media*, p. 85.
86. Ibid., pp. 258–259: "For centuries, the woodcut and the engraving had delineated the world by an arrangement of lines and points that had syntax of a very elaborate kind. . . . Syntax, the net of rationality, disappeared from the later prints [made with the halftone process], just as it tended to disappear from the telegraph message and from the impressionist painting. . . . [William Henry Fox Talbot] was quite aware of photography as a kind of animation that eliminated the syntactical procedures of pen and pencil."
87. *McLuhan Unbound*, #19, p. 7.
88. Ibid., p. 12.
89. Ibid., p. 8.
90. NAC, MM to Mark Slade, 19 April 1979, emphasis added.
91. *Laws of Media*, p. 3.
92. *Understanding Media*, p. 85.
93. Ibid., p. 25.
94. NAC, MM to Philip E. Slater, 12 December 1963.
95. NAC, MM to Marshall Fishwick, 17 December 1975.
96. NAC, MM to Elio Flatto, 12 June 1975.
97. NAC, MM to James M. Curtis, 27 September 1972.
98. NAC, MM to Ray di Lorenzo, 5 April 1974.
99. NAC, MM to Philip E. Slater, 12 December 1963.
100. MM to Peter Drucker, *Letters*, p. 270.
101. NAC, MM to Bill Jovanovich, 14 December 1965.
102. NAC, Max Nanny to MM, 3 June 1971.
103. NAC, MM to James M. Curtis, 12 September 1972.
104. Ibid., 27 September 1972.
105. NAC, MM to Mark Slade, 3 May 1973.
106. NAC, MM to Fritz Wilhelmsen, 28 January 1974.
107. NAC, MM to D. S. Berlyne, 23 November 1972.
108. NAC, MM to William Massee, 13 June 1974.
109. NAC, MM to Cleanth Brooks, 16 May 1977.
110. NAC, MM to James M. Curtis, 12 September 1972.
111. NAC, Fritz Wilhelmsen, 28 June 1974.

112. NAC, MM to Joe Foyle, 12 June 1974.
113. NAC, MM to Barbara Rowes, 29 April 1976.
114. NAC, MM to Claude de Beauregard, 19 December 1978.
115. *Laws of Media*, p. ix.
116. Ibid., p. 98.

REFERENCES

ABBREVIATIONS

Letters: *Letters of Marshall McLuhan* (see Secondary Sources and References below)
MM: Marshall McLuhan
NAC: National Archives of Canada

WORKS OF MARSHALL MCLUHAN

"American Advertising." In W. Terrence Gordon, ed., *McLuhan Unbound* (Corte Madera, CA: Gingko Press, 2005), #9. Repr. from *Horizon*, 93–94 (October 1947), 132–141.

"G. K. Chesterton: A Practical Mystic." In W. Terrence Gordon, ed., *McLuhan Unbound* (Corte Madera, CA: Gingko Press, 2005), #11. Repr. from *The Dalhousie Review*, January 1936, 455–464.

The Classical Trivium: The Place of Thomas Nashe in the Learning of His Time, W. Terrence Gordon, ed. Corte Madera, CA: Gingko Press, 2006 [1942, unpublished].

Culture Is Our Business. New York: McGraw-Hill, 1970.

"Footprints in the Sands of Crime." *Sewanee Review* 54 (1946), 617–634.

The Gutenberg Galaxy: The Making of Typographic Man. Toronto: University of Toronto Press, 1962.

"The Humanities in the Electronic Age." In W. Terrence Gordon, ed., *McLuhan Unbound* (Corte Madera, CA: Gingko Press, 2005), #7. Repr. from *The Humanities Association Bulletin* (1961), 3–11.

"Inside Blake and Hollywood." In W. Terrence Gordon, ed., *McLuhan Unbound* (Corte Madera, CA: Gingko Press, 2005), #10. Repr. from *Sewanee Review* 55, October 1947, 710–715.

The Interior Landscape: The Literary Criticism of Marshall McLuhan, Eugene McNamara, ed. New York: McGraw-Hill, 1969.

"James Joyce: Trivial and Quadrivial." In Eugene McNamara, ed., *The Interior Landscape: The Literary Criticism of Marshall McLuhan* (New York: McGraw-Hill, 1969), pp. 23–47.

"Laws of the Media." In W. Terrence Gordon, ed., *McLuhan Unbound* (Corte Madera, CA: Gingko Press, 2005), #19. Repr. from *et cetera/ETC.: A Review of General Semantics,* Vol. 34, No. 2, June 1977, 173–179.

McLuhan Unbound, W. Terrence Gordon, ed. Corte Madera, CA: Gingko Press, 2005.

The Mechanical Bride. Corte Madera, CA: Gingko Press, 2002 [1951].

"New Media as Political Forms." In W. Terrence Gordon, ed., *McLuhan Unbound* (Corte Madera, CA: Gingko Press, 2005), #14. Repr. from *Explorations* 3, Toronto: University of Toronto Press, August 1954, 120–126.

"Notes on the Media as Art Forms." In W. Terrence Gordon, ed., *McLuhan Unbound* (Corte Madera, CA: Gingko Press, 2005), #15. Repr. from *Explorations* 2, Toronto: University of Toronto Press, 1954.

"Pound, Eliot, and the Rhetoric of *The Waste Land.*" *New Literary History* 10, 3 (1979), 557–580.

"Pound's Critical Prose." In Eugene McNamara, ed., *The Interior Landscape: The Literary Criticism of Marshall McLuhan* (New York: McGraw-Hill, 1969), pp. 75–81.

"Printing and Social Change." In W. Terrence Gordon, ed., *McLuhan Unbound* (Corte Madera, CA: Gingko Press, 2005), #1. Repr. from *Printing Progress* (1959), pp. 89–112.

Understanding Media. W. Terrence Gordon, ed. Corte Madera, CA: Gingko Press, 2003 [1964].

"Wyndham Lewis: His Theory of Art and Communication." In Eugene McNamara, ed., *The Interior Landscape: The Literary Criticism of Marshall McLuhan* (New York: McGraw-Hill, 1969), pp. 83–94.

With Jerome Agel. *War and Peace in the Global Village.* Corte Madera, CA: Gingko Press, 2001 [1968].

With David Carson. *The Book of Probes.* Corte Madera, CA: Gingko Press, 2003.

With Quentin Fiore. *The Medium is the Massage: An Inventory of Effects.* Corte Madera, CA: Gingko Press, 2001 [1967].

With Eric McLuhan. *Laws of Media: The New Science.* Toronto: University of Toronto Press, 1988.

With Barrington Nevitt. *Take Today.* Toronto: Longman, 1972.

With Harley Parker. *Through the Vanishing Point: Space in Poetry and Painting.* New York: Harper & Row, 1968.

With Bruce Powers. *The Global Village: Transformations in World Life and Media in the 21ˢᵗ Century.* New York: Oxford University Press, 1989.

With Wilfred Watson. *From Cliché to Archetype.* New York: Viking, 1970.

SECONDARY SOURCES AND REFERENCES

Bates, Ronald. "The Medium is the Message." *The Tamarack Review* 33 (1964), pp. 79–80.

Berthoff, Ann E. *Richards on Rhetoric. I. A. Richards: Selected Essays (1929–1974).* New York: Oxford University Press, 1991.

Berton, Pierre. *The Cool Crazy Committed World of the Sixties.* Toronto: McClelland & Stewart, 1966.

REFERENCES

Boon, James A. *From Symbolism to Structuralism.* New York: Harper & Row, 1973.

Burnett, Ron. *How Images Think.* Cambridge: MIT Press, 2004.

Davis, Erik. *Techgnosis.* New York: Harmony Books, 1998.

Eco, Umberto. *Travels in Hyper Reality.* San Diego, CA: Harcourt Brace Jovanovich, 1983.

Feigen, Gerald M. "The McLuhan Festival," in George Sanderson and Frank Macdonald, eds., *Marshall McLuhan, The Man and His Message* (Golden, CO: Fulcrum, 1989) 65–69.

Fekete, John. *The Critical Twilight: Explorations in the Ideology of Anglo-American Literary Theory from Eliot to McLuhan.* London: Routledge, 1977.

Ford, Joseph. "Letters to the Editor," *Time,* 10 July 1964.

Fox, C. J. "Our Mass Communications." *Commonwealth Review,* 16 October 1964.

Frye, Northrop. *Anatomy of Criticism.* Princeton: Princeton University Press, 1957.

Frye, Northrop. *Fearful Symmetry: A Study of William Blake.* Princeton: Princeton University Press, 1947.

Gorak, Jan, ed., *Northrop Frye on Modern Culture.* Toronto: University of Toronto Press, 2003.

Gossage, Howard Luck. "You Can See Why the Mighty Would Be Curious," in Gerald Emanuel Stearn, ed., *McLuhan Hot and Cool* (New York: Signet Books, 1969), 20–30.

Hass, Hans. *The Human Animal.* New York: Putnam, 1970.

Innis, Harold. *The Bias of Communication.* Toronto: University of Toronto Press, 1951.

—. *Empire and Communications.* Rowman & Littlefield, Lanham, MD, 2007 [1950].

Joyce, James. *On Ibsen.* Copenhagen: Green Integer, 1999.

Kroker, Arthur. *Technology and the Canadian Mind: Innis/McLuhan/Grant.* Montreal: New World Perspectives, 1984.

Krugman, Herbert E. "Electroencephalographic Aspects of Low Involvement: Implications for the McLuhan Hypothesis." *The Journal of Advertising Research,* volume 11, 1 February 1971.

Lee, Nanci. "New Year's Resolution: All Things Awkward." *The Coast,* Halifax, Nova Scotia, 27 December 2007.

Lewis, Wyndham. *Time and Western Man.* Corte Madera, CA: Gingko Press, 1993 [1927].

Miller, Jonathan. *Marshall McLuhan.* New York: The Viking Press, 1971.

Molinaro, Matie, Corinne McLuhan, and William Toye, eds. *Letters of Marshall McLuhan.* Toronto: Oxford University Press, 1987.

Muggeridge, Malcolm. *Christ and the Media.* London: Hodder & Stoughton, 1977.

Neill, S. D. "Books and Marshall McLuhan." *The Library Quarterly* 41, 4 (1971), 311–319.

—. *Clarifying McLuhan: An Assessment of Process and Product.* Westport, CT: Greenwood Press, 1993.

REFERENCES

Ogden, Charles Kay, and Ivor Armstrong Richards. *The Meaning of Meaning*, W. Terrence Gordon, ed. London: Thoemmes/Routledge, 1994 [1923].

Parker, Douglas. "Reverse Canadian," *Riverside [California] Press–Enterprise*, 24 May 1964.

Petroski, Henry. *The Toothpick: Technology and Culture.* New York: Knopf, 2007.

Pirsig, Robert. *Lila: An Inquiry into Morals.* New York: Bantam Books, 1991.

Poe, Edgar Allan. "A Descent into the Maelstrom," in *The Complete Tales and Poems of Edgar Allan Poe* (New York: The Modern Library, 1935).

Poster, Mark, ed., *Jean Baudrillard Selected Writings.* Stanford, CA: Stanford University Press, 1988.

Richards, I. A. *Practical Criticism: A Study of Literary Judgment.* London: Kegan Paul, Trench, Trubner & Company, 1929.

Ricks, Christopher. "Electronic Man." *New Statesman*, 11 December 1964.

Russo, John Paul. *I. A. Richards: His Life and Work*. Baltimore: Johns Hopkins University Press, 1989.

Saussure, Ferdinand de. *Course in General Linguistics*, trans. Wade Baskin. New York: Philosophical Library, 1959. [The earlier of two English translations from the original French and the one read by McLuhan.]

Solan, Lawrence. *The Language of Judges.* Chicago: University of Chicago Press, 1993.

Stamps, Judith. *Unthinking Modernity: Innis, McLuhan, and the Frankfurt School.* Montreal: McGill-Queen's University Press, 1995.

Starobinski, Jean. *Words Upon Words: The Anagrams of Ferdinand De Saussure.* Translated by Olivia Emmet. New Haven: Yale University Press, 1979.

Stearn, Gerald Emanuel. *Hot & Cool: A Primer for the Understanding of and a Critical Symposium with a Rebuttal by McLuhan.* New York: Dial Press, 1967.

Teilhard de Chardin, Pierre. *The Phenomenon of Man.* New York: Harper and Row, 1959.

Thomas, Alan. "Misunderstanding Media." *Toronto Telegram*, 22 August 1964.

Tyler, Parker. *Magic and Myth of the Movies.* New York: Henry Holt, 1947.

Wershler-Henry, Darren. "Picky, picky, oh so picky . . ." *The Globe and Mail*, 12 January 2008. Review of Petroski, above.

Willmott, Glen. *McLuhan, or Modernism in Reverse.* Toronto: University of Toronto Press, 1996.

Wolfe, Tom. "Suppose he is what he sounds like . . ." in Gerald Emanuel Stearn, ed., *McLuhan Hot and Cool* (New York: Signet Books, 1969), 31–48.

FURTHER READINGS

Most undergraduate university students at the turn of the twenty-first century—and some of their younger professors—were born after McLuhan died in 1980 and have not been exposed to his ideas. They belong to the generation that McLuhan predicted would demand a curriculum adapted to a world retribalized by the dominance of electronic technology. But in the experience of this writer, exposure to McLuhan's ideas can still act as an irritant, even to young people. They greet with skepticism his notion that they share a tribal encyclopedia, fail to recognize the satire of *Adbusters*, shrug off the question "What if *how* is more powerful than *what*?" That is the question McLuhan challenged the world to ponder when he said that the medium is the message.

Some intrepid academics rise to the challenge of teaching McLuhan in contexts as diverse as media studies, philosophy, semiotics, and management studies. But McLuhan is not a domain or a discipline; his intellectual legacy—still waiting to be fully realized—is not so much about any thing (a what) as it is a way of thinking (a how) about everything. Had he been asked in which field he hoped to have the strongest and most enduring influence, he would likely have replied *education*. But more than half a century after his interdisciplinary team conducted controlled experiments comparing the efficacy of four different teaching media, a half century that spawned countless more media with teaching potential, the results of those experiments have received scant attention or follow-up. (They are available as an appendix to the 2003 edition of *Understanding Media.*)

Surprisingly, the most dynamic and burgeoning current research is being conducted by the scientists who refused to take McLuhan seriously during the closing years of his career. He had turned his attention to brain hemisphere research with his hallmark approach—free-wheeling, tentative, imaginative, creative. Like all his other investigations, it bore the marks of the integrated trivium. When he spoke to audiences steeped only in neurological science, the exclusively dialectical underpinnings of their specialty made the trivium look trivial. McLuhan was greeted with everything from polite skepticism to impolite guffaws. The situation has changed radically.

Some current literature in the field now known as *neuroplasticity* makes no mention of McLuhan. *iBrain* (Small and Vorgan, 2008) is subtitled *Surviving the Technological Alteration of the Modern Mind*, suggesting to anyone familiar with Poe's story of the navigator of the Maelstrom that the survival in question is no longer a matter of developing a strategy against a hostile environment—that the enemy is within. The book's first chapter, "It's All in Your Head," reinforces that notion. McLuhan's definition of technology as extensions of the human body, his notions of media as environments, media as "outerings," and the radical formulation of the latter as the idea of humans wearing brains outside their skulls, all of these radically deconstruct the deliberate cliché-archetype interplay of the rhetoric at work in *it's all in your head* and open up avenues unexplored by Small and Vorgan.

Don Tapscott, *Grown Up Digital* (2009), focuses in on McLuhan: "Does the medium affect the way we absorb the information? Back in the 1950's, Marshall McLuhan argued that it does. The way we receive information—by reading a book, watching a movie, or listening to someone on the telephone—has a big impact on the brain, and that impact is even more important than the actual content of the message. In other words, McLuhan said in his famous but somewhat oblique line, 'the medium is the message'" (p. 104).

Various passing references to sequels to McLuhan's work given by Tapscott are discussed in greater detail in Norman Doidge, *The Brain that Changes Itself: Stories of Personal Triumph from the Frontiers of Brain Science* (2007):

> Most people think that the dangers created by the media are a result of content. But Marshall McLuhan, the Canadian who founded media studies in the 1950s and predicted the Internet twenty years before it was invented, was the first to intuit that the media change our brains irrespective of content, and he famously said, "The medium is the message." McLuhan was arguing that each medium reorganizes our mind and brain in its own unique way and that the consequences of these reorganizations are far more significant than the effects of the content or "message."

Erica Michael and Marcel Just of Carnegie Mellon University did a brain scan study to test whether the medium is the message. They showed that different brain areas are involved in hearing speech and reading it, and *different comprehension centers* in hearing words and reading them . . .

Each medium leads to a change in the balance of our individual senses, increasing some at the expense of others. According to McLuhan, preliterate man lived with a "natural" balance of hearing, seeing, feeling, smelling, and tasting. The written word moved pre-literate man from a world of sound to a visual world, by switching from speech to reading; type and the printing press hastened that process. Now the electronic media are bringing sound back and, in some ways, restoring the original balance. Each new medium creates a unique form of awareness, in which some senses are "stepped up" and others "stepped down." McLuhan said, "The ratio among our senses is altered." (pp. 308–309)

Doidge goes on to report the results of an experiment with a video game at Hammersmith Hospital, London, England, the results of which showed the reward neurotransmitter dopamine, also triggered by addictive drugs, released in the brains of subjects while they play the game. This is an echo of an observation made by McLuhan even in the earliest drafts of *The Mechanical Bride* from the 1940s about what he would later call mankind's first technology, spoken language: the word is now the cheapest and most universal drug.

But neuroplasticity is not the only domain currently offering sequels to McLuhan's work. From a steadily growing bibliography of literature inspired by McLuhan, here are a few titles chosen specifically because they examine his thinking and apply it in a variety of ways.

Cavell, Richard. *McLuhan in Space: A Cultural Geography.* Toronto: University of Toronto Press, 2002.
The author identifies McLuhan as a forerunner of critical cultural geographers, hence the title, evoking the link between McLuhan's distinction (acoustic space/visual space) and the body of work by thinkers who ground their analysis in the organization of space as a determining force in political, economic, cultural, and social structures.
Federman, Mark, and Derrick de Kerckhove. *McLuhan for Managers: New Tools for New Thinking.* Toronto: Viking Canada, 2003.
A systematic application of the whole range of McLuhan's thinking tools to business culture.

Genosko, Gary, ed. *Marshall McLuhan: Critical Evaluations in Cultural Theory*. London: Routledge, 2004.
This 3-volume collection features reprints of critical writings about McLuhan spanning the period from the 1960s to the dawn of the twenty-first century. Genosko's own critical essays open each section. Contributors include some of the commentators discussed in the present work, such as Jean Baudrillard and Umberto Eco, as well as others such as James Carey, Derrick de Kerckhove, Raymond Williams, and Tom Wolfe.

Genosko, Gary. *McLuhan and Baudrillard: Masters of Implosion*. London: Routledge, 1999.
Genosko examines the influence of McLuhan on the work of Jean Baudrillard and advances the case for McLuhan's ideas being more far-reaching in the development of postmodern theory than most commentators acknowledge. Genosko traces both the survival and the distortion of McLuhan's percepts in Baudrillard's writings, concluding nevertheless that it is through Baudrillard's influence that McLuhan has left his mark on contemporary cultural thought and practice.

Kroker, Arthur. *Technology and the Canadian Mind: Innis/McLuhan/Grant*. Montreal: New World Perspectives, 1984.
This book remains, after twenty-five years, one of the most insightful works on McLuhan in relation to his sometime mentor, political economist Harold Innis, and to social philosopher George Grant.

Kroker, Arthur, Marilouise Kroker, and David Cook. *Panic Encyclopedia: The Definitive Guide to the Postmodern Scene*. Montreal: New World Perspectives, 1989.
Describing itself as "the dark, reverse and imploding side of all the modernist encyclopedias," this book makes only one concession to convention by alphabetically arranging its entries. These do not deal with facts but with post-facts in entries ranging from one to seven pages over sociology, physics, technology, politics, and economics. The authors are as bold as McLuhan himself in their use of metaphors (camp is postmodern spirituality, shopping malls are liquid television), and though the stamp of McLuhan's modes of thinking are visible throughout, the book's predominantly bleak mood-line moves it away from McLuhan's technological optimism and toward George Grant's technological determinism (see preceding entry). The panic referred to in the title carries both its conventional sense and that of the inverted panic of inertia—a reaction to the numbness induced by the technological age.

Kroker, Arthur, and Michael A. Weinstein. *Data Trash: The Theory of the Virtual Class*. Montreal: New World Perspectives, 1994.
The authors occasionally offer explicit commentary on McLuhan in his own aphoristic style ("McLuhan is the moment of *positivistic* emergentism."— p. 143; "The age of soft sex . . . is also the time of the softening, and sudden reversal, of McLuhan."—p. 152) but sustained throughout the work is a subtle and imaginative application of McLuhan's thought that consistently respects its dynamic and coherence.

Levinson, Paul. *Digital McLuhan: A Guide to the Information Millennium*. London: Routledge, 1999.

FURTHER READINGS

Explication and application of McLuhan's ideas in systematic fashion, including use of McLuhan's four laws of media, brings the whole body of his thought seamlessly from the age of television to the age of the Internet.

Marchessault, Janine. *Marshall McLuhan: Cosmic Media*. London: Sage Publications, 2005.

A lively, accessible, and broad-ranging treatment of essential McLuhan.

Strate, Lance, and Edward Wachtel. *The Legacy of Marshall McLuhan*. Cresskill, NJ: Hampton Press, 2003.

The editors of this volume contribute their own essays to those of other commentators uniformly infected by the spirit of McLuhan at his exuberant and exploratory best. The result is robust writing under such titles as *Hold the 21ˢᵗ Century! The World Isn't Ready; The Invention of Lasagna Made the Pullman Car Obsolete; A Catechism of McLuhanisms for Unbelievers; Way Cool Text Through Light Hot Wires and Cellphones.*

INDEX

INDEX

St. Bonaventure 56, 59, 63, 65
Steiner, George 24
structuralism 143–7
Superman 71, 72
Swift, Jonathan 65
Swinburne, Algernon 31
symbolist 146, 149

tactility 9, 16, 32, 110
taste 111
technological determinism 5–6,
    24, 128
technological optimism 5–6, 22, 24
technological realism 6, 24
technologies
    electronic vs. mechanical 109
telegraph 40, 87, 89, 92, 107, 108, 126
telephone 89, 126
television 6–12, 39, 85, 87, 89, 90,
    95, 101, 111, 114, 115, 116,
    126, 130
    iconic quality of 7, 12
tetrad 20, 64, 132, 141, 142
    see also laws of media
tetrad structure 19
text messaging 90
Thomas, Alan 112
Thomas, Dylan 87
Thomas, E. C. 61
Thomist philosophy 43
touch 111
Toynbee, Arnold 27, 93
transformation theory of
    communication 128
transformation/transportation 115,
    116
trivium *see* classical trivium
Trudeau, Pierre Elliott 10, 79
Turner, Joseph 120
Tyler, Parker 45, 46, 47, 48

understanding as process of
    translation 22

Varro 41
Vico, Giambattista 47
videocassettes 116
visible environment 86
visual-auditory bias 72
visual bias 92, 108, 130
visual culture 119
visual orientation 90
visual sense 117
vortex 31, 32, 33, 35, 70,
    97, 136
Vorticism 31, 32, 33, 34, 35

Warhol, Andy 118
Warren, Robert Penn 102
Warton, Thomas 57
Watson, Sheila 120
Watson, Wilfred 118, 120, 121,
    122, 123
Wayne, John 75
wheel 106
Whitehead, Alfred North 33, 76,
    79, 80, 81
White, Vanna 10
Wiener, Norbert 96
Wilde, Oscar 120
Williams, Carl 127
Willmott, Glen 25, 26, 27
Wilson, Leon 103, 104, 112
Wimsatt, William 17, 123
Wolfe, Tom 6
word magic 60
    see also power of words
writing 107, 108, 122

Yeats, W. B. 122
Yogi, Maharishi Mahesh 11